D1604107

Hutchison, Robert A., 1938-
    Danger--heavy goods : driving the
toughest, most dangerous roads in the world
/ Robert Hutchison. -- 1st U.S. ed. -- New
York : Morrow, c1987
    288 p. : ill. ; 25 cm.
    Includes index.
    ISBN 0-688-06756-5

    1. Trucking--Middle East. 2. Trucking--
Europe.   I. Title.

DANGER—
HEAVY
GOODS

ALSO BY ROBERT HUTCHISON

Vesco
Off the Books

DANGER—HEAVY GOODS

Driving the Toughest, Most Dangerous Roads in the World

ROBERT HUTCHISON

WILLIAM MORROW AND COMPANY, INC.
New York

Library of Congress Cataloging-in-Publication Data

First Published in Great Britain in 1987 as: *Juggernaut*
by William Heineman Ltd.

Hutchison, Robert A., 1938–
    Danger—heavy goods : truckers race the devil and the clock on the toughest, most dangerous road in the world / Robert Hutchison.
        p.   cm.
    Includes index.
    ISBN 0-688-06756-5
    1. Trucking—Middle East.   2. Trucking—Europe.   I. Title.
HE5688.2.H88   1988
388.3′24′0956—dc19   87-35099
                                                                      CIP

Printed in the United States of America

First U.S. Edition

1 2 3 4 5 6 7 8 9 10

BOOK DESIGN BY BERNARD SCHLEIFER

This book is dedicated to Chris
Lawrence and the other victims
of the *Herald of Free Enterprise*
disaster in March 1987

CONTENTS

8   *CONTENTS*

1. DOVER DOCKS

GRAHAM Davies lit another cigarette, pushed his empty tea mug across the kitchen table, and looked at his watch. As an international freight driver, he saw his family less than a week in every month, and getting back on the road again was never an easy matter. Once under way, though, he knew he would slide back into the routine of the road soon enough and everything would be all right. But the first few miles and the last few of every trip were always the most difficult because they seemed the longest.

Graham owned and operated his own truck, but contracted his services to a major freight forwarder, Whittle International Freight Limited of Preston, northwest of Manchester. The pressures of being a long-distance driver were as weighty as some of the cargoes he pulled, and the financial insecurity that seemed a part of being a diesel gypsy was turning his wife, Madeleine, into a nervous wreck. Earlier that summer, while Graham had been on the road, I had seen Madeleine sit for hours in their darkened front room, wondering how they were going to keep it all together. She blamed herself for the fact that they were hard up, but also she regretted that Graham had given up the taxi business. At least the taxis had paid good money, while it was a constant battle just to keep the truck on the road, with no cash left over at the end of a trip to pay off debts. Nor could she hide her apprehension about Graham's next trip with me. She knew it would be more dangerous than his usual runs to Greece or Morocco. And she fretted, too, that as Graham would be away longer than normal, the bank manager might cancel their seven-thousand-pound overdraft.

Angela, who was fourteen, and Jennifer, twelve, liked it when their father was at home. Mum was happier then and didn't nag them as much. Of the five Davies children, they were the only ones still living with their parents. Their eldest sister, Stella, with two young boys of her own, was divorced and living near London. Martin was in Auckland with his New Zealand wife and baby. Julian, the manager of an exhaust repair shop, was married to a Blackpool girl and they had recently moved into their own home.

Around 3:00 P.M. Graham decided he could defer our departure no longer. We walked to the lane by Stanley Park where he parked his Scania 111 and drove it around to the house so that we could load our gear. Jennifer was crying. She didn't want her father to leave.

"Silly goose. Dry your tears," he told her. Graham was as sparse with his words as he was with his emotions. But I could tell she was tugging at his heartstrings. "That Jennifer," he said later, "she's as daft as they come."

We were in the Northwest of England, where people undulate their voices like the sound of the sea, flattening vowels and rolling syllables, all the while deforming words and their meaning in ways that foreigners, whether from Cornwall, Connecticut, or the Charente-Maritime, find difficult to comprehend. For example, they call police cars *jam butties*. Now try and figure that one out, I told myself.

"Why?" I asked Graham.

"Why what?"

"Why jam butties?"

"Because in Lancashire a *buttie* is a sandwich. A police car is a *jam buttie* because it is white and has a red stripe along its side," he explained, as if it were something everybody should know.

Another example was the *Illuminations*. It took me a long time to understand what Graham was referring to when he asked if I had seen the Illuminations. "They reckon it's the greatest free show on Earth."

At first I thought it might be a local football championship—the Eliminations—or maybe a collection of medieval manuscripts. But no, to attract Scottish tourists during the autumn off-season, Blackpool lights up its eight miles of seafront promenades, piers, and its tower with multicolored garlands, displays that explode in electric orgasms, and dancing laser beams that paint the sky. They can probably see the lasers bouncing off the ionosphere over in Ireland, and a good number of the Scottish tourists get so boozed they no doubt see the whole thing double. We had been the night before and, apart from the annoyance of being caught in an eight-mile traffic jam, watching the Scottish women sort out their menfolk had been as entertaining as the lights themselves.

Back in the front corridor of the Davies home, I handed boxes of food and equipment to Angela, who carried them to her father. He stored them on the lower bunk of the Scania, behind the two seats: twenty-four boxes in all, plus the bags and briefcases containing our personal gear. Although the cab was seven feet wide and the bunk almost four feet deep, that didn't leave us much room. Graham would sleep on the upper bunk; I had brought a sleeping bag and some foam rubber insulation and was planning to sleep under or on top of the trailer, depending on the weather.

Unlike the French, who buy most of their food en route, British long-distance drivers buy everything they need for the trip from their local supermarket. Hence Graham and I had spent most of Saturday afternoon purchasing supplies of condensed milk, Spam, Irish stew, canned vegetables, more Spam, canned potatoes, packages of ersatz hamburgers, still more Spam, instant noodles, black pudding, bacon, cookies, chocolate, sliced bread, tea bags, and all the other things that British drivers like. The only concession I wrung from him was to add to our meager store of utensils a pressure cooker, which, French drivers swear, next to the jack, tire iron, and gas cooker, is a trucker's best friend. I was determined to buy fresh produce along the way.

Another perversity I had noted about truckers is that invariably they named their beasts of burden after a woman, or at least something feminine. Graham called his Scania simply *Old Girl* because, he said, she was a good, steady creature. To be more precise, *Old Girl* was really a tractor. Once she had a trailer behind her, she became a juggernaut. The British press gave the name to these forty-ton contraptions; it conjures up an image of some mighty, irresistible force, and that was exactly how I saw these rigs as they rushed along the narrow byways and highways of Europe.

We left Blackpool at 4:00 P.M. on September 14, 1986, and bullied our way south through two hundred miles of Sunday traffic to pick up our trailer at the Infrasystems factory in Luton, thirty miles from London. We reached Luton just before 9:00 P.M.

''Damn,'' Graham said on our first pass in front of the factory. ''They haven't sheeted the tilt, have they?''

A tilt in the language of British truckers is a type of trailer built to international specifications. It can carry up to twenty-five tons of cargo on three back axles, and its metal frame is covered by canvas sheeting.

Once loaded, the sheeting is drawn over the frame and laced to the bottom of the trailer by a single cable that runs from the front along both sides and joins at the back so it can be sealed by Customs officers for bonded transit through foreign countries.

Our tilt was standing in the shadows in front of the factory on the far side of the road. It was loaded with eight big pieces of loose cargo and assorted cases containing motors, jigs, conveyors, and a cardboard tube full of plans. Our manifest described it as "the dismantled parts of one automatic flood coater, one LPG-fired preheat oven, one automatic dip-coating device with fluidized bed, and one LPG-fired postheat oven." The total weight was listed as five and a half tons.

"Just enough to hold her on the road," Graham commented, referring to the lightness of the load. "*Old Girl* should like that."

In fact we were pulling half of an industrial oven system. It was a one-off model, designed for coating and baking plastic pipes that would run through it on a conveyor belt. The unbaked pipes went in one end and thirty minutes later came out the other all shiny and orange. Our job, together with another Whittle International truck, was to deliver the complete system to the Saudi Conduit & Coating Company at Al Khobar, an oil port halfway down the Persian Gulf coast, opposite Bahrain. The other truck, driven by twenty-six-year-old Steven Walsh, was to join us in Belgrade on Thursday.

We anticipated that the trip to the Persian Gulf would take three weeks. We were going through Eastern Europe to Yugoslavia, into Greece, then Turkey and Iraq, and finally to the Tapline across the Saudi desert. Counting our return through Jordan and Syria, we would transit fourteen countries and cover more than ten thousand miles. We would travel along trade routes that had been used for thousands of years—the same roads over which Persian armies and Roman legions had marched, and for control of which Crusader princes fought Arab caliphs, and that in some places are still being fought over by Turks and Kurds, Arabs and Iranians. We would pass through the city of Tarsus, where St. Paul was born; Edessa, where Abraham was thought to have rested on his way from Ur to Canaan; and traverse valleys where the Assyrian hordes had once spread havoc.

A Total gas station stood next door to the Infrasystems factory, and to foil stickup artists the woman at the cash register was locked inside a bulletproof glass cage. As Graham backed *Old Girl* up to the trailer, I noted the woman was selling diesel for 1.66 pounds a gallon. In Saudi Arabia, we would buy it for ten pence per gallon, cheaper than the price of water there. Graham eased the "fifth wheel," a greased circular platform, over the back axle of the tractor, onto the trailer's locking pin. The mechanism snapped shut with a loud click, but still he gave the trailer a tug to make sure it had locked properly. It had. We were now—tractor and trailer—fifty-six feet long, twelve and a half feet high, with five axles, twelve wheels, and a gross weight, supposedly, of twenty-three tons, seventeen less than the maximum allowed on European roads.

The trucking industry in Europe, as Graham would later complain, is highly regulated—much more so than in the United States. Restrictions on such things as gross tonnage, maximum length, and axle weights are severely enforced and, along with the dimensions of the roads themselves, have had an effect on the design of the heavy-goods vehicles that ply the European cargo routes. The other major consideration in European truck design is economy. Taken together, these factors have meant that European trucks are quite different from their American cousins. Design in Europe has sought operating efficiency and maneuverability over the long-haul power of American vehicles.

The maximum length allowed in Europe is fifty-four feet, while in America the only length restriction is on the trailer; an American tractor can be any dimension. In Europe this has meant the development of short tractors, with cabs over motor, in order to cram as much loading space as possible on the trailer, while in America most tractors are long-nosed jobs with their motors in front of the cab and a sleeping compartment behind, sometimes even a toilet and shower. European cabs are cramped, and the driver's narrow bunk is behind his seat.

Another major difference between American and European trucks is their motor size. In Europe fuel has always been more expensive because it is imported and, in addition, it is heavily taxed in order to finance the development of national road networks. Therefore running economy is more important than in the United States, where fuel is relatively cheap.

The Swedes, with their Scanias and Volvos, have been leaders in developing the most efficient motors because their fuel costs are the highest. They were the first to introduce the turbo charger now used on all European trucks. The Scania, for example, has a six-cylinder turbo-charged motor that develops 280 horsepower and consumes thirty-five liters per one hundred kilometers, or almost seven miles to the U.S. gallon when fully loaded. All European tractor units run on deisel.

So European trucks are generally sleeker, more maneuverable, and more fuel efficient than American trucks. They are the thoroughbreds of the industry, but few can meet the stringent American pollution-control standards. Running economy means dirtier exhaust. They can turn on a radius equal to their own length. Because of weight restrictions, they have more axles, usually five or six, with up to twenty-six wheels. Some tractors have two drive axles, with four tires each. Most heavy-duty trailers have three axles, sometimes with four wheels on each axle. While some metal box trailers exist, most are canvas-covered for easier customs inspection. The British prefer step trailers to flatbeds and have fewer "road trains"—twenty-four-foot trucks with twenty-foot trailers—than continental cargo operators. The British long-haul fleet is almost exclusively tractors pulling forty-foot trailer.

Once we had *Old Girl* coupled to the trailer, our next task was to ensure that the load was safely secured so it would not shift during the journey. We climbed up the trailer's side gates and shook some pieces of galvanized paneling. They swayed back and forth like sheets in the wind.

"That won't do, will it? We'll have to secure the lot," Graham announced.

We got the cargo straps and started tying down the bigger pieces. This would cost us a good hour of driving time, and we were anxious to get to Dover. After straightening everything away, we pulled the canvas back over the top of the tilt and were preparing to "zipper" it up when an Infrasystems engineer drove up. He asked if everything was in order. We allowed that it was. He knew we were to pick up the trailer sometime after midday, and he had been driving by every hour or so, keeping an eye on it.

Once we got the oven to Al Khobar, the engineer and some of his assistants would fly out to assemble it. "The only one like it in the world," he said. Infrasystems had designed and built it in the record time of three months. Graham retracted the trailer legs as I connected the air hoses and electric cable between the tractor and the trailer. When we finished, our friend remarked: "Don't worry about the whiskey. They'll never find it. We've really hidden it well."

We thanked him, thinking this a joke. After all, he was laughing when he said it, wasn't he? Back in the cab, we waved good-bye. It was now 9:50 P.M. and we were happy to be back on the road. It took about twenty minutes for the implications of the engineer's remark to sink in. "Oh, shit," I finally said with a gasp. "Do you *really* think he was joking?"

"Why?" Graham asked.

"Saudi is a dry country," I reminded him. "No spirits, no beer. You get thrown into prison, even lashed, for breaking the law."

I didn't mention that we also risked having the truck confiscated. This would be no small disaster for Graham. *Old Girl* had been freshly painted for the trip in Whittle International's yellow livery and looked like a company wagon. But she was in every sense Graham's only means of livelihood.

This was our first trip to Saudi. The year before, we had driven together as far as Baghdad, carrying a dismantled banqueting kitchen for the Iraqi president, Saddam Hussein, who was remodeling the presidential palace in the midst of his costly war with Iran. Al Khobar was fully one third as far again.

Graham said nothing, weighing this potential dilemma in his mind. As the navigator and occasional codriver, I could sit back and relax, watching the night lights flick by, half listening to the citizens' band radio for warnings of "heavy metal" and "pick-and-shovel" meaning traffic jams and road works. *Old Girl* offered a bumpy ride. "It feels heavier than what's marked on the manifest," Graham said. "Probably more like eight tons back there." Just then we blew an air hose.

"Damn," he said. "We've lost the back brakes." But he was determined to roll on till we came to a traffic circle with a diner on it, where we could stop for a cup of tea.

Graham was an oddity among long-distance truckers in that he rarely swore. The men who risk their lives on the Middle East run pride themselves on being among the roughest, raunchiest, most ornery drivers in the world. Many enhance their image by sporting tattoos, earrings, beer bellies, and accordion wallets attached by a chain to large-buckle belts, and almost all have a vocabulary that would make a trooper blush. It is equally true that most are romantics at heart who become instant pushovers when treated with anything approaching respect; in fact, their hearts are often bigger than the turbos that run their trucks. Graham's need for peer identity stopped with the accordion wallet. He had no chain, earrings, tattoos, or large-buckle belt, though he did own a collection of exotic T-shirts. These also are part of the uniform.

The most remarkable thing about Graham, as I had come to know him during the past year, was the image he cast of calm stoicism. Or

was it just plain old stubbornness? For that, too, was a feature of his
character. He stood perhaps five feet, eleven inches, with a sturdy
build. But because he was wedged behind the wheel of the Scania for
long hours, he was not at a peak of physical fitness. The lack of
exercise and the pounding from the road had given him a paunch. He
kept his dark hair short; as it was bushy and straight it didn't need a lot
of brushing. His skin, I noted, was easily irritated, which meant that
in idle moments he would shave off any hint of stubble with an electric
razor run off batteries. In the morning he groped about till he found his
thin-rimmed glasses. But once awake, his eyes became quick with
movement that matched an often wry smile. I imagined he must have
been impish at school, giving his teachers a difficult time. He was
rebellious, but to change rather than toward established authority,
which made him a political conservative.

He had learned well the routine of long-distance freight driving,
as, for example, in clearing customs. At each border the procedures
were basically the same, though some of the wrinkles changed. When
we arrived at Dover Docks he knew exactly what to do and in which
order, like a jet pilot running down a checklist before takeoff. It was
midnight and hundreds of trucks were being disgorged from cross-
Channel ferries, water pouring off their roofs. While the moon was
still darting in and out of clouds over Dover, it was evidently a
stormy night in Europe. Few trucks, we noted, were heading for the
Continent.

Our first concern was to fill the belly tank under the trailer with
three hundred gallons of diesel. It took an hour to raise the Dover
Diesel Sales operator, and then he charged us a pound a gallon for the
tax-free diesel. This was no bargain. At least, though, we could
proceed to the freight agent's office.

As it was illegal to transport more than forty-five gallons of diesel
in an open tank through West Germany, we had to fill out a T-form,
which normally covers the transport of goods inside the Common
Market, stating that the diesel in the belly tank was part of the cargo
we were delivering to ourselves at Folmava, a town on the Czech side
of the West German border.

So much for Common Market bureaucracy. We drove *Old Girl*
into the Customs bay where we presented the T-form, an eight-page
TIR carnet, and our cargo manifest to a Customs inspector. He placed
lead seals on the back of the tilt and around the belly-tank spigot, then
stamped our TIR carnet, removing the first *volet* or paper stub from this

essential document issued by the International Road Transport Union (IRTU) in Geneva, Switzerland.

TIR stands for *Transport International Routier,* an international convention, regulated and managed by the IRU, that covers all TIR traffic. The convention guaranteed our cargo's passage in bond through the seven IRU member states we would transmit on our way to Al Khobar. As Iraq and Saudi Arabia do not subscribe to the TIR convention, separate documents were needed for these countries. Customs officers in each of the IRTU member countries were supposed to inspect the seals to make sure they had not been tampered with, and if the seals were intact, then stamp our TIR carnet and remove two stubs—one upon entering and the other when leaving the country. These stubs would eventually be sent to IRTU headquarters in Geneva. After the journey, when all the stubs were reunited with the used carnet, the IRTU would then retire the document, thereby liberating the Customs bond.

Only once the cargo papers had a Customs stamp on them, signifying the freight had been cleared for export, would the Townsend Thoresen ferrymaster sell us a ticket. He booked us on the 5:30 A.M. freighter to Zeebrugge in Belgium. With nothing more to do but wait, we went to The Barnacles, a truckers' grub shop at the end of the docks, for a cup of tea and a toasted cheese sandwich. No sooner in the place than we noticed the mood was sullen.

"What is it?" Graham asked the girl who took our order.

"Consternation," she said.

"Consternation over what?" I asked.

"For 'im what died. 'Ee was missing two days. They found 'im this morning."

It took a while, but finally we dragged the story from her. " 'Ee was a right beefy lad," she said. "Good-looking an' all. Never 'ave suspected 'ee was queer, like."

The consternation, we gathered, was not over the fact that the fellow was now dead, but rather over the manner in which he had died. Not that foul play was suspected. Far from it. He had returned from the Continent late on Friday and logged in with Customs, after which he went to The Barnacles for a meal and then disappeared. His vehicle was parked, curtains drawn and the doors locked. Customs agents hunted all over the docks for him to clear his load. When they pounded on his door, no one answered.

The harbor police finally pried one of the doors open. Inside, a macabre sight confronted them. The driver was stretched out on his bunk, behind the two seats, wearing a woman's negligee and black silk stockings. He had a self-applied garrote around his neck and apparently had accidentally strangled himself in an act of kinky self-abuse.

"Twisted, he was," Graham quipped.

"What do you mean?"

"A real head-banger, wouldn't you say?"

I agreed.

We finished our tea and decided it was time for a few hours' sleep. The wind was rising, with sand blowing across the docks, heralding a change in the weather. We had parked beside Ossie MacIntosh's cream-colored Ford Transcontinental. Ossie was a black giant of a man, with shoulders the size of an ox but as gentle as a pussycat in a fur slipper. In fact, Ossie could be downright taciturn. But he was thoughtful of others, which made him one of the more respected drivers on the run to the Balkans and Greece.

2. MOSAIC OF TRADE

THE ferry crossing took the normal five and a half hours—time for a meal, a shower, and sleep. As it turned out, Ossie MacIntosh was the only other TIR driver we knew on board. The rest were either T-form Charlies—truckers whose routes are within the Common Market and are so called because their cargoes are covered by T-forms rather than TIR carnets—or foreigners, mainly Turks. Over breakfast, Ossie asked if we wanted to run together to Belgrade. As we had to pick up my Czech visa in Bonn, we regretfully said no. It was always good to run with a mate like Ossie; he was solid, considerate, no hassle.

It was raining hard when we rolled off the ferry in Zeebrugge. We handed in our TIR carnet to Belgian Customs, and had it stamped and the second *volet* lifted, all in a matter of ten minutes. We stopped at the Total service station a mile from the docks, where Graham debated long and hard about whether to buy a twenty-four-volt refrigerator small enough to fit on the engine cowling inside the cab. It took about an hour for the sensation of thirst brought on by desert heat to win over cool reason and then, purchase made, we carried the trophy back to the patiently waiting *Old Girl* and installed it between the two seats. We now had a 150-mile drive to the West German border, where we would pick up the next series of stamps in our TIR carnet.

It rained all day as we drove along the Belgian motorway, by-passing Brussels, then Liège, and crossing the Ardennes near Aachen, one of Germany's oldest cities. Leon Ashworth, Whittle's operations manager in Preston, had given us the broad outline of our routing, leaving Graham to fill in the details.

"Don't transit Kuwait," he said. "Too risky round Basra. You

must enter Saudi through Ar'ar, and come back Jordan-Syria. I've
alerted our agent in Ar'ar to be on the lookout for you.''

"Ar'ar," Graham repeated, like he was trying to fit his teeth
around the word and chew it. " 'Ow do I get there?''

Leon did a double take, looking pointedly at Graham for a moment
till he realized that Blackpool's star long-distance driver was putting
him on.

"Out the gates, down to the end of the road, then turn right at the
traffic lights. You'll have no trouble finding it,'' Leon said.

No trouble at all, I thought. That was a fine one. Leon winked at
Pam Aspden, his assistant. She was usually the one who had to
contend with Graham's special brand of humor.

"Ah, aye, he's a hard one, that Leon,'' Graham later said. "But
when you get back from a trip, he always has the check waiting for
you, right on his desk. That counts a lot in this game. Not all of 'em
are like that.''

King Leon, the other drivers called him. But at least they felt they
had a rapport with Leon Ashworth; they could talk to him, whereas
they could not talk with Michael Whittle, the group's chairman.
Michael Whittle's grandfather Joseph had founded the business in
1880. The Whittle firm in those days hired teamsters who drove the
freight to and from the railyards and docks in wooden wagons called
sling vans drawn by draft horses that were stabled at Bolton, off the old
A6 road from Preston to Manchester. "Our motto is 'Keep moving,' "
Joseph Whittle used to tell staff and clients. And for more than one
hundred years the Whittle family has been doing just that.

Graham and I were well into the routine of boredom by now. The
280-horsepower motor was humming monotonously, one of the three
giant windshield wipers occasionally sticking on its backward swing,
thereby confusing the others, and water was spraying out from the ruts
under our wheels in fifteen-foot jets onto either side of the roadway.
The rain-soaked countryside had sufficiently deadened my visual
curiosity to allow my imagination to play with a notion that international trade was a delicate mosaic of which we were now a subatomic
particle.

Aachen, I remembered, had its place in that mosaic. Almost
forgotten by modern travelers, it nestles in the Eifel Mountains, still a
textile city but removed from the major trade routes. Even our route,
the E5 autobahn, steered well to the south and east of it. But for almost
one hundred years, beginning in the eighth century, Aachen was the

capital of Europe. Charlemagne had installed his court there in a remarkable Roman-looking palace and made it a focal point of international trade. He exchanged embassies with Harun-al-Rashid, the great Arab ruler of Baghdad, and with the emperor of eastern Byzantium. For a brief few decades trade again flourished on a scale that had not been seen in Europe since the days of Augustus. Aachen remained at the center of European trade until two tiny pieces of the mosaic changed, contributing to the collapse of Carolingian society.

The Carolingian monarchs earned most of their revenues from taxes levied on Flemish wool. Bruges was the capital of Flanders, and Zeebrugge, where the continental part of our journey began, became its port after the North Sea inlet leading to Bruges had silted up. Flemish woolens were at the time considered the finest in the world. They were exported as far afield as Baghdad and Bohkara.

After Charlemagne's death, the empire became burdened by internal strife. To keep the royal finances afloat, Charlemagne's successors increased the wool tax until the Flemish merchants could no longer compete in world markets. Trade shrank and revenues declined. Finally the empire split into three. Its breakup seemed proof that nations, like corporations, can live beyond their means for as long as their savings last or for as long as they can borrow the savings of others. But in Charlemagne's time, as in Roman times, international lending had not been invented, so nations that lived in chronic deficit were doomed to collapse.

The Flemish wool merchants had more resilience than Carolingian monarchs. Aachen withered to insignificance while Bruges rose to become one of Europe's great entrepôts of trade, and, together with Florence, remained a flourishing textile center for hundreds of years.

Another factor that sealed the fate of the Carolingians was the rise of the Northmen. By then these Scandinavian warriors and traders had expanded their dominions into Muscovite Russia. From there they carried their commerce down the great rivers of central Russia to the gates of Constantinople and Baghdad, at the time the two wealthiest cities in the world and therefore the largest marketplaces for northern European goods. Among the articles these ''Russ'' traders brought with them were Baltic amber, brocade, furs, Frankish swords, and slaves. Flemish merchants began using the Northmen as their middlemen in trade with southern Europe and the East.

The mosaic was ever-changing—a living mechanism as complex as life itself. Major trends often evolved slowly and were at the time impossible to discern. As the Northmen ferried their furs and textiles south, traffic on the great caravan routes from the East was disrupted. These routes had been the bloodline of international trade, bringing silk, spices, perfumes, and other luxury items to the Mediterranean and taking precious metals, glassware, *objets d'art,* alabaster, Flemish cloth, and Byzantine wares back to the East. But in the turmoil of the Dark Ages, traffic along the overland caravan routes virtually ceased. Muslim rulers who succeeded Harun-al-Rashid tried to monopolize the East–West caravan traffic and charged exorbitantly to match their monopoly. This did not sit well with the Norman and other Christian princes.

At this point, virtually all overland trade from the East was diverted to sea routes. Maritime shipping was less costly, and ships could handle bulkier cargoes than the two-humped Bactrian camel. But again events changed the mosaic. In 1291 the pope forbade Christians to trade with Egypt, through whose ports the Ceylon and Malabar coast traffic passed, and at about the same time the Egyptian sultan began to look upon the Red Sea as his private preserve.

Trade with the East was all but stifled. Goods still got through, mainly in the hands of Jewish and Levantine merchants who were not bound by papal bulls nor averse to dealing with Arabs, but it was on a restricted scale. The mosaic remained more or less unchanged for another hundred years, until the magnetic needle revolutionized navigation and made the longer sea routes around Africa into the Atlantic viable alternatives. Long-distance maritime transport, however, required greater investment for the building of sturdier vessels and larger port facilities. Merchants overcame these problems by pooling their capital to operate shipping fleets, and governments raised Customs and excise duties to build new sea terminals. But whenever trade outstripped investment, overland transport filled the gap.

This was most recently demonstrated in the 1970s, when Middle Eastern ports became too congested or simply were not equipped to handle the increased trade brought on by a quadrupling of world oil prices. Overland routes again became predominant. The modern caravans were the forty-ton juggernauts such as Graham's *Old Girl.* They were relatively cheap to run and didn't require a large capital investment. One juggernaut could carry as much cargo in weight as one hundred camels. These forty-tonners, using extendable low-loader trailers, can transport steel girders and machine presses, or, with forty-foot refrigerators, chilled pharmaceuticals, temperature-controlled computers, and frozen foods. Of course, some trucking enterprises did less well than others; their rates were undercut by better-placed competitors, and traffic patterns changed. This, too, was part of the mosaic.

We reached the outskirts of Bonn at around 8:00 P.M. that first Monday and parked off the autobahn in a small village square. Next morning I took a taxi to the Czech embassy, got my visa, and we were under way again by 10:00 A.M., destination Prague. Graham preferred the Czech-Hungary route to Austria because there were no road taxes to pay. Austria was the most expensive country in Europe to transit— a tax of 105 pounds for three hundred miles.

It was still raining when we left the outskirts of Bonn on the A61 to Koblenz and Heidelberg. Toward the Hockenheim-Ring exit we noticed that two trucks had telescoped together in a paved shoulder on the right side of the autobahn. The first truck had overturned, and it looked like a car was pinned underneath it; of the other, only a portion of its cab remained visible. Because of the rain, everything was blurred. Once past, something familiar about the front truck struck us, and Graham, who was on that side, as *Old Girl* had right-hand drive, tried to look back, but it was too late. When you have twenty-three tons behind you, you don't stop on a penny.

"Wasn't that Ossie's Transcon lying on its side?" he asked.

I had thought the same but, as I hadn't seen clearly either, I wasn't sure.

"Damn," Graham mumbled. We kept steaming into the rain. His mood was as grim as the weather.

We stopped at a service area for lunch of Lancashire black pudding sandwiches and a pot of tea. While eating, Graham disconnected the CB radio and hid it at the back of the overhead rack. It was illegal to use CB's in Czechoslovakia, and to be caught operating one would risk all sorts of unpleasantness we didn't need.

After the town of Walldorf we swung east toward Nuremberg and Amberg, which for us was the end of the autobahn. The rain had become intermittent, but was still heavy at times, as we wound through the Bavarian hills. Graham was attempting to make up the few hours we had lost that morning while obtaining my visa. Realizing a long and arduous road lay ahead of us, I was for taking it easy. But Graham had the overhead of his truck and an impatient bank manager to consider.

By midafternoon we had heard the same news report a dozen times about the seventeen people killed and 112 buildings destroyed by an earthquake in southern Greece. Its epicenter was at the extreme southern end of the Peloponnisos, far from where we were headed. Between the newscasts, it seemed like the U.S. Armed Forces network was playing only cowboy music that Tuesday, and it was starting to wear on our nerves. Whenever the miles start dragging and time gets heavy, drivers invariably think of the women they have left behind. I suppose it's the same with soldiers and sailors. But I knew Graham was worrying about Madeleine and how she would cope in his absence. Would he telephone her from a roadside phone booth to find out? Never, not Graham. He would call only when back on Dover Docks to let her know he had returned safely.

Above the windshield, running the length of the cab's interior, was a shelf about ten inches deep with six inches of space between it and the ceiling. On the driver's side Graham had installed a new touch-selector radio and self-reversing cassette deck acquired from a Blackpool discount house. Two speakers were wedged into each corner of the shelf— one over my left ear and the other over Graham's right ear. He was proud of the system's stereo effect, and so that he might enjoy the full benefit of the stereo sound over the rumble of the motor he turned the balance hard left. This meant that I received a jolting number of decibels while Graham was lost in musical memories—Lonnie Donegan, Petula Clark, Buddy Holly, the Spinners, Dinah Shore, and the Kinks.

As the miles clicked by, Graham would forget to change the cassette so that his favorites of the sixties would keep repeating themselves *ad infinitum*. My only defense was to put on earphones and turn on my Walkman. Listening to a competing cassette, but at lower decibels, I would try to read or just daydream. Graham would finally wonder what I was up to, look over at me, and at first register no reaction. After a few minutes he might start singing out of tune with the music. At last he would ask a question—any question—just to get my attention. He didn't like Walkmen.

"They're antisocial," he once complained.

"What did you say?" I was being unkind; I had heard perfectly well.

"Those things are antisocial—"

"I can't hear you."

That would get him mad. Finally he would turn the sound system down and begin again.

Other items on that shelf included the CB radio and rolls of paper towels and toilet paper. On my side I tried to wedge in a few books:

a Cadogan guide to Turkey, Layard's *Nineveh and Babylon,* and Colin Thubron's *Mirror to Damascus* among them. There wasn't much foot room because a blue gas bottle for the cooker was on the floor, together with a ten-gallon container of motor oil. A toolbox that wouldn't shut was down on the left side of the seat. I could rest my right arm on the refrigerator, but had to keep on adjusting the cooker in front of it, which vibrated back and forth. Sometimes the cooker slid off the cowling, causing much confusion, as it usually happened on a turn. Its lid rattled so annoyingly that we had to jam the atlas of road maps under it. At all times we had to ensure that we had turned off the gas. Once we forgot. When we realized the cock was open there was enough propane floating around the cab to blow both of us through the windshield had Graham decided to light a cigarette.

I had a list of things to do that I knew were helpful, and tried to remember them, like wiping the left wing mirror clean of mist or rain, making sure it was properly adjusted, or that I didn't obstruct Graham's view of it. And above all not to kick the fusebox in front of me with my cramped feet.

Then, without warning, bang! Startled, Graham jumped in his seat. My heart skipped a beat. My books had fallen from the overhead shelf. Sheepishly I replaced them, working hard to fix them securely back in place.

The second time they came down, Graham got mad. "You're going to make me have an accident with those bloody things." He couldn't understand why I had so many books anyway. What did I need them for? "Stick 'em behind," he suggested.

But behind, on the lower bunk, there was hardly a spare inch of space. The food and motor parts were stored there; on the top bunk were my knapsack, bedroll, and Graham's battered suitcase. Occasionally these items ended up in our laps as well. If the road surface suddenly became corrugated you literally had your hands full.

Graham complained unceasingly about my large amount of gear, which embarrassed even me. He also complained about the flies, the weather, and above all about my ability, in those cramped conditions, to lose things. He could be a tyrant if ever I took him seriously. But most of the time I sensed he didn't mean it. He was only testing me, trying to provoke a reaction. It was a game I learned to play with him. It gave us something to do. He would be amused by my lapses into alleged Americanisms. "I'm going to the bathroom," I would sometimes tell him.

"The bathroom," he would retort, stretching the "a." "That's American. What's the matter with the toilet?"

"But you refer to *Old Girl* as a truck. Surely that's American?"

"You can also call her an artic." "Artic" was short for "articulated vehicle," I learned.

"But not a lorry?" I asked.

"No, she's not a lorry."

I was confused. Another driver we met tried to clarify it for me. "Anything that goes abroad is a truck. If it stays at home it's a lorry." I became even more confused.

What really pleased him was when I dusted the dashboard and helped clean the cab, or washed the tea mugs, frying pan, and our other utensils. "My mate's doing the housecleaning," he said, beaming, picking at a scab on his forearm.

After topping the motor with oil, blowing diesel into the running tanks, or other hand-soiling chores, he would clean himself with detergent applied to an old rag he kept behind the seat and more often than not neglect to rinse off the detergent. I was sure the raw detergent was giving him that sore on his forearm.

Graham turned taciturn again. I looked out at the trees. Hidden in the forest on either side of us were the gun emplacements and observation posts from which NATO and Warsaw Pact forces eyed each other. Separating the two was an electrified wire-mesh fence built by the East Europeans to prevent their citizens from fleeing to the West. The fence was not far away—off to our right—but in the dark we couldn't see it. From the Baltic it runs at least to the Danube and maybe even farther, though I have never seen sign of it beyond the hills around Bratislava. I know for sure it doesn't exist along the Hungarian-Yugoslav border. In the sector through which we were presently driving it was guarded by Czech soldiers carrying Kalashnikov rifles, and they meant business. They scrutinize every inch of the truck as you drive through the checkpoint at Folmava, and if they turn even mildly suspicious they can keep you immobilized for hours.

Curiously, a little while back we had passed a large floodlit furniture supermarket in the middle of nowhere. I wondered if it had been placed there and lit up like a Christmas tree to remind the Czechs that over here it was consumer heaven, the land of plenty, while over there it was drabsville.

Counting the two rest stops, Graham had been driving for ten hours, and he was getting pretty cranky. You could see his eyes were heavy, and he was chain-smoking. I estimated up to sixty cigarettes a day. He lit another as we rolled up to the West German Customs post. For some reason the border crossing point was in darkness. Rising out of the east an almost full moon, partially shielded by clouds, filtered silver light onto the eight trucks lined up ahead of us: mostly Turks, but I could see one Romanian and a single Brit, so we were not alone. We parked, got our documents together, and took them to the Customs post. Besides the TIR carnet, at each border crossing we were required to produce seven different sets of papers: our bill of lading, a consignment note known as a CMR;* the truck registration; the *carnets de passage,* also known as triptychs, which ensure that both truck and trailer can be temporarily imported into a country; third-party insurance papers; and, of course, our passports.

It took twenty minutes to clear West German Customs and one hour and twenty minutes to get through the Czech side of the border. While still on the German side, we had a drink and a bite to eat with John Hodges, who was on his way to Istanbul with a load of diesel engines. John was taking it easy. He had parked for the night and planned to cross into Czechoslovakia in the morning. He wanted to get to the Hotel Wien, on the outskirts of Budapest, by the following night. Hotel Wien is a noted brothel favored by British truckers because of the high-class hookers who hang out there. There was another motel-*cum*-brothel down the road from Folmava, at Rocky-cany, but the Brits don't go there anymore because the Turks have taken it over.

"You just wait and see," John said. "There'll be so many awbies parked up there you won't be able to get near the place. I stay clear of Rockycany now, I tell you I do. Don't want no AIDS or anything like that."

Hodges was in his late thirties. He started as a Middle East driver in 1973 but now only went as far as Turkey. "I've had enough of the Middle East. The hassle's not worth it," he said, expressing a view that was increasingly common among British drivers. He had a broad Essex accent. His sister, a quiet-spoken blonde with the looks of a fashion model, owned a stylish boutique called Special Occasions on High Street, Kelvedon, in Essex, forty-five miles northeast of London.

---

* CMR stands for *Convention relative au contrat de transport international de marchandises par route,* the so-called CMR convention. A CMR consignment note confirms the contract of carriage and is made out in three original copies signed by the sender and carrier. The first copy remains with the sender, the second accompanies the goods, and the third is retained by the carrier.

Housed in an eighteenth-century corner cottage, the shop sold five-hundred-pound Pierre Cardin *ensembles,* slinky lingerie, and knee garters to the yuppie wives and mistresses from the stockbroker belt centered in nearby Coggeshall, a village that has had more than its share of society murders. An apartment over the shop was John's *garçonnière* when he was not on the road.

By 11:30 P.M. we were rolling again, this time in another world, almost another century: The narrow roads were built in the 1930s for lighter traffic, the villages were poorly lit, and the streets were nearly empty. On the outskirts of Plzeň we were stopped at two different police roadblocks. They examined our passports, then waved us on.

"Something's happening. Must be looking for someone," Graham said. Two weeks before, the Czech secret police had arrested seven leaders of the Jazz Section, an unauthorized group that was dissatisfied with state-controlled culture. It was another clear sign that the Helsinki Charter of Human Rights was not about to be implemented in Czechoslovakia, even though the Czech government was one of the charter signatories. But nobody imagined that the hard-line government of Gustav Husak was about to adopt more liberal policies, especially not John Hodges, who at that very moment was seated in his cab, watching an eerie light show as Czech troops chased through the forest, which they floodlit by sectors, trying to locate a car and its passengers who were attempting to flee to the West.

"It was really strange. All those soldiers crashing through the woods looking for a carload of obviously misguided citizens wanting to leg it to freedom," was how John described it when we met him again in Belgrade.

The Skoda works looked like something out of Kafka. They were darkened and idle, their overhead hopper lines and cranes but silent shadows when we passed them before the right-hand dip into the center of Plzeň. We drove through the city on damp cobblestones and turned right again on the road to Prague, under a bridge with suspended tramway lines overhead. The sign said 3.80 meter's clearance, which gave us only four inches' headroom, assuming this took into account the tramway cables. I had visions of the truck tearing out a whole section of the cables, bringing darkness and chaos to our lives and half the city of Plzeň.

"She's always passed before. Don't see why she won't tonight," Graham commented drily. The roads were greasy. Going up the incline out of Plzeň, *Old Girl* slipped on the cobbles, her back wheels spinning. Two more police checks, then straight road and more rain.

At about 1:00 A.M. we rolled into the paved shoulder at Rockycany. Just as John Hodges had predicted, scores of Turkish trucks were jammed into the parking lot outside the motel. "These bloody Turks," Graham said grumpily. "As soon as they get onto something, they spoil it, don't they?"

We had stopped because our running tanks were empty and we needed to blow some diesel through from the belly tank. First Graham broke the Customs seal on the belly-tank spigot and opened the valve. Then he ran a length of hose from the valve to the running tanks. Next he disconnected the brake line and coupled it onto a nozzle that fed into the belly tank. Finally he used the air compressor for the brakes to build up enough air pressure in the belly tank to move the diesel forward. It was ingenious.

While Graham was supervising this operation, a Turk stumbled out of the motel and lurched toward us. East European police are severe about drinking and driving. If they find a truck driver has even the slightest trace of alcohol in his blood they not only confiscate his license but also see to it that he is banned for life from driving in Eastern bloc countries.

"*Eh, kollege, hast du die Polizeikontrolle weiter oben auf der Strasse gesehen?*" the Turk asked in good but halting German. His truck was facing west, toward Furth-im-Wald.

"A forest of them," I told him.

He grunted and turned back to his truck. "*Besser dass ich schlaffen gehe,*" he said.

"*Ja, dass ist eine sehr gute Idee,*" I remarked.

We set out again into the night. Crossing the road ahead of us were two fawns and a buck. They stopped and blinked, then disappeared over a hedge. Finally, after skirting Prague on the new bypass and climbing the hill to the main Prague–Bratislava expressway, we arrived at a services area and parked for the night. It was 2:20 A.M., and Graham could no longer keep his eyes open.

3. DRIVING WITH THE DEVIL

NORTH of Brno, in the Czechoslovakian hills, we saw our first rays of sunshine in three days. We were steaming along the expressway, soon to take the detour for heavy vehicles over the mountain behind Bratislava, a portion of the road that all drivers hate.

Pulling around a sweeping left-handed bend on top of the mountain, we spotted two British trucks on the paved shoulder and pulled in. It was 2:00 P.M. and time for lunch anyway. The two drivers were Bob Hedley, an owner-driver pulling for Astran, on his way back from Muscat, at the extreme eastern tip of the Arabian peninsula, and Gordon Durno, driving for Falcongate. Gordon was taking a load of spare parts to Athens.

Hedley had been on the road for seven weeks and had only twenty pounds left in his pocket. Durno, a kindly Scot in his midfifties who once did only Middle East work, had just given Hedley enough diesel from his belly tank to get him back to Dover.

Hedley had been delayed at Kafji, on the Saudi frontier with Kuwait, on his outward journey because as he arrived there the Customs administration closed for four days to celebrate the Muslim New Year. When the holiday ended, the Saudis announced that a new decree had gone into effect on the first day of the new calendar limiting all trucks entering the country to one diesel tank only. This cost him another two days of pleading with the Customs manager not to remove his belly tank. As Hedley was transiting Saudi Arabia for Muscat, the Customs manager relented and did not molest the truck more than to cut open the diesel tanks to peer inside for contraband. "But that's it, mate. No more belly tanks. They burn the fuckin' things right off with a fuckin' blowtorch," Hedley said.

30

"Bloody hell," said Graham, "I can't let them do that."

"You won't have no choice. They're raving maniacs down there."

Hedley, who weighed 250 pounds and was known as the Animal, was one of the original Middle East drivers. He had been on the run for almost as long as Dick Snow, a former Royal Navy radio operator who also drove for Astran. Snow, at fifty-two, was regarded as the dean of British long-distance truckers. He had made his first trip down the line twenty years before, when Astran ran not only to Kabul but also crossed the Khyber Pass to places like Rawalpindi and Lahore. Because of the seven-year-long civil war in Afghanistan and problems with the Iranians, that kind of driving had ended, at least for the moment.

Hedley's red and black Ford Transcon looked like it might have just come over the Khyber and had taken such a pounding that it needed to be Scotch-taped together. Bob's clothes were covered with grease, and he was unshaven, but he was smiling.

"Two drivers?" he said, looking at me. "Which route you going?"

"Ar'ar," I said.

"They won't be having that, either. Two drivers aren't allowed in Saudi. One of you'll have to stay behind."

Graham looked at me, and I at him, wondering whether to laugh or cry.

"Well, if they allow only one of us through, we know who it's going to be, don't we?" he said.

"Oh, I don't mind taking *Old Girl* to Al Khobar on my own," I replied.

Graham was not in a mood for jokes.

While Gordon was shutting the valve on his belly tank and storing the hose, we asked Hedley if he had seen Ossie MacIntosh anywhere along the line. We were hoping someone might have passed him. Hedley had not. It was still conceivable, however, that Ossie and Hedley had taken different routes. Nevertheless, we feared the worst for Ossie, and it did nothing to brighten Graham's mood.

"Bob's a walking disaster. I dunno how that man keeps driving," Gordon said after Hedley left us.

We sat and talked for a while, building cheese-and-onion butties. Gordon was going through Budapest to see what he could find and was in no hurry. He was on salary; Graham was not. Graham wanted to take a more direct route, across the Hungarian meadowlands to the

Yugo frontier near Subotica, and then on to Belgrade. After leaving Gordon, we descended into the Danubian plain, heading for Medvedov. The corn was being harvested in the warm September sun and the fields were broad and flat, with dark, loamy soil. The roadsides were lined with cherry and chestnut trees, and children were busy picking the chestnuts. The farmers here seemed more prosperous than those in the North of the country. Their cottages had well-kept gardens and the lawns around them were carefully groomed. Some had little castles and brightly painted gnomes standing in the grass.

In spite of the light traffic, at Medvedov we found two dozen trucks in front of us, waiting to get into the compound shared by both the Czech and Hungarian Customs services. Entering the compound, we rolled over our first weighbridge, slowly, slowly so as not to disrupt the scales. No other country on the Middle East run is as strict as Hungary on axle weights. The maximum gross weight for five-axled articulated vehicles is the same as in the United Kingdom: thirty-eight tons. But the maximum allowed on any one axle is eight tons. Should the weighbridge show nine tons, the overweight fine would be one Deutschmark for every excess kilogram, or the equivalent of 260 pounds sterling. Nobody came out of the weighbridge house to challenge us, confirming that we were within the limit on all axles. If, however, a problem had existed, chances are it could have been solved with a bribe, though the profferer must be very careful. Everyone in the Eastern bloc likes their own cache of hard currency, and the Hungarians are no exception.

A Czech Customs officer collected our passports. Three hours later a Hungarian Customs officer returned them. Finally, at 8:15 P.M., we left the compound and headed for Győr, only ten minutes away.

"Don't you find you get a good idea of a country's character during the first few miles on its roads?" I asked Graham.

"Oh, aye, sometimes the difference from one country to another can be like night and day, though only a line on the map separates the two."

The change between Czechoslovakia and Hungary was immediately noticeable. We could see that Hungarian roads were better maintained; homes and factories had a more prosperous air; even the car and truck parks were filled with new vehicles, a fair percentage of them imported from the West or Japan. The streets of Győr were wide, well lit, well marked, and above all spotlessly clean. Life, also, seemed to move at a faster pace.

Györ is on the right bank of the Danube, where the Raba River flows into it, and the Raba's name has been given to the city's major truck works as well as to an immense new sports stadium. Emperor Augustus was the first to bring an organized army through the town, which, because it sits astride a well-trodden passage, has been burned and rebuilt many times. In the older sections, many fine baroque and rococo houses still exist, though we saw none, skirting the city's industrial suburbs.

"It's just like Switzerland," I remarked.

Graham said he didn't know whether it was or not, as Switzerland was one of the few countries he had never motored through. But the faster pace on the better-surfaced roads interested him. He was hoping to make up the time lost at the border, not by pushing *Old Girl* faster than the forty-mile-per-hour limit (fifty miles per hour on expressways), but by extending her hours on the road. This can be done in Eastern Europe, Turkey, and the Middle East, where no limit on driving hours is imposed. In the Common Market, however, truckers are not supposed to drive more than nine hours a day, with rest stops required at specified intervals.

We cut through the heart of Hungary in the middle of the night. There was a full moon rising, and some ground mist in the valleys. Graham was pushing *Old Girl* through corners, down hills, and into the foggy hollows, my cassette of Beethoven's Second Symphony blaring from the roof speakers. Where normally we might have slowed for a bend to, say, thirty miles per hour, Graham held her at forty miles per hour. *Old Girl* rattled, her brakes hissed, the gears grumbled as he moved them up and down the ten-speed transmission, and sometimes they jumped into neutral of their own accord. We felt like a train, and the engineer was driving her as if the devil himself were sitting in the caboose. We had hoped to reach Belgrade by midnight, but our late start from Prague and the delay at the Hungarian frontier had excluded any possibility of that.

"We're a funny lot," Graham finally said, looking over to see if I was listening. He had lit another cigarette, and the glow from it reflected off his glasses like snake eyes in the night. "We're a breed unto our own, really. We have to look after ourselves. Nobody else does. Once out of the Common Market we've got to drive sixteen hours a day to make the job pay."

Graham started explaining his driving philosophy, which included a lesson in road economics. "Put it this way," he continued. "I've got to clear twenty-three hundred pounds this trip. That means I've got to do it in five weeks. If I don't, I start losing five hundred pounds a week.

"It's a game, you know, where it's all go. You haven't got a moment to live. And it's all about money. Certainly no pleasure job. But it gets into your blood, and once it does you can't get it out."

Ivor Graham Davies was born in the village of Biddulph, in the West of England, on November 22, 1936. He was the eldest of three boys. His father, Garnet Davies, was a motor engineer who had a garage at Stoke-on-Trent, in the Potteries, where Dalton and Wedgwood china are made. In 1948 his father sold the garage and moved the family to Blackpool, where he bought a rooming house. But the tourist trade didn't appeal to him and after a few years he sold the rooming house and became a foreman at Platt's Engineering Company in Blackpool.

"He was a brilliant mechanic, but very quiet. You would never hear him boast about work, yet he could rebore anything you wanted. In those days you really repaired motors to make them last. Today they just put on a new piece, throw the old one away, and call themselves mechanics," Graham explained.

Graham had done his national service in the Royal Engineers, becoming a sapper-mechanic. He learned to repair Bedfords, Commers, AECs, and Land-Rovers while serving in Cyprus and North Africa. Back in Blackpool he went to work for Morris Motor Company's commercial vehicles agent. In 1962 he married Madeleine Pomfret. They invited old Mr. Platt to the wedding. During the reception, Mr. Platt drew Graham and his father aside and asked if they wanted to take over the business.

"We ran it for six years. But then we figured it wasn't producing enough, so we closed it and I went into the taxi business."

Graham made money in taxis. At one time he owned three radio cabs and had nine drivers working for him. He ran the cabs twenty-four hours a day. In the midseventies he sold them and bought a fleet of four trucks. He figured bigger wheels, bigger profits. With the cash left over from the sale of the last taxi, he made a down payment on a thirty-thousand-pound house on South Park Drive, in a quiet neighborhood off New Preston Road. They had five children by then, while the two-story red-brick home had only four bedrooms. But Madeleine had fallen in love with it. They did the renovating themselves, giving it a warm atmosphere that reminded me of the house where I had lived as a boy in Montreal.

Soon after, Graham was hit by an unfavorable income-tax assessment. The Inland Revenue said he owed them twelve thousand pounds. To meet the claim he sold his trucks and ever since has been fighting to come back from near-bankruptcy. He bought *Old Girl* secondhand in 1982 for twelve thousand pounds from an Ipswich haulier who did mostly container work inside the United Kingdom. With *Old Girl* running seven weeks out of every eight he just managed to meet his monthly mortgage payments of 170 pounds and service the bank overdraft. Madeleine worked part-time at The Saddle, a local pub, and covered household expenses with her earnings. Besides the house and *Old Girl,* Graham owned a Morris 1100 that had belonged to his father, who died in 1983. The car was in almost mint condition. Madeleine preferred to use public transportation. They rarely went out and spent most evenings watching television. Madeleine occasionally reads; Graham never, except trade journals.

Graham's overheads eat all of his earnings. He has to pay thirty-one hundred pounds a year in U.K. road taxes, three thousand pounds in insurance, and eighteen hundred pounds in vehicle maintenance. The road tax upsets him because he drives his truck in the United Kingdom less than six weeks a year. In addition, he has to rent the trailer, which costs another 105 pounds a week, and he is liable for any damage done to it while on the road, including punctures or ripped sheeting.

For the Saudi trip, Whittle International had contracted to pay him forty-five hundred pounds. Of this he drew twenty-five hundred pounds in running money, and a check for the balance, minus the ferry charges, would be waiting when he returned. Every penny counts and is carefully spent. The backload from the Continent, which usually pays another fifteen hundred pounds, might make the difference between whether he breaks even, shows a loss, or comes up with a respectable profit for the trip. Any unforeseen problems along the way, such as an accident, mechanical breakdown, or delay due to bad weather, shifting war zones, diplomatic upheavals, or Customs hassles, could literally mean financial disaster. The pressures are therefore immense. I was beginning to understand why he was driving like the very devil was on our tail. This precarious situation, I learned, was common among the owner-drivers who make up the majority of long-distance road haulers in the United Kingdom.

Added to Graham's list of worries was Bob Hedley's report that belly tanks were no longer allowed in Saudi Arabia. He was counting on making the run back home with cheap Saudi diesel, which would save him maybe five hundred pounds. But if he had to abandon the belly tank at the Saudi frontier, not only would he lose that opportunity but he also would have to pay the trailer rental company for the abandoned material. The question was whether we should remove it ourselves in southern Turkey and pick it up again on the way home. Or should we risk going in with it, claiming ignorance of the new decree, and trying to bluff our way through? Problems, problems.

"You always have problems on this job. What makes it interesting is that no two trips are ever the same," Graham said.

Try as hard as he could, there was no way to push *Old Girl* any faster along these country roads. We were still a good 150 miles short of Belgrade and realized we would not get into Yugoslavia that night. Exhausted, at 11:00 P.M. Graham pulled into a parking lot behind a Euroshell service station near the town of Dunaföldvár.

We had the lot to ourselves. Neither of us was what you might call hungry, but as we hadn't eaten anything since the Bratislava mountain, Graham decided to try some instant noodles. The instructions said, "Remove tin foil from top of goblet, add boiling water, and stir." We did just that and it frothed and bubbled away for what seemed like a couple of minutes. I assumed, perhaps unjustly, that there were more chemicals than noodles in the designer-smart plastic container. I was reflecting on this when Graham suddenly startled me with a cry of, "My God, there's a mossie in the cab!"

It took me some moments to realize what he was talking about. But when he demanded, "Where's the DDT spray?" I knew it was war. The mosquito was zapped out of its socks by a squirt of Aroxol and fell onto the dashboard. I decided the time had come to spread out my sleeping bag on a strip of grass at the edge of the parking lot. I bade Graham good night. He checked that the windows were rolled up, locked the doors, pulled shut the curtains, and I was sure I noticed *Old Girl* shake with delight as he rolled into his bunk.

4. NATIONAL HOTEL, BELGRADE

NEXT morning I was woken by two military helicopters hedgehopping across the Danubian cornfields. Graham and I had guessed by the military traffic the night before that the Czechs and Hungarians were holding joint military maneuvers. It was impossible to see what markings these whirlybirds carried, but they were making low-level haste toward the Danube, where I supposed the imaginary invaders were attacking.

Graham slept through the raid and was still sleeping an hour later when I banged on his door. After a tea-and-toast breakfast, we left our parking lot at 9:40 A.M., soon turning onto a shaded road along which our progress was slowed by horse-drawn carts. The corn waiting to be harvested had turned brown and the trees were already tinged with orange and yellow, as the first timid frosts had struck early. Not a cloud was in the sky, and peasant women were decorating the roadside shrines with flowers.

We crossed the Danube a second time before reaching Tompa Customs, where the Yugoslavs collected a hundred pounds in transit tax, which they assessed on our manifest weight. We cleared Customs shortly after midday. Again, the character of the country made itself felt in the first few miles. Not only were the roads narrower and less well maintained than Hungarian highways, but they also were littered with trash that spilled over into the ditches and hedges.

We stopped on a paved shoulder for lunch twenty-four miles north of Novi Sad. Minutes later, Gordon Durno pulled in and parked beside us. He had taken a longer route through Budapest and, even though his truck was more heavily laden, still caught up with us. I told Graham

37

there was something wrong with the Davies driving strategy. Of course, he didn't appreciate that remark.

"You're needlessly pushing yourself. You end up completely worn out, start late next morning, and you're just not operating as efficiently as you might," I tried to tell him. I was sure a more rational work schedule would enhance his driving capacity and increase the number of miles we could cover in a day.

"Look at Gordon. He drives a longer route but doesn't overpush it, and he gets here at the same time as we do." I was annoyed, because I had wanted to go through Budapest and Graham had said it would take too long. Gordon could sense the dissension and was only too happy to add his own brand of mischief.

"I'll tell you how I did it," he volunteered.

When he got to Budapest, he said, he decided to give the Hotel Wien a miss and, feeling good, kept on heading south. I had to admit, once he launched into his narrative, the schedule sounded far from rational. "Got to the Windmill at half-past one this fuckin' morning," he said. The Windmill is a restaurant outside Kecskemét, in the orchardlands of Hungary. It had become a favorite British trucking stop, replacing Rockycany to some extent.

"I would have been there about midnight, like. But trust me, a proper bright cunt, like, ain't I? I normally come out of Budapest onto the expressway, and up the expressway. I thought, well, it'll be quiet tonight so I might as well go up the old road to see if anything's cooking: Bits of stuff going about, like.

"I had just come out of Budapest, like, fuckin' hell, there's a roadjam, isn't there? Flashing lights. They're washing the fuckin' road, like. There's a body in the road! There's a dead horse in the road! Something must have run into the horse, like. That's why they're washing the fuckin' road."

Graham and I were doubled up in laughter by now. Gordon was wandering about in front of the two trucks, hands in his pockets, telling the story like he was the one doing the bleeding. When he finished describing the mopping-up operation, he announced that the Windmill had been empty and no British trucks were around. "It's queer, this. Nothing's happening."

Graham agreed.

Evidently Gordon had seen no sign of Ossie MacIntosh, but we asked anyway. None, he said. Graham told him we feared that Ossie's

Ford Transcon had been hit from behind while parked for the night on the paved shoulder.

"Jeezus, was it bad?" Gordon asked.

"Oh, right as can be," Graham said. "The other bloke came right through his back door, didn't he."

Graham looked at his watch. Gordon caught the gesture and suggested we have some sandwiches.

"What you having—anything good?" Graham wanted to know.

Gordon thought he might make a few cheese and jam sandwiches. Graham decided we would have fried-egg butties. Not bad. While we were tending to our respective menus, Gordon explained that on his last trip to Saudi he had to drop his belly tank at Haditha, a Customs post on the frontier with Jordan, and pick it up again on the way out. "It just knocks the arse out of the job, like, doesn't it?" he complained.

That started Graham worrying again. "I can see what's going to happen. It'll bloody well bankrupt me, this one. I'd have been on my way back from Greece by now."

"How long have you been away, like?"

"Sunday. But I was home nearly two weeks waiting for this job to come up. I'd have been gone before if I'd taken another Greek job." Graham and *Old Girl* were Greek specialists. They had made over fifty trips to Athens in three years, which wasn't bad going.

"I left on Sunday, too, and you know, like fuckin' hell, it'll take me till Thursday to get to Belgrade. It must be failing me."

"A week to get to Athens," Graham said.

"Aye. I won't get my papers to the agent now till Monday. That's it: Forget about the rest of the day. Won't get loaded up till Tuesday. Geordie, you know, got there two weeks ago. On the Monday he sees the agent and he didn't get loaded up till Thursday. Because they put Piraeus on his paperwork instead of bloody Athens."

When drivers start trading stories a degree of paranoia always seems to creep in. To anyone not accustomed to hearing truckers kibitz about life on the road, Gordon, who was from Aberdeenshire and spoke with a rolling brogue, might have sounded like an uncouth redneck. Certainly he was no gentle-mannered pilgrim. He did have a slightly twisted smile, even an occasional evil glint in his eye, and he also rubbed his overly round paunch with the kind of satisfaction that suggested more beer and lager had swilled through it in the past week than most men might consume in a year, though he was by no means an inordinately heavy drinker. In fact, like most truckers we met, he adhered to a kind of code of chivalry that made him, in addition to being naturally warmhearted, an especially considerate user of the road.

"Yeah, it's some game, isn't it?" Graham remarked.

"Oh, aye," Gordon replied. "The trip before, I'd unloaded and went to bed on a Monday night. You know when I next got to bed? Fuckin' Thursday night. And the foreman says, 'Keep your tachos right. Drive legal, like.' "

All heavy vehicles are required by law to have tachographs fitted onto their speedometers. The tachos record the speed of the vehicle and the number of hours it has been driven. This is done on a circular graph known as a tacho disk or tacho card, which is inserted under the speedometer gauge. Drivers must insert a new disk every day their truck is on the road. Also called "spy in the cab" and "expressway Frisbees", they are detested by the drivers.

"Driving legal" is a constant concern. Not only do drivers have to know about such things as axle weights, gross tonnage regulations, legal dimensions, maximum driving hours, and diesel restrictions, they also must be equipped with the right road permits and make certain their *carnets de passage* have not expired, that their insurance coverage is valid for the countries they run to, whether war risk is exempted, and whether weekend driving bans exist for all or part of the year in the countries they transit. "There're so many rules and regulations in this job you've got to be a lawyer to work 'em all out," Graham said.

"You know they tried to nail me for a careless-driving charge on the M6 the other day," Gordon announced. We were talking window-to-window while eating our sandwiches. "Well, it wasn't fuckin' me. They said it was fuckin' truck No. 123 for a start. Our boy at the office went through the tacho cards, right. Truck No. 123 on that date was in fuckin' Saudi Arabia. He wrote to the police and said, 'You'd better check your fuckin' facts, because that truck 123 was in Saudi Arabia on that date. You'll have to come again.'

"What does this fuckin' copper do? Well, he comes back and says it was truck No. 122. Well, I was the only one in the fuckin' area on that date, see. So we wrote back again and said there was still some mistake. Now the head copper in Liverpool got involved. He gave me the shout to come in. When I got back the next time around, I said fuck this, we've wasted enough time on this thing already. So I went to see this copper in Liverpool. He says to me, 'What's all this carrying on about?'

" 'Fucked if I know, mate,' I said. 'Maybe you can tell me, like.'

"So he started hassling me. This other cunt was fooling him. I was supposed to have been out in the middle lane with three trucks in front of me and I moved into the outside lane and fuckin' overtook the three of them and he was behind me, ass wet and all. It was at midnight, you see, on the twenty-sixth.

"We got the tachos out again and I was fuckin' parked up at Willows services at like half-past five on the twenty-sixth. I'd unloaded at Bradford and had Wigan to do next. But the foreman at Bradford said, 'Stop somewhere en route and go up to Warrington in the morning and pick up a pallet of fuckin' paper on your way back to the yard.' So I didn't even leave Willows till seven-thirty in the morning. I was counting the fuckin' hours off, like. Also, I had the parking ticket from the Willows services, see.

"So I had to go back and see the copper, like. So fuck me, it was not even on the M62. I was on the M62, see. It was the M6 at Knutsford where this offense supposedly took place. So I gave him my tacho cards and parking ticket and he put them all away. So I bet there's a letter waiting at my house saying, 'Sorry, there's been a mistake.' "

"But was it you?"

"No. But the copper at Knutsford has been after us for a while because we made a cunt out of him twice, like. Called him a liar in court and he didn't like it."

"Yeah, they don't, do they."

"And then last Christmas Eve our foreman was out in one of the trucks. On his way back to the yard, his tacho was right and everything, this same fuckin' copper stopped him. He says, 'Right, the next time I see one of your trucks I'm going to stop it. And the next one, and the next one. I'm going to stop you all till I put you off the fuckin' road.' So we fuckin' filed a complaint against him."

"Ah, they don't like being buggered about, do they?"

"Oh, no."

"Smithie's painted one of his yellow now. He keeps changing bloody colors so the police can't find him."

"Yeah, at least ours are properly taxed."

"Has Robbie been caught for that yet?"

"No."

"It's bloody frightening, really. Something should be done about it."

"They should take a tax on diesel, or on the number of days a wagon remains in the country—the way the Swedes work it. Either that or we should start leaving our tractors in Belgium, like Astran and Priors are doing now."

"I mean, to pay thirty-one hundred pounds a year in road tax— that's diabolical. We're only on the roads in Britain about fifteen days a year."

We rinsed our kitchenware and as it was getting on to 3:00 P.M. decided we'd better head out. "On you go," said Gordon. "I'm heavy. I'll follow you."

North of Novi Sad, on the E5 motorway, we were pulled over by a policeman on a motorcycle. He wanted to see our tacho. Graham is a stickler about driving within the seventy-kilometer-per-hour (forty-five-mile-per-hour) speed limit. His tacho had not wavered once above the seventy-kilometer-per-hour line. The policeman handed it back and waved us away again. There was a time, however—and not so long ago—when Yugo police would not have given back the tacho until an appropriate ransom, such as a D-mark note or a pack of Marlboros, had been paid. Now they don't bother. This indicated to me that their standard of living must have improved one hell of a lot.

An hour later we crossed the Danube for the third and last time, heading for Zemum, a town on the right bank of the Danube where the Sava River joins it. I got out the notes of an interview I had before leaving with Miroslav Lazovic, a director of the Museum of Art and History in Geneva, and read them aloud for Graham. Zemum, Lazovic had told me, used to be an important economic and trade center. The town is directly across the Sava from Belgrade, which in the eighteenth century marked the northern limit of Ottoman expansion into Europe. Although part of the Austro-Hungarian Empire, the people of Zemum were Serbs, and because of its strategic frontier location it became an important Austrian Customs post through which trade with the Ottoman Empire was channeled. In those days, Serbia's principal export was pigs. They left Zemum on their trotters for slaughterhouses in Budapest and Vienna.

The oldest building in Zemum is the eighteenth-century Karamata House. It belonged to a merchant family of Greek origin who had fled the Ottomans with a sackful of gold ducats. One of the Karamatas revolutionized the pig trade. He built a series of pigsties at intervals of one day's march along the road from Zemum, through Budapest, to Vienna. He then dispatched herds of piglets along the road in the charge of lowly paid herders. The pigs rested each night in one of the Karamata sties and fattened themselves during the day on roadside grass, arriving nicely plump in the two great cities, where they were sold for such profit that the Karamatas soon became bankers. They founded the Danube & Adriatic Bank, which grew into one of the largest private banks in the Balkans until nationalized by Tito. When the emperor of Austria visited Zemum in the eighteenth century, he stayed at Karamata House. No longer was it the modest home of pig merchants but a banker's mansion. The imperial arms that are today still displayed on its façade testify that the Karamatas became one of the empire's most influential families.

"You ever thought of transporting pigs?" I asked.

"Not bloody likely. Can you imagine the mess they'd make?"

"And the squeals."

"Oh, aye, and the stink."

"But you might become a millionaire," I suggested.

"Are you out of your mind, or what?"

"Me?"

He scowled, then laughed. "You're crazy. Absolutely crazy."

Today the frontier between East and West was no longer along the Sava, and Zemum, like Aachen, had been forgotten by history. The town had been virtually swallowed by Neo-Belgrade, with its drab high-rise apartment blocks, concrete consumer palaces called shopping centers, a giant conference facility, and at least two modern American-style hotels, which together combined to make it a socialist dream city. Strange, I thought, how much Neo-Belgrade resembled the urban sprawl around many American or British cities: gray, matchbox architecture that was impersonal and uninviting. I would have preferred Karamata House, but it was down by the river, and our route didn't take us that way.

The National Hotel, where we were headed, is on the outskirts of Neo-Belgrade. A rather more modest establishment than the nearby Hilton, it is run as a model of Yugoslav socialism by its employees who are also its shareholders. Because of the business it receives from the international trucking fraternity, the National Hotel not only has become notorious but also a small gold mine. Its restaurant is first-class by trucking standards, and rooms can be rented by the half hour so that greasy drivers can shower if desired and generally clean up there.

The National Hotel's shareholders have assured themselves much popularity among the fraternity by serving typically English fare such as steak and chips and London mixed grill. The drivers indiscriminately call the personnel George. The personnel retaliate by calling the drivers George.

We arrived there at 4:30 P.M. to find a squadron of other British trucks already in the parking lot. One of them was Steve Walsh's Volvo F12 painted, like *Old Girl,* in Whittle's colors. Steve came over and asked, "Where you been?"

"How long you been here?" Graham wanted to know.

"Yesterday. Took it nice and easy, like."

Graham looked disgusted. "My mate here says I'm doing it all wrong. Don't you start in on me now."

Steve winked at me, smiling. I was beginning to like him. Maybe we could yet instill some discipline in Graham. To say he didn't have any would not have been right. He had a lot. He had to in order to survive in this game. But if I could be pardoned for passing judgment, I feared the tension of the road and the pressures of his bank manager were getting to him. Only later, as our problems increased, did Graham give the impression of being at ease. Steve, on the other hand, went the other way—from euphoria to depression.

Steve was perhaps young for the job—twenty-six—but a steady driver, superb really, and as a mechanic he came well equipped to the calling of a long-distance trucker. His youthful enthusiasm, ginger hair, crooked nose, and inquisitive eyes gave him a Tom Jonesian air. In another age he might have been a highwayman's apprentice. In this age he was an American pop culture freak. He liked country and western music, Bruce Springsteen and John Denver, and had a Stars and Stripes flag hanging at the back of his bunk. Like me, he was a Gemini.

As we got to know him better, it became apparent that Steve, in spite of his outward cockiness, was really quite shy. He regarded driving juggernauts as a *macho* occupation, and driving them to the Middle East was *mucho macho.* He identified strongly with the *macho* aspect of the profession. He was in search of an idol, preferably someone with a barrel chest, fists of steel, quality tattoos, and a million miles of driving experience on the toughest, most dangerous roads in the world.

Truck driving is a subculture with a devoted following in Britain and on the Continent. At the Peter Forde Garage in Blackburn,

England, where the company for which Steve drove was headquartered, there is a mechanic called TIR John. He is crazy about trucks and dreams of becoming an international freight driver, although at twenty-six he does not have even an ordinary driver's license. He wears blue jeans with a large-buckle belt and a chain attached to an accordion wallet, has a Volvo jacket, Londra Camp T-shirt, and a pair of the Swedish clogs that many TIR drivers wear. Truck manufacturers promote a European truck racing championship, which TIR John follows and which has become a big sport, and he buys the two or three trucking magazines that come out monthly.

TIR drivers are not Clint Eastwood characters out of a TV serial, nor do they ride the wheels of adventure with carefree abandon. Their job is packed with tension and can be soul-destroying. They are forever courting tragedy. Danger of road accidents stalks them at every moment once they leave Western Europe, and the odds of a mishap, as well as the consequences, increase as they head south and east. By and large, they lead lonely lives. Many suffer from broken marriages, poor nutrition, lack of physical exercise. They are always fighting fatigue, and they get "the munchies" for candy, which gives them sugar rushes.

The requirements of the job make TIR drivers the jacks of many trades. They have to be part engineer, part banker, part diplomat, and part psychologist, linguist, and foreign-exchange expert, but above all they must have a bottomless mine of patience. Those who do not have all of these qualities in some degree will never remain long in the game. A garbled manifest, for example, is an affliction that can cause a truck to be turned back at a frontier or require the posting of an additional bond, causing days of delay. Steve had been confronted with such a problem at Dover; he played it cool and got away with it.

"Do you have a control panel on board?" he asked.

"Dunno. What's it look like?" Graham replied.

"Supposed to be a big mother with two red lights on top."

"Oh, yeah. It's on our trailer. Why?"

"They fucked it up, didn't they? It's on my manifest."

Graham said nothing. I thought, "Oh, shit, here's a problem."

"I got down to Dover on Monday, like, and the bloke at Customs looked at me manifest. He said, 'Aw right, then, let's have a look at this 'ere piece,' pointing to where it said I had this control panel. I suppose he wanted to see if it were electronic tackle or something. So I opened her up and he looked in. Weren't bloody there, were it? So

I called Leon, and he called Infrasystems, then he says, 'Well, Steve, we'll have to tread carefully with this one.'

"Leon explained to the Customs bloke that we were two trucks going out together, only I'd been delayed a day. He said they'd fucked it up at the factory and loaded the other trailer with the control panel. Finally the bloke threw his arms in the air and said, 'Aw right, only 'cause it's Whittle,' and tells me, 'Zipper 'er up.' Fucked if he didn't put a seal on her. Finished, like. Poof, I'm off, thinking, bloody hell, if the trip begins like this, what's the rest of it going to be like?''

"Hope nobody else wants to look inside. Otherwise we might have a spot of explaining to do,'' Graham said.

"Only too right, mate. Fucking hell!''

Steven Richard Walsh came from a town near Blackburn, about twenty-five miles southwest of Blackpool. At seventeen he began an apprenticeship as a mechanic, working for a national package delivery firm at their depot near Blackburn. He became a foreman with them and then passed his HGV test. (HGV stands for Heavy Goods Vehicle. All British juggernaut drivers are required to have a Class I HGV license issued by the Ministry of Transport, for which they must pass a test. Normally, insurance companies will not cover a driver for foreign risk, particularly on the Middle East run, unless he has had two years' domestic HGV experience.) He married at twenty-two and, drawn by the prospect of higher wages, went "mechanicking" with two other firms, stopping nine months with one and ten months with the other before deciding to go into business for himself.

He bought a garage and called it Truck Stop Repairs.

"I had loads of work, but the problem was getting paid. Sometimes I had to wait seven to nine months to get me money. Some still owe me. Mostly owner-drivers.

"I did that for twelve months and decided to get out while still afloat. I had a new home at the time and my wife was panicking.''

He drove a cattle truck after that and said it paid good money. Then about a year ago Steve got a call from the Blackburn haulers Howell & Taylor. "How would you like to do the Middle East?'' this fellow asked him. They ran a service called Middle East Express.

"I said, 'Oh, hell, why not?' '' His marriage was on the rocks and he wanted a change.

His first job was to recover a truck that had been left in Greece. It was the famous blue Mack we would hear about later. The gearbox had gone at Evsoni, and it had to be towed to a garage in Salonika. "I drove it to Munich and picked up a trailer. Loaded the trailer and took it back home.''

Steve later transferred to Peter Forde Transport, which took over from Howell & Taylor after it went out of business, and ever since had been pulling Trans-Arabian trailers from Northampton to Iskenderun. The trailers were loaded mainly with personal effects of Iraqi and Syrian students returning home.

The other drivers at the National included Terry Grant, "off" Grangers, pulling a forty-foot refrigerator with a load of chilled meat for American military bases in Turkey; Bob Anderson, another of the Falcongate crew on his way to Baghdad and Qatar; and Chris Lawrence, a Scot who drove for John Gaskell, the Blackburn owner of a six-truck fleet. Chris, who was returning empty from Athens, had picked up an English hitchhiker named Karen. After spending a year in Greece, she was returning home for her sister's wedding. One of the first questions Graham asked was whether anybody had seen Ossie MacIntosh. No one had any news of him. Graham explained what he thought had happened.

We also mentioned Sunday's consternation on Dover Docks. None of the lads had heard about that, either. This surprised me. I would have thought the news of a silk-stockinged driver found dead in his cab, tool in hand and a garrote around his neck, was something that would have traveled down the truckers' bush telegraph at very near the speed of light. Perhaps we weren't making such bad time after all.

Terry, a tough cockney who had been driving to the Middle East for more than ten years, was disturbed by the story. "Fucking hell," he said, "this is going to give us truckers a bad name."

We moved to the restaurant terrace, where we continued the ritual telling of war stories, Chris Lawrence assuming the chair. The session moved into high gear. Lawrence had a peppery tongue and a deep voice that commanded attention. Sitting back, relaxed, his shirt was open to his navel, showing a chest covered with tattoos. He sounded like a Scottish W. C. Fields. "George, be a sport and bring some more beer," he called to the head waiter.

"Yes, George, coming right away."

"I got told one the other day and I don't know whether you've heard it, but the fellow reckons it were a true story," Chris began.

"This Englishman was driving down to London and he breaks down. He can't get the wagon started again. So, coming down the road behind him was Paddy in one of those green Kelly Freight fridges. The

Englishman signals Paddy to stop and says, 'Will you do us a favor, mate?'

" 'And what will I be doing for ya, now?'

"He said, 'Are you empty?'

"He says, 'Ya.'

"He says, 'I got a load of penguins on board. Will you take 'em down to the zoo for me? There's forty quid in it for you. I can't get the fuckin' thing going.'

" 'I'll be sure, bejesus. Now throw them in the back.'

"So he gets these penguins in and off goes Paddy. In the meantime the Englishman gets his lid pump working and he's off down the road as well. But on the outskirts of London it's night now, he comes to a halt, jumps down, and has a look. Across the road are these fuckin' penguins. So he thought, 'What's going on?' Paddy is leading the penguins along the pavement. So he goes up to Paddy and says, 'Fuckin' hell, I told you to take 'em to the zoo. I gave you the forty quid.'

" 'I did take 'em to the zoo,' says Paddy, 'and there's some change, so now I'm taking 'em to the pictures.' "

After the groans and catcalls had died down, Bob Anderson reported that Paddy had a bit of trouble last week in Calais. "He called the foreman and said, 'Boss, I missed the ferry.'

" 'Well, what's the problem, Paddy? Take the next one.'

" 'But boss, you don't understand. I missed it by six feet.' "

Another chorus of groans was cut short when Chris announced, "Well, here comes Mr. Crack." John Hodges had pulled in and parked his blue Transcon. He was smiling like a Cheshire cat when he arrived at the table. "The one last night was a bit tasty," he confided. "I met her at the disco and went back to her apartment on the other side of Budapest. It cost me a hundred deutsche marks. But beautiful she was. I can tell you I wouldn't be doing this job if it wasn't for the crack." He took out his wallet and handed me two snapshots of girlfriends he had met along the road in Romania. "Oh, naughty, naughty they were, but lovely." He kissed one of the naughty ladies right between the legs. "Gotcha," he said before replacing her in his wallet.

John travels with a Polaroid camera so he can take pictures of the girls he makes love to in his cab. Then he saw Karen. They smiled at each other.

"They know what the game is, don't they?" Chris said when

Karen went for a shower. "They don't come out here on their mother's arm and expect Pullman service. I had to tell her, 'Keep your fuckin' feet off my dashboard.' I don't want my truck to end up like Hedley's wagon. There's so much grease on the floor you have to wipe your feet when you get out of the thing."

"George, where are those beers?" Bob Anderson asked.

"Coming, George."

Terry wondered what had happened to "that left-hooker Mack."

"The blue one that had the pipe go through it?" Steve asked.

"Oh, aye, that was Jag Joe," Chris answered. "He went off the road seven miles north of Belgrade, down into a big ditch, and they're just putting a pipe down, aren't they. One of those steel water pipes and it went through the front. Passed right under the seat. Would have taken his legs off it had been a right-hooker. He was in fuckin' anguish. He calls the foreman and says, 'I got a problem with the wagon. There's a pipe stuck in it.'

" 'What's that, Joe?' the foreman asks.

" 'I can't move the wagon because there's a pipe stuck in it.'

" 'Well, take the fuckin' thing out. Throw it away and get going, lad,' the foreman says.

" 'But,' Joe says, 'you don't understand. It's seven miles long, the fuckin' pipe.' Seven miles of water pipe. He would have fuckin' drowned if they'd turned on the water.

" 'Are you drunk, or what?' the foreman asks."

By this time everyone was limp from laughing. "That was Smithie's wagon," Steve said. "It got fixed, broke down again, and I drove it for a while afterward. Fucking breezy, it was."

"I would have walked first before I'd have got into that thing," Chris said. "It was like getting into a personnel carrier and driving over a minefield. It wasn't a truck. It was an embarrassment."

We moved inside and ordered dinner. George beamed benevolently at us. The bill was adding up to many thousands of dinars and more profits for the shareholders.

Over chunks of mixed grill, Graham asked Chris how his brother was. "Fine, now," Chris said. "But he doesn't enjoy coming out here anymore."

"Did they ever get the Greek who ran him over the cliff?"

"Oh, aye, at the frontier."

"I was coming along the road near Pretty Jane"—Pretty Jane was a Yugoslav town whose real name was Predejane—"and I saw this cab sticking straight up in the air. 'That's English,' I thought. And this fellow was staggering up from the ravine, blood all over 'im. It was Chris's brother, on his first trip to Athens.''

''You see,'' said Chris, taking up the story, ''I was in front, and when I saw my brother was no longer behind me I pulled up by the hotel on the bend at Pretty Jane to wait.''

''When I got to him,'' Graham continued, ''he kept on about this bloody Greek who had cut in front of him. He had to get so far over that his back wheels caught on the shoulder going around an inside corner and pulled the whole truck into the ravine. All Chris's brother had, fortunately, was fifteen stitches. A tree saved the whole thing from rolling down the cliff into the river.''

''Oh, aye, the tree pushed the front of his motor in. Almost killed him,'' Chris said.

''Was a good job for him that the hotel manager spoke English. I remember him telling you, 'Will you just do as I say. I'm trying to help you.' ''

''That's right. He and the magistrate were doing all this boozing and then we had to give them this grub job. Finished up we had to pay for the whole bleedin' lot. 'Thank you very much. It was a nice meal. You can take your wagon now and go. It's down the mountain.' They went home full of grub and pissed as rats.''

While Chris was explaining how they got his brother's truck back on the road, John was talking to Karen about crack. Chris was eyeing this and getting madder by the minute. John was trying to convince her to ride down to Istanbul with him. The only problem was that John had to go the Bulgie route, and Karen had no Bulgarian visa. Finally, about midnight, Chris left the table, announcing he was leaving early in the morning. He told Karen her gear would be on the back of the tractor. She had been evicted. John was delighted.*

---

* The Lawrence family was struck by a double tragedy over the next five months. Chris Lawrence's eighteen-year-old son was killed in a road accident in Greece in November 1986. Three months later, returning from a particularly difficult winter run to Athens, Chris Lawrence was trapped belowdecks and drowned when the Townsend Thoresen ferry *Herald of Free Enterprise* capsized off Zeebrugge on March 6, 1987.

5. "WE UNDERSTAND. YOU'RE BRITISH."

WE left Belgrade the next morning at 7:00 A.M.: six trucks rolling in convoy across the Sava and through the city of Belgrade on the Trans-European Expressway. Steve Walsh was in front. We were followed by the two Falcongate trucks driven by Gordon Durno and Bob Anderson. After them came Norman Martin, a third Whittle driver who had pulled into the National during the night. Norman was driving his own Leyland Roadtrain with twin axles on the back of the tractor. Terry Grant, with his Granger refrigerator, was at the back door.

Chris Lawrence had already left for Zagreb when we departed and John Hodges, who was going Bulgie to Istanbul, was still asleep, curtains drawn. There was no sign of Karen.

The rain had caught up with us again, leaving the roads greasy. In the left lane going north we noticed a car had run up the back of a truck. A mile farther down the road another Yugo truck was immobilized in one of the northbound lanes. Its back axle had fallen off, and traffic was backed up for miles.

We were heading for Evsoni, a town across the Yugo frontier in northern Greece. We were traveling along one of Europe's earliest trade axes, the Morava–Vardar corridor. The part of it we were now on was known to the Serbs as Czarigradski Drum, literally the Way to the City of Emperors. The Romans, in all their wisdom and engineering might, had used it, as had the Goths, the Huns, the Crusaders, and the Ottomans. All morning we drove south along it, through the Serbian hills. Covered with patchwork fields and hardwood copses, they formed a suggestive landscape that for four hundred years had witnessed the skirmishing between East and West. Thirty-six miles

51

from Belgrade and to the east of our route stands the Danubian town of Smerderevo. In the fifteenth century it had been the site of a decisive Serbian defeat.

I was rummaging around, looking for my notes. "My mate's always losing something," I had overheard Graham complain to Bob Anderson at the National.

"But Graham," I protested, "what do you expect? You've got everything in that truck but the kitchen sink. I mean, there's the cooker, the fridge, the pots and pans, a ton of food, even a dented teapot."

"Whatcha lost now?" he wanted to know, noticing my agitation.

"Nothing," I said obstinately.

"Come on, you can tell me," he coaxed.

"My notebook."

"It's there, behind the fridge," he said, delighted.

So it was. Relief. I turned to the notes of my interview with Miroslav Lazovic. "You want to hear?" I asked.

"Sure, go ahead." It was a change, after all, and Graham, though he knew a lot about the history of Lancashire, didn't have much idea about the history or culture of the countries he drove through. He never had time. It was always drive, drive, drive.

The Serbs, I began reading aloud, had filtered south from Galicia along the river networks of central Europe to settle in the Balkans in the sixth and seventh centuries. Except for a brief spell of a hundred years around the time of Stephen Dushan, who strangled his father to become the grand *zhupan,* they never really had a kingdom of their own. They traveled along the routes of commerce, from market to market, living in tented encampments that grew ever more elaborate.

In earliest times Serbia was called Rassi, so it is speculated that they might have had a chief city called Rass, but no trace of it has been found. Their history is tragic. They were a mobile people who converted to Christianity in the ninth century. Some of their princes traveled to Jerusalem and brought back artists to decorate their churches. But all through this period they were under constant pressure from the Bulgars and Ottomans. In 1371 the Serbs fought their first major battle with the Turks on the banks of the Maritsa, in the heart of the Balkans, and were defeated. They fought a second battle eighteen years later on the plain of Kosovo, farther to the west, and killed Sultan Mohammed Suliman. For a time the Turks withdrew, but soon returned, and by 1459 had pushed the Serbs into the notch of land between the south bank of the Sava and the Danube. At Smerderevo, the fate of the Serbs was decided for the next four centuries. Repression and massacre followed their frequent rebellions.

At Nis, the corridor split in two. The eastern fork, being the most direct route to Constantinople, now Istanbul, went through Bulgaria. This was the continuation of the Czarigradski Drum. The southern fork descended to Salonika. At this strategic crossroads the Turks had built a tower in which was imbedded nine hundred Serbian skulls. In Serbo-Croatian it was called the Tyele Kula (Tower of Skulls) and was intended to discourage other Serbs from rebelling against the Ottoman might.

Norman Martin left us at Nis. He was taking the Czarigradski Drum to Istanbul. The rest of us continued south. We were also going to Istanbul, but by the longer "touristic" route along the Aegean coast.

Nis dominates the Morava Valley, down which we had been driving since bypassing Smerderevo. Where the valley broadens into a rolling plain, in the third century the Romans destroyed an Ostrogoth army, thereby assuring the empire's survival for another hundred years. Twenty years later, the future Emperor Constantine was born within the city's walls. We had no interest in Nis other than it happened to be where the expressway ended and a tollgate barred our unimpeded passage onto the old two-lane highway that was no joy for juggernauts to travel.

We were heading for Leskovac, where in early summer British refrigerator trucks sometimes backloaded cherries for English supermarkets. The parking lot behind the YugoPetrol station, next to the Atina Motel, was an habitual lunch stop for British trucks. When we arrived there at 11:30 A.M., the weather was still overcast but not raining, and the roads were dry. We brewed tea, made sandwiches, and relaxed for an hour before setting out again. Terry took the lead. He wanted to get to the border ahead of us to see "the doctor." The refrigerated meat he was carrying had to be inspected by a vet, even though it was in transit under Customs seal. More bureaucratic nonsense.

The Morava flows north to the Danube. It rises near Skopje, the capital of Yugoslav Macedonia. Skopje itself is on the Vardar, which we picked up after sighting our first mosque and minaret, a sign that the Orient was approaching. The Vardar flows south to the Gulf of Salonika. Its gorges can be treacherous. Just how treacherous was demonstrated when we rumbled out of a sharp S-bend before the first

tunnel to find a Yugo tractor-trailer heading in the same direction as
ourselves, over on its side on the left shoulder, its snout almost
touching the tunnel entrance.

The driver was standing beside his cab, looking dazed. He had
bandaged his arm and removed a few things from the cab through the
broken windshield; they were piled neatly by the roadside. We slowed
and raised our hands, as if to ask what had happened and whether he
needed help. He gave us a thumbs-up signal, so we drove on. There
was a strong wind gusting through the gorge, which at that bend had
hit us sideways. The Yugo driver had undoubtedly come into the curve
too fast and, possibly top-heavy, had been flipped onto his side by a
sudden gust.

South of Titov Veles, once a Roman military post, the wind was
pushing us from behind. Graham was pleased. "Helps save diesel,"
he said. "Strange, you know. If your wagon gets tired, you get tired.
If there's a headwind, you can hear her groan. The motor strains, and
so do you."

We were all in a better mood after letting off steam at the National
Hotel the night before, and we were also into a more rational routine.
When we arrived at the Yugoslav border post of Gevgelija, the
Customs police passed us through without checking our seals. We set
our watches ahead one hour to Greek time—6:15 P.M.—and entered the
line of trucks waiting to clear Greek Customs. We had no problems.
The Greek Customs inspectors were good-natured, and by 7:00 P.M. we
were parked outside the Shell service station at Evsoni.

"Did you see that Yugo changing his wheels?" Gordon asked as
he swung in beside us. "Funny bloody way to go about it, don't you
think?"

"How did he manage it?" I asked.

"Too bloody fast into the corner, and his fuckin' load shifted. Or
else had one too many plum brandies."

We assembled upstairs, over the service station and truckers' shop,
and ordered beers and grub. The place used to be called Chris's, but
Christos, the chef, had recently opened a restaurant down the road,
next door to the BP station. Maria, his sister-in-law, who still worked
at the Shell station, said Christos had made a mistake. But from what
we heard Christos didn't seem to be doing too badly. Each month he
drew more business away from the new owners of the Shell station. On
the way home we planned to pay Christos a visit and see for ourselves.

After dinner, a first round of Metaxa, the pungent Greek brandy, was followed by many more, and the conversation turned, as inevitably it does, to the problem of how to keep driving and make it pay. This had become the No. 1 concern for British owner-drivers. They have not seen a rise in freight haulage rates in eight years. Not only that, but British rates were being systematically undercut by the Turks, Hungarians, Bulgarians, and Romanians. The Bulgarians, with five thousand vehicles, have the largest TIR fleet in Europe. It is operated by the state-owned So-Mat company, with headquarters on the outskirts of Sofia. The orange So-Mat trucks are mainly Mercedes, Volvos, DAFs, and Scanias. They haul freight for half the normal price in order to earn hard currency. The Turks are just as competitive. They do it to keep alive.

The only thing that keeps the Middle East route viable for the Brits is that Saudi Arabia will not allow Communist-bloc vehicles onto her territory. With oil prices falling, the Gulf war, and economic crisis throughout the Middle East, truck traffic was drying up. Not only had it been hit by war and recession, but also the sea routes, with improved terminals, had again become competitive in shipping time and rates. We had been through one of those phases in Middle Eastern trade when overland transport was more efficient than sea transport. For a decade after the 1974 oil boom, British and other North European trucks had carried to the Gulf the dismantled infrastructure needed to build modern ports for handling maritime cargo. Now that the ports were built and the harbors were no longer congested, a container ship took only two weeks longer than a juggernaut to reach a Gulf destination.

What the drivers found most difficult to accept was that British freight forwarders like Davies Turner and even Whittle, whenever they could, used Bulgarian or Turkish trucks to ship British goods to Middle East and Balkan destinations.

"There's no sense in it, and there's certainly no bloody future. They're just cutting their own throats as well as ours. I tell you, the job's fucked," Terry Grant said.

Falcongate drivers going to the Middle East are forbidden by their foreman to take the touristic route through Greece because of a seaside spa called Kavala, where drivers have a tendency to lay over and spend a few days on the beach, trying to pick up the Australian girls who ride the double-decker "magic buses" from Singapore to London. Gordon was telling Bob Anderson he should have gone through Bulgie with Norman Martin. But Bob, who already had two blowouts on this trip and was short of money, insisted that the Yugo Customs officer at

Tompa, where he had entered the country, refused to let him exit via Gradina on the Sofia–Istanbul route. The Yugoslavs and Bulgarians have been insulting each other for centuries, and no love is lost between them.

Bob said the Customs officer told him: "Mister, if you go Yugo, you go Yugo all the way," and taxed him to exit at Gevgelija, which is more expensive, as it requires driving an additional two hundred miles on Yugo roads. Although short of cash, Bob kept ordering more Metaxa. "You're a *get*," Gordon kept telling him. *Get* in Gallic, I learned, is similar to *nebbish* in Yiddish. Gordon kept squinting at Bob, a Geordie from south of the border, near Hartlepool.

"Ask Bob who hung the monkey," Graham kept prompting me.

"Why?"

"To see how he reacts."

Legend has it, Graham later explained, that in the seventeenth century a foreign ship foundered during a storm off Hartlepool and the only survivor was a monkey. The people of Hartlepool, according to this tale, had never seen a monkey before, especially not a half-drowned one. After much debate over what to do with the creature, they finally hung it as a spy, and this to the town's eternal shame.

"If you go into a pub in Hartlepool and ask, 'Who hung the monkey?' sure as anything you'll get a punch on the nose," Graham said.

Terry, who had been listening to this, said the last time he stopped at Evsoni he had been quietly eating his dinner and almost got punched on the nose without mentioning a monkey. He and a mate were watching a table of old Middle East hands, including the dean, Dick Snow, reminisce about the pioneering days on the route. The reminiscers were celebrating Snowie's supposed last trip, and it went on till the early hours of the morning. The party finally degenerated into a donnybrook, with Snowie turning Terry's table upside down. Terry's friend was cut on the arm by a flying ashtray. Snowie passed out. Next morning Terry tried to apologize to Maria for the upset. "It's all right," she said coldly. "We understand. You're British."

6. KAVALA

ON Saturday morning we said good-bye to Gordon Durno and set sail for Kavala beach. Bob Anderson was repairing a tire and said he would join us at Kavala. Terry had left ahead of us, and everyone seemed to think we would be in Istanbul by midnight. I doubted it, knowing the attractions of Kavala.

One of the first things anyone who wants to become a long-distance trucker must learn is that there's a big garbage can, and it's situated right outside your window. The British are especially renowned for throwing their trash into the big garbage can, and Graham engaged in some housecleaning this morning as we rolled down the fifty miles of expressway to Salonika. He tossed empty cigarette packs, Coke cans, paper towels, used teabags, everything, out the window as he sang along with a tape of "My Old Man's a Dustman, and He Wears a Dustman's Hat." The sun was out, the little twenty-four-volt refrigerator was working a dream, and Graham was in a good mood.

We passed Pella, the ancient capital of Macedonia, and circled around the back of Salonika, following a Greek military convoy. We also saw what happens when a trucker tosses a lit cigarette out of his cab. A ferocious grass fire had been burning on the city's outskirts for three days and, according to the previous evening's TV news, had gutted six outlying factories. The military convoy, followed by the Whittle convoy, trundled through the midst of the flames, which were licking at our tires, and we had to roll up the windows to keep out the smoke.

Salonika had been founded in 316 B.C. by Cassander, one of Alexander the Great's generals. Cassander had named it for his wife,

57

who was Alexander's half sister. When the Romans conquered
Macedonia, they made Salonika the capital of a province. The city, on
the most direct route from Egypt and Palestine to Rome, enjoyed seven
hundred years of prosperity under Roman rule. Travelers who landed
in Salonika's port embarked on the Via Egnatia to the Adriatic coast,
where it was but a short hop across to the Italian mainland at Brindisi.
And as it was at the gateway to the Morava–Vardar corridor, it
commanded access to the shortest land route into central Europe.

From earliest times Salonika had a large community of Jewish
traders. St. Paul, who counted many of them among his converts,
addressed two epistles to the Thessalonians here. When the empire was
split between East and West, Salonika rose to become the largest
metropolis in the East after Constantinople, eclipsing even Antioch and
Alexandria. This lasted as long as Byzantine warships remained
masters of the Mediterranean. When the Saracens became a sea power
they spread chaos through the Aegean. In 904 they sacked Salonika
and sold twenty-two thousand of its citizens into slavery. For the next
three hundred years the city of Cassander slept.

When the leaders of the Fourth Crusade humbled the Byzantine
Empire in 1204, they proclaimed Baldwin of Flanders the first Latin
emperor of Constantinople. Baldwin's largest fief became the Kingdom
of Thessalonica, which he awarded to Boniface, Marquis of Montfer-
rat. Boniface, however, didn't keep his crown very long. Three years
later, returning to Salonika along the Thracian coast from a meeting at
Ipsala with Henry of Flanders, Baldwin's brother, he was captured and
beheaded by a Bulgar raiding party. Twice sacked by the Turks,
Salonika finally fell to them in 1430 and remained an Ottoman city
until British and French forces liberated it in December 1915.

Under the Turks, Salonika was not permitted to grow. The
Sublime Porte preferred the Czarigradski Drum from Constantinople to
Nis and neglected the old Via Egnatia. The hinterland fell into ruin,
and the hills overlooking the main highways became the haunts of
bandits. But the Greeks to some extent promoted this state of
decadence, because they found that the number of Turkish visitors
diminished in ratio to the inconveniences of the route. If the roads were
in good repair, the Turkish janissaries appeared only too frequently to
exact the sultan's tribute. If the roads were badly maintained, the
janissaries put off their visits, sometimes indefinitely.

When Salonika was returned to the Greeks in 1919, its population
was one hundred thousand. The population doubled in the early 1920s,

absorbing refugees expelled by the Turks from eastern Thrace and Asia Minor. The refugees brought with them skills for development, and today Salonika is Greece's second-largest city and seaport. The seaport is used by Yugoslavia for imports of Egyptian cotton, U.S. grain, and Asian tropical products. Altogether the port handles eight million tons of dry and bulk cargo a year, which is not an enormous amount compared to northern European standards. But the Vardar is not the Rhine, and Salonika will never be a Rotterdam. Cassander's city, like all urban centers, is a prisoner of her geography and hinterland.

The truck route goes nowhere near the seaside promenade or port, so we saw nothing that day of the Gulf of Salonika. Instead, the road to western Thrace and the Turkish frontier turned left beneath an underpass and climbed into the hills to the east of Salonika. Kavala was one hundred miles distant and the road followed the course of the old Roman military highway, the Via Egnatia, cutting across the top of the Chalcidice peninsula. We traversed to the Gulf of Orphani, reaching the coast at a place where a school founded by Aristotle had supposedly stood. Opposite the ruins were hot springs in which Alexander was said to have bathed when a student. A strong east wind rippled the sand along the beach.

"We've got to watch these Greeks," said Graham after a five-ton refrigerator truck raced by us, almost putting his outer wheels over the edge. "They're devils for running you off the road." Both of us were thinking of Chris Lawrence's brother and how he had been pushed off the road in the Vardar gorges by just such a maniac. We were coming to the head of the gulf, still following traces of the Via Egnatia.

Nobody seemed to know the origin of the name Egnatia. The highway, which runs six hundred miles from the Adriatic to the Bosporus, was built soon after Macedonia capitulated to the Romans in 148 B.C. For half a millennium thereafter history was made on the Via Egnatia. Caesar marched along it with his legions in search of Pompey and was reported to have covered one hundred miles a day for days in succession. Roman dispatch bearers could cover one hundred sixty miles in twenty-four hours. After hurrying across it in 42 B.C., Augustus defeated Brutus and Cassius at nearby Philippi. Nero built a chain of inns along it. And Emperor Aurelian, who defeated Queen Zenobia of Palmyra, was murdered on it by a secretary whose name was Eros. When Rome was divided between East and West, the highway remained a key artery in the final struggles of the empire. The fact that we were two juggernauts rumbling along it some two thousand years later, on our way to the Middle East, seemed almost a banality. We were bowling around a left-handed bend just before a bridge over the Strymon River when we were confronted by a magnificent carved lion sitting erect on a stone pedestal, perhaps eight or nine feet tall, on the left side of the road. It was the most handsome lion I had ever seen: elegantly slim, majestic, powerful, with an almost contemptuous sneer.

"Did you see that?" I asked Graham.

"What?"

"That lion?" Of course he hadn't had time to see it. A car was behind us, a narrow bridge ahead, and we were bearing down on a sharp right-hander to get onto the bridge.

"Can we stop?" I asked. The question was right off the wall, but the lion had taken me by surprise.

"Are you daft? Can't stop here." He checked his mirrors and concentrated on the swing into the rickety bridge. Our back right wheels just made it around the concrete abutment at the end of the bridge, which was certainly not wide enough for two vehicles. "Besides, we gotta keep up with Steve."

"Then on the way back," I badgered him.

"On the way back, maybe."

I suspected he knew that if he put me ashore here he'd have trouble getting me back again. I was left with my imagination, wondering from where this creature might have come. I learned later that it had been pieced together from fragments found in the immediate area by French archaeologists in 1936. Once it had been reassembled, they placed the creature on a makeshift pedestal salvaged from the foundations of an early Greek bridge over the river. It had become known as the Lion of Amphipolis, a city whose ruins lay over the hill on the left. We clattered across the narrow bridge and started to climb into the Pangeon Mountains. I looked backward for signs of the ruins, but with no luck.

We were traveling on a winding road to the south of Mount Pangeon, retracing the route taken by Xerxes the Persian on his march to Thermopylae and Athens in 480 B.C. We were temporarily off the Via Egnatia because it circled to the north of Mount Pangeon, whose precious metal deposits were already exhausted when the Romans became masters of Macedonia. A green valley lay on our right, and Mount Simvolon barred our view of the sea.

The hills around Kavala had been scorched the year before by a brush fire, reducing a forest of pines to charcoal. A bit of green underbrush had grown back, but much of the natural beauty was gone, perhaps forever. Before descending to the port we pulled over to the side of the road to admire the view of the bay, with the island of Thasos in the distance and the citadel seemingly at our feet. The sea was deep blue, the sky was bright, and Graham had suddenly forgotten we were in a hurry. It was 3:00 P.M. when we wound our way down into the town. The Kamares Aqueduct, built in the sixteenth century by Suliman the Magnificent to carry water to the citadel, runs through the center of Kavala. We drove under it, down to a sandy beach that arches around the bayshore for several miles to the east, and parked in front of a restaurant opposite the main cemetery. Terry was waiting for us together with two other British drivers and a Frenchman with a stainless steel tanker that Graham admired longingly.

"Hmmm," he said in apparent seriousness, "that fellow's got a big belly tank, hasn't he?" The Frenchman laughed. He was on his way home, full of Turkish chemicals, and he had two English girls with him.

"There's no justice," Steve complained of the Frenchman's good fortune. He was about ten years older than Steve, looked fit, and had a moustache that accentuated his well-sculpted Gallic features. He had just come in from the beach, and one of the English girls was rubbing the sand off his back.

Terry was sitting at a table inside the cafe with Stanley Mills, the original Mr. Bad Luck Driver. "Stanley's had his HGV license for ten minutes and says he's been everywhere, knows everybody," said Victor the Frenchman when we met him in Ankara two days later.

Victor was being unkind. Stanley is about the gentlest person anyone could hope to meet. He has large, sad eyes, is of medium build, and, like everyone else in the game, was trying very hard to make a living at it. Stanley was an owner-driver who, when I first met him the year before, was pulling a forty-foot fridge for Ryders, since bankrupt. This year he was pulling for Grangers, the same company that Terry worked for. Stanley was on his way back from Turkey and had been fined two thousand drachmas (ten pounds) for speeding.

"Unheard of," Graham said. "Nobody ever gets done by Greek coppers." They are regarded by truckers as the most consumer-friendly on the Middle East route. But it had happened to Stanley. The year before, after we had met him down the road at Frenchman's

Corner, he had jackknifed* going over a Greek mountain, and a motorist ran under his trailer.

"What happened to the motorist?" I asked.

"He wrote himself off," Stanley said without emotion.

When Stanley was brought before a magistrate, he explained that the accident occurred in the rain and he had lost adhesion on the marble chips the Greeks mix into their asphalt. The chips render the road surface extrahard and therefore more wear-resistant, but as soon as it rains, the chips turn the road into a bobsled run for vehicles. This road-surfacing technique has been abandoned. Stanley, at the time on his second trip abroad, was let off with a fine, but he did have a dead Greek on his conscience.

"Now I park when it rains," he said. "It's safer."

We had a quick bite to eat and decided to go for a swim. A bus was parked at the beachside in the camping site half a mile down the road, and Steve wanted to check out the passengers. We wished Stanley a safe journey home. Terry said he would wait for us at Frenchman's Corner, six miles this side of the Turkish frontier. The Customs post at Ipsala closes at 6:00 P.M., so we realized we would not arrive in Istanbul that night.

We pulled into the BP station at Frenchman's Corner after 9:00 P.M. In addition to Terry, three Dow Freight and two Dutch trucks were parked outside, and their drivers were in the Frenchman's cafe having a meal. They were on their way home, empty.

Leon Woltman, a large barrel-chested driver who had made his first run to the Middle East in 1973, was sitting in the far corner, apart from the others, quietly smoking his pipe. He was from the Wirral, in Cheshire, England. An ex-merchant seaman, he had jumped ship to work as a waiter in San Francisco. He planned to settle there until a U.S. marshal served him with draft papers. As he didn't relish serving with the U.S. Army in Vietnam, he spent the next six months in Australia at the home of a girlfriend. But when her father suggested that marriage might be the decent thing, Leon returned to the United Kingdom and learned to drive a tractor-trailer.

The two Dow Freight drivers were Eric Wall and Brian Hirst, both from Manchester, England. While parked at Londra Camp in Istanbul, Eric had picked up an attractive eighteen-year-old girl from County

---

* Jackknifing is when the tractor swings around onto the trailer. This occurs when the momentum of the trailer becomes greater than the momentum of the tractor, generally as a result of overbraking on the drive axle.

Clare in Ireland and was taking her home. He was busy fending off approaches from Terry, who had showered while waiting for us and was looking so spick and span I hadn't recognized him. Brian Hirst was getting drunk and baiting Leon with crude insults. We ordered pork chops and Greek salad and listened to the war stories whiz around.

Leon had news of a friend of his, Roger—"last names don't count in this game"—that had left him feeling blue. Roger, a veteran owner-driver, had almost been killed as a result of a blowout in Saudi. His truck turned over and he had a good part of the windshield imbedded in him. "But that's not all," said Leon. "He was pinned under the cab, unconscious. The Saudi police wanted to drag the wreck off the road and worry about getting Roger out later."

The local townspeople wouldn't let the police back their wrecker up to the truck until they had jacked up the cab and unpinned Roger. Once freed, he was bundled into a police cruiser and taken to the next town, where, instead of being admitted to the emergency ward of the local hospital, he was thrown in jail. This is standard procedure for any Westerner who has an accident in Saudi. He probably would have died had not some British medical staff working at a local hospital heard about it and been able to treat him as best they could while he was still detained in the holding cell. He was kept there for three weeks before the British embassy was able to arrange his repatriation. Leon said Roger would spend the next four months in the hospital.

"I won't drive to Saudi any more," Leon said. "They're crazy down there. It's too much hassle. You never know what's going to happen."

About midnight it came time for the bill. Brian suggested everyone should leave an extra hundred drachmas (fifty pence) for the waitress. Leon said to count him out. Brian, his eyes wild and bulging, took offense. He started yelling at the top of his voice that Leon was a disgrace to the profession. "I won't run with that cheap fucker ever again," he said. Leon was unperturbed. When it looked like things might get serious, four unsuspecting French drivers who were on their way to Istanbul walked in the door.

"Oh, shit," said Eric, "here come the Kermits."

Brian looked around, thinking it might be trouble. Leon calmly got up and walked away from the table. The rest of us followed. Brian was still muttering, "I'll never run with that fucker again."

7. LONDRA CAMP, ISTANBUL

SUNDAY morning, September 21, was cold and overcast. We had now been out a week and were beginning to show some wear and tear. Graham had burned his pants on the cooker, while I was feeling dusty after another night by the side of the road. With the rising sun we pulled away from Frenchman's Corner without breakfast in order to get to the border before Customs opened and traffic began to build up. Terry and Steve were in front. We brought up the rear. We parked in the middle of the road at 7:40 A.M. and had fifteen minutes during which to brew a pot of tea. There was a strong west wind blowing along the Thracian hills, bringing with it what looked like a stable weather front. Only one other truck, a Jordanian, was ahead of us.

We stayed in Greek Customs for half an hour, then crossed the long bridge over the Maritsa River into Turkey, setting our watches ahead one hour. The Maritsa rises in the hills near Sofia and runs eastward to Edirne before turning south to the Aegean. In the last part of its three-hundred-mile course it forms the frontier between Turkey and Greece and is heavily fortified on both sides. Turkish soldiers in full battledress, with bayonets fixed to their Korean War-model rifles, guarded the Customs compound, reminding us that Greece and Turkey, two NATO allies, were at bitter odds over Cyprus and control of the Aegean continental shelf. They looked even meaner than the Czechs.

After a five-minute wait on the bridge, an officer came out of a boxlike gatehouse and walked over to my side of the cab.

"Hello, meester. Passports, pleez." I handed them down and he scrutinized them carefully before returning them, then waved us forward. We rolled through a foot-and-mouth bath and moved into the outside of three lanes where eight other trucks were already parked.

We took our documents and passports to the *gumruk* house. *Gumruk* is Turkish for Customs and has become part of the *lingua franca* of truckers. While Graham waited to pay 210 pounds in road tax and have our TIR carnet stamped, I changed money, had a quick wash in the *gumruk* men's room, and then headed for the small bistro tucked into the northwest corner of the compound for a glass of *chai*—the long-leafed green tea that Turks delight in drinking. The only other driver in the compound whom we knew was Wolfgang Myer, the German Geordie, who pulled for Dow Freight. He was on his way home from Istanbul. The French brigade from the night before moved in behind us.

TIR trucks transiting Turkey (to Iran, Iraq, Syria, and the Soviet Union) are required to use one of two TIR routes, and no deviation from them is permitted. Drivers are asked to state through which frontier post they will exit, and this is marked on a pink sheet called a *Check Form for International Transport Vehicles with Foreign Licence Plates to Transit Turkey.* This form must be stamped at seven TIR *kontrol* posts across the country. Failure to do so brings a fine at best but also could entail a considerable delay in obtaining an exit visa. Should a driver lose his control sheet he is in big trouble. Other restrictions on TIR traffic exist and are strictly enforced. No stopping is permitted on roadsides; trucks must park in authorized TIR camps; the speed limit is fixed at seventy kilometers per hour (forty-five miles per hour) for foreign-registered vehicles, while Turkish trucks, which are much more dangerous, are permitted to go at eighty kilometers per hour.

Once the paperwork was completed, we returned to the truck to wait for "cabin control." After a few minutes a guard appeared and climbed into the cab. He looked distastefully at the boxes of food on the lower bunk. "What's dat?" he asked.

"*Camion* restaurant," Graham replied. In the *lingua franca* of the road, *camion (kamyon,* in Turkish) has become the universal word for truck.

The guard smiled. "No food box?" Many long-distance trucks carry a locker on the side of the trailer in which the driver keeps his food, cooker, and sometimes a refrigerator.

"No food box," Graham repeated.

The guard caught sight of an unopened pack of Marlboros lying on the cooker, placed there for him to see, and pocketed it. "Okay," he announced, and climbed down. We waited for the Customs inspector to place another seal on the tilt. The practice was to give him a fifteen-hundred-lire (1.50-pound) bribe. The inspector moved up the line, pocketing his 1.50 pounds in *baksheesh* at the back of each truck. Not to pay the *baksheesh* would risk hours of delay over some trumped-up hassle. The economics of this operation were interesting. We estimated that sixty trucks passed through Ipsala during a normal eight-hour day. If the inspector worked one week on, one week off, his rake off would be 1,260 pounds a month, which he would have to split with the other Customs officers on the same shift. By comparison, the minimum monthly wage in Turkey was fixed in 1985 at 41,400 lire, equivalent to just over 40 pounds, while the average monthly wage for a government functionary was somewhat over twice that amount. So even if ten other officers shared in the split, each probably managed to double his monthly salary.

By the time we moved out of Turkish Customs at 11:00 A.M. we had already said good-bye to Terry, who would turn right after Ipsala on the road to the Dardanelles, where he would catch the ferry to Izmir. We stopped at the first service station for another brew of tea. Crazy Steve, however, roared past and turned left into the second service station because he had spotted another Volvo F12 belonging to Peter Forde Transport, the Blackburn company for which he drove, taking on diesel. He circled between the pumps and told his friend, Fred Williamson to join us for tea.

The French brigade pulled in soon after, but they went across the road for a sit-down lunch with a bottle of decent Turkish red wine—*"un bon petit Pinot,"* said Janot Richin. He and Pascal Berger were on their way to Baghdad with construction material. Janot looked at me again. "Two drivers? Saudi Arabia! The Saudis won't let the French in with two drivers. Do the British have special privileges?"

"No," I assured him. "There is no anti-French conspiracy. But I have a valid visa and I don't see how they can leave me standing in no-man's-land."

"Don't be too sure. The Saudis are capable of anything. *Bonne chance, mon vieux.*"

We left Ipsala at 1:00 P.M., and once again the first few miles of a country told us a lot about its character. The landscape had completely changed. The countryside was vast, emerald-green in spring, brown in autumn, often snow-clad in winter. There were straight telegraph and electricity lines but no fences. Not much cultivation—mainly grazing land, some cornfields, and lots of horse-drawn carts. The road went straight over the low, rolling hills, often several feet higher than the surrounding countryside as new roads were built atop old ones, generally without a shoulder, which presented a problem if you fell asleep. The result was frequently fatal.

British drivers call Turkey Marlboro country. We soon found out why. Hardly fifteen minutes after leaving Ipsala, Steve was steaming up a hill when he was pulled in by a *trafik polisi* waving a "lollipop"—a wandlike stick with a round reflector with red on one side and green on the other. By the time we reached the hillcrest, Steve had pulled out again and the policeman directed us to stop. "Tacho, meester," he demanded. Our tacho was okay, but he asked for a pack of Marlboro anyway, which we had to give him to get the tacho disk back.

"Bloody scrounger," Graham remarked as he put *Old Girl* back into gear. Later we asked Steve how he got away so fast. He said he told the policeman he didn't smoke, which was true. But he added mischievously, "*Kollege* behind smokes Marlboro." The copper was only too pleased to let Steve go so he could catch us before we steamed by.

Each village we passed had its own mosque, and the minarets could be seen from afar. On one long incline we were overtaken by a herd of cars with flags flying and horns blaring. It was a wedding party. They were all over the road, even on the left shoulder. When we next passed them, they had pulled into a motel parking lot and were dancing in three large circles.

"They're having a whale of a time," Graham observed.

The wedding party, waving their flags, clapping, and stamping the beat for the dancers, cheered as we drove by and made signs for us to join them. They were full of the exuberance that has given this region of Turkey a special place in the country's aspirations. Although it comprises only 3 percent of Turkey's total land surface, Thrace offers the rest of the nation the hope of being able to distance itself from the squabbles of the Middle East.

Turkey has made large strides toward integrating into the European Economic Community. The first national trait of a Turk may be his hospitality, but the second is industry. Turks are hard workers. "Good bodgers," said Alan Wood, another English driver. "They can mold new motor parts with the most primitive tools, but the parts always work."

Industrious, they are. You have the feeling after spending time with them that they want to pull themselves by their bootstraps into the twenty-first century alongside Britain, West Germany, and France. Turkey has asked to become a full member of the Common Market. The European Economic Community in Brussels has been dragging its feet. Turkey's agriculture is among the most productive in the world. It grows more wheat than Canada and is the fourth-largest exporter of cereals. If Turkey is admitted, Western Europe, watch out! Turks have already colonized West Berlin with their migrant workers. The so-called Turkish *Gastarbeiter* are now hard at work colonizing the rest of West Germany, as well as Belgium and Holland. Most Dutch TIR trucks are driven by Turks. Another fifty million of them are still at home. The Turks actually want to work. The Arabs do not. And in spite of leftist agitation or Muslim fundamentalism, they are the West's staunchest ally in this strategic corner of the world.

Since time began, Thrace has been on the mainland route for Asian conquerors bent on subjugating the West and for European adventurers bent on conquering the Orient. According to some historians, the Hittites crossed into Asia Minor from this triangle in about 4000 B.C. Darius and Xerxes came the other way to do battle with the Greeks. The Romans bisected it with the Via Egnatia to speed their legions to the Eastern marches. Thrace has known other armies, including the Goths, Bulgars, Avars, Crusaders, Russians, and Greeks. But on this particular autumn Sunday, in spite of the exuberance of a colorful wedding party, Thrace seemed to us a lonely place, with only a few tumuli and some Osmanli bridges to show for the great events that have swept it by.

We descended into Tekirdag, ancient Bisanthe, reaching the Sea of Marmara coast by 3:00 P.M. To the south, the road went to Gallipoli. Gelibolu, as the Turks know it, holds a special place in their history. In 1354, one hundred years before the fall of Constantinople, Suliman Pasha acquired the Ottomans' first toehold in Europe, capturing Gelibolu fortress, and in 1915 Mustafa Kamel Pasha, who became known to the world as Ataturk, architect of the modern republic, successfully checked a British-led invasion of the Dardanelles by Australian and New Zealand troops in a battle that cost 252,000 Allied casualties.

Two hours later we reached the urban sprawl of Istanbul. On a hillside to our left giant earthmovers were scarring the countryside, scooping from the landscape the roadbed for a six-lane expressway that will link the Trans-European Expressway with the new Bosporus Bridge, scheduled for completion in 1992. Minutes later we were at the gates of Londra Camp.

The Londra Camp gatekeeper had us surrender one passport to ensure that we would not leave without paying the overnight parking charge of 1.50 pounds. The day had turned warmer and we churned up dust even though we crawled to the lower level of the five-acre TIR parking lot. Dust, I had learned, was an essential ingredient at truck stops across Europe, along with the odor of diesel and urine. Rather than use roadside facilities, which are generally disgusting, drivers prefer to piss against their back axles. Turkey, a country as large as France and the United Kingdom combined, is a land of many surprises, and its roadside lavatory facilities are no exception. Turkish lavatories, though only a hole in a tiled floor with a tap for water, are kept clean by attendants around the clock. For this you are expected to leave a five-pence tip and are roundly insulted by the young attendant if you do not.

Although we had already traveled 2,235 miles, the overland route to the Middle East really begins at Londra Camp. Here the European road net is siphoned into a single artery leading onto the Bosporus Bridge. When we pulled into the camp, some two hundred trucks were already parked and yet the place appeared empty. Some of the trucks had been there for days, waiting for backloading instructions, transfer of funds, spare parts, or simply their "empty papers," without which they could not depart. They were from all over Europe and the Middle East, and most were painted in distinctive livery.

They included the orange-and-red trucks of Pekaes, the winged-horse line from Warsaw, the green-and-yellow Hungarocamion trucks from Budapest, blue-and-white Finnwheels from Helsinki, the dirty blue Bar-Speed International heavyweights from Tehran, red-with-black-trim Iochum Transports from Marseilles, yellow-and-red Schenker Fracht from Salzburg, rust-colored Dow Freight Services from Swindon, and smartest of all, the Simba Transport Volvos from Gothenburg: white-with-blue-trim cabs, reversed to blue-with-white-trim trailers. The Bulgarians and Romanians shared their own Mo-Camp down the road.

Hungarocamion trucks were lined up along the western boundary, and maybe fifty Iranians with their big Macks, Whites, and long-nosed Volvos were grouped along the eastern wall. British drivers always parked in the same row in the middle of the camp, sometimes sharing it with the French, Dutch, and Swedes. John Hodges's Ford, bearing a sticker that said "Humpty Dumpty Was Pushed!" on a side window, was already parked, the curtains drawn, alongside a Scania 82M marked International Transport, Manchester, and a beat-up blue Volvo belonging to Eastern European Freight Limited, Haywood, Lancashire. Beside them were five Iranian Macks, leaving barely enough room for Steve and us.

"What the hell are they doing here?" I asked, referring to the Iranians, who had moved into British row. Last year the Iranian trucks had been concentrated in the eastern corner of the TIR park. Now they were spread all over the place.

"Dunno. We'll have to complain to the management," Graham answered, throwing *Old Girl* into reverse and backing her into the slot until—thud!—we hit the wall.

"Sorry about that," he apologized. We jumped down into the dust. A quick shower, our third of the week, which was not too bad, was No. 1 on the agenda, and then off to the self-service restaurant for an *Efes kontrol*.

When they get to Turkey, Middle East drivers joke about *Efes kontrols*. Efes Pilsen is the local Turkish brew, and about four of them in a row should knock any ordinary person onto the ground. Its precise strength in terms of alcohol by volume is a closely guarded secret, as are the ingredients, which magically turn your head into a cobbler's workshop the following morning. But it seems that British drivers can drink a score of them at a sitting and still find the way back to their trucks.

Londra Camp, so named because it borders the Londra Asfalti, for many years one of three asphalted trunk roads in Turkey, was opened in 1964 by Mehmet Döyme, who ran an import-export business in Switzerland before returning to Istanbul. His sons thought he was making a mistake and advised against it. But Father had a vision of expanding tourism and so bought what was then a cabbage field on the outskirts of Istanbul and turned it into a campsite for European tourists, who were beginning to explore Turkey as a cheap and out-of-the-way vacation experience.

The sons were astonished when a first-year trickle of holiday-seekers became a torrent, and in 1968 the Döyme family added a three-story motel and swimming pool to the campsite.

"Few TIR trucks were on the road then," said Mustapha Döyme, Mehmet's eldest son, who now runs the camp. Once the motel was completed, four Astran drivers started stopping at Londra. They included Dick Snow and Trevor Long, a former RAF wing commander who once was almost lynched by a mob in Baghdad and who was later expelled from Saudi Arabia for being "disrespectful," factors that contributed to his retirement from the game.

Astran is the pioneer in intercontinental trucking, and its drivers used to be considered the "princes of the road."

"That was before they hired Bob Hedley," commented Victor the Frenchman, an inveterate gossiper.

"They're still snotty buggers," Graham confirmed.

Astran was founded by two graduates of Guy's, London's famous teaching hospital. "It started as a lark, really," Bob Paul, one of the cofounders, told me when I met him at the Astran depot in Kent, south of London. "Mike Woodman, by then an RAF dental surgeon, drove back home with his family from Singapore in the summer of 1963. Coming through Afghanistan, a landlocked country, Mike noticed all this Russian and American aid pouring in. He wondered how it got there.

"Back in London, he talked to me about it. We'd been classmates at Guy's and played cricket together. He was convinced that overland trucking to Asia was viable. 'What do you think? Shall we give it a try?' he asked. I said it sounded exciting. And so we decided to go into business.

"At first people laughed. Neither of us had driven a truck before. Then, one day in January 1964, Linotype called us and said they had three printing presses to be delivered to Kabul. We said, 'Great!' and went out and bought a secondhand Guy Warrior: top speed, thirty-five miles per hour."

The first trip took three months to get to Kabul and back. They did it twice more. On the second and third trips, they backloaded Afghan carpets to sell in Hamburg and London. That was the beginning. They proved that overland transport to Asia was both possible and viable.

"The business was different then," Mustapha said, taking the tale a few years' farther down the road—in fact, to 1969, when Snow and Long started coming to Londra Camp. "British drivers dominated the route, and it wasn't so cutthroat. Sometimes they'd stay a week in Istanbul and relax. There was never any hurry."

The TIR drivers used to do most of their drinking across the highway at a brothel called West Berlin, since closed, and occasionally there would be fights. "But on the whole, I found there was comradeship that bound them together," Mustapha added.

He remembered Dick Snow and one of the Swedish drivers betting who could drink a beer faster underwater. They both plunged to the bottom of the swimming pool, fully clothed, with beers in hand. The Swede won. Mustapha personally favors the British, which is perhaps understandable, as his wife is English.

The first Bosporus Bridge opened in October 1973. It was also the year of the Yom Kippur War and the Arab oil embargo. Overland transport to Asia and the Middle East boomed, and with it the fortunes of the Döyme family. "Soon we were getting five hundred trucks a night," Mustapha said. Londra's record of nine hundred trucks was set during the winter of 1978, when the road to Ankara was blocked for ten days by snow.

Before the Bosporus Bridge existed, trucks had to wait half a day—or during periods of bad weather, up to three or four days—to cross the straits by ferry. They formed lines through the streets of Istanbul, and the Stambulis cursed them mightily for the traffic jams they caused. To the geographical barrier of the Bosporus was added the psychological barrier of having to wait for the ferry in an increasingly hostile environment: This was the ticking meter that slowed development of overland transport to Asia.

The bridge, built by an Anglo-German consortium at a cost of fifteen million pounds, took three and a half years to complete. Its 3,542-foot main span was at the time of its inauguration the fourth-longest suspended span in the world, after New York's Verrazano Narrows, San Francisco's Golden Gate, and the Mackinac in Michigan. A total of twenty-two thousand vehicles were expected to cross it daily. Fifteen years later, the traffic was estimated at more than thirty-eight thousand daily, necessitating the construction of a second, larger bridge five miles farther north on the Bosporus at thirty-six times the cost.

When it was opened on October 30, 1973, President Koruturk and half a million jubilant Turks walked from one continent to the other, shouting, singing, and dancing to the music of pipes and drums. It was not only a national event but also an intercontinental one, provoking immediate changes in the mosaic of trade.

For one thing, the 110-mile Suez Canal, the once-vital maritime link between the Mediterranean and Red seas, had been closed since the 1967 Six-Day War, and at that point in time it seemed unlikely to reopen in the near future. To reach the Persian Gulf, maritime traffic had to take the longer Cape of Good Hope route around the tip of southern Africa. But the Shah of Iran's insistence on quadrupling the world price of oil following the Yom Kippur War produced such a boom in oil royalties for the Gulf states that they started spending those petrodollars on extravagant development schemes—so-called petro-dollar recycling. It was either recycle or risk provoking the collapse of the international monetary system. And so recycle they did.

What followed was the golden age of the Persian Gulf. It lasted a decade. Development took off like a rocket, and ports that had seen their last major improvements in the days when the Ottoman Empire stretched from the Danube to the Arabian Sea were unable to cope with the cargoes they received. Ships lay at anchor in their roadsteads for months at a time before being offloaded. In desperation, attempts were made to offload ships waiting off the port of Jeddah by helicopter. Cargoes of perishable foodstuffs had to be jettisoned overboard. Quickly it was discovered that trucks coming overland from Europe could get the goods there faster, more efficiently, and at less cost. The Bosporus was the last major obstacle to unimpeded overland transport to the Middle East—apart from the roads themselves—and when the Bosporus was bridged it was like a dike had been unplugged.

The Döyme family benefited enormously from the boom in intercontinental trucking. They were at the right place at the right time to provide an essential service. As they remain at the intersection of the overland trade routes, they are sensitive to changes in the flow of traffic. "During the past year," said Mustapha, "TIR traffic has decreased by at least 50 percent. You can smell recession in the air. Because of the Gulf war, Iran and Iraq have no money. This affects Turkey because both countries used to be our largest trading partners. It means that we, too, must tighten our belts, so we have cut back our imports."

Goods ordered by Iran and still in the pipeline were being picked up by the Ayatollah's trucks when and as Tehran had the money to pay for them. It was done on a piecemeal basis. Tons of mechandise were standing in Turkish warehouses waiting for the letters of credit to release them. Iranian trucks sometimes had to wait five or six weeks in Istanbul. Because of settlement problems, Turkey had virtually stopped exporting to Iran, representing a trade loss of two billion dollars per annum.

Iranian drivers stranded at Londra Camp had become the Döyme family's biggest headache. Some of the Iranian drivers bring their families with them and live in their trucks like Gypsies. They get into fights. They traffic contraband. They fall ill or have accidents. In recent months, two Iranian drivers were arrested for transporting drugs. Their trucks were impounded. A third was arrested for blackjacking his colleague to death. Their two trucks were still standing in the lot.

Another aspect of the Döyme success story was that they had become so successful they were criticized for neglecting their clients. This put them in danger of losing their trade. During the winter of 1985–86, it is said that seventeen British drivers had to be repatriated because they came down with typhoid fever while stopping at Londra Camp. A number of German and Dutch drivers also took ill and had to be sent home without their vehicles. French drivers now avoid staying at Londra if they can. "The sanitary conditions are disgusting," Janot Richin said. "It's become so bad that we prefer to drive through to Ankara."

The medical upsets could have been caused by any number of hazards, from contaminated food and poor hygiene in the kitchen to impurities in the beer. The French tend to quench their thirst on wine, which if it becomes contaminated turns to vinegar and therefore is undrinkable. But not that Efes Pilsen. The ankle-deep mud in the TIR parking lot during the rainy winter season was another problem. The mud is mixed with a fair quantity of human garbage and waste as truckers are more used to the garbage can outside their window than the one at the far end of the yard, and they prefer the back axle to a distant toilet.

The locale that serves as the Londra Camp restaurant and bar is quite sinister—cold marble-chip tiles on the floor, bare tables and chairs, and stone walls, only two of which have windows. When we entered, a delegation of German drivers—whom the British call The Gas Company—sat in one corner, drinking beer. Their number included one woman built like a snub-nosed Mack and who is, I believe, Germany's only female long-distance truck driver. In another corner sat two Englishmen, a suicidal Dane, some Dutch, an Irish poet with an Australian mistress, and two teenaged British lovelies trying to hitch a ride home. There was an absence of French.

It must be said that British long-distance drivers are rather cliquish. They don't even like T-form Charlies. They have adopted a repertoire of names for their foreign colleagues. Austrians are called Alpine Turks and are not much appreciated because of their lack of road manners. The French are Kermits, after Kermit the Frog of Muppet fame. The Bulgarians are known as Wombles after *The Wombles of Wimbledon Common,* a kids' TV series in which one of the characters is Great Uncle Bulgaria. The Romanians are F-Troop, taken from an American TV comedy of the same name. The Dutch are the Tulips. The Turks are Awbies, a deformation of the Turkish word for *sir,* and Arab drivers are Ragheads because of the *kaffiyehs* they wear. Reference to the Germans as The Gas Company has provoked many a barroom brawl. The Germans retaliate by calling British drivers Island Monkeys.

British drivers also delight in bestowing zany nicknames on each other. Seated around a table in the bar at Londra Camp you might find yourself in the company of Egg-on-Legs, Daft Peter, Slippery Mick, Kidney Bass, Cat Weasel, Depression, Ratchetneck, Flying Pharaoh, Sex Machine, Safecraker, or Muleskinner.

Hanging out with the suicidal Dane was Tony Taylor, co-owner of the Eastern European Freight Volvo. Taylor had unloaded his shipment in Istanbul and was waiting for empty papers before heading back home. Alan Larsen, the Dane, had traded T-shirts with Taylor because Larsen wanted the one with ''The Highwayman'' written across it. ''See that,'' Larsen said with a snarl, pointing to the writing across his chest. ''It's my name. I'm The Highwayman.''

We asked Taylor if he had seen John Hodges.

''Not once. He pulled in last night, drew his curtains, and that was it.''

Probably down on Pig Alley, we surmised. Nobody knew whether he had a girl with him.

Larsen was in his middle forties, with cropped hair, a bristly gray beard, bulging biceps, earrings, and some quality tattoos. He claimed to have been a trucker for twenty years, though this was his first time as far as Istanbul. He was on some sort of a midlife ego trip and it had turned terribly bad. At six in the afternoon he was already pissed. He acted like an alley cat with his tail in the air, looking for a screw and a fight, but as soon as anyone reacted, he backed away.

''You're nothing but a fuckin' wet sock,'' he told Steve, who the first time around ignored him. Steve, in truth, was more interested in the two hitchhikers.

''You're a fuckin' wet sock. Not a goddamn driver,'' Larsen

insisted. "Here, read my name! What's it say? I'm The Highwayman. I'm tough. I'll kill you, son-of-a-bitch."

Steve finally told him to stuff it. Larsen threatened to land one on the button. Steve and Larsen were well matched: both of medium height and stocky in build. But Steve was twenty years younger, sober, and surer of himself. He quietly stood up and asked Larsen to repeat what he had said.

"I'm buying. What'll you have?" The Highwayman asked.

"Thanks. A beer," Steve replied.

When Larsen returned with the drinks he at once tried to reestablish his credibility. He said he had talked to the British driver being held by the police at the Romanian border with Bulgaria. "He's been there about two months."

We had heard over the bush telegraph that the Romanian police had detained a British trucker whose name we did not know. Apparently he had run over a Romanian peasant. We knew that other British drivers visited him on the way through and that the British embassy in Bucharest was trying to have him released.

"He's not in prison," Larsen confirmed. "He's sort of under truck arrest—not allowed to leave the country."

On his way through Bulgaria, Larsen had, from what we could gather, consumed one beer too many and was himself arrested. He went berserk when told to leave his truck and head for the cells. He picked up one of the Bulgarian policemen and was about to wrestle with him when two other policemen drew their guns and told him to get moving. He was fined nine hundred deutsche marks, released after twenty-four hours, and told never to come back to Bulgaria. He said, "If they try to stop me on my way home, I'll drive the fuckers down. At least I'll die with a smile. I'm The Highwayman."

Larsen drove a white MAN with green trim—a refrigerator truck with a refrigerator trailer, which is different from a tractor-trailer. He had unloaded on Thursday, reloaded Friday with five hundred kilograms of fresh flowers, and had been sitting at Londra Camp for two days, getting drunk. He had a bad case of shot nerves and couldn't get himself back on the road.

"It happens," Graham said. We never did hear how he made it home.

We decided the Efes Pilsen was all right but that rather than tempt Fate, we would try the "World-Famous Pudding Shop" in downtown Istanbul for supper. With the two hitchhikers we hired a taxi for the twelve-mile ride into town. The Pudding Shop grub was awful. Once a truckers' hangout, it is now cluttered with hippies on the road, modern-day pilgrims with bloodshot eyes and vacant faces. We decided to cross over Galata Bridge to a nightclub in Karakoy, passing on the way the Neve Shalom synagogue, where two weeks before, Arab terrorists had killed twenty-three Jews during their Sabbath services.

The clip joint we ended up patronizing charged us two pounds per beer, which is not within a trucker's wage. They refused to drop the price even though management was attempting to hire our two hitchhikers as "models." We returned to Londra Camp. The girls moved in with Steve for the night. I tried the Döyme establishment. At 4:00 A.M. I was woken by a mosquito standing on my chest. He was wearing tennis shoes. Soon a pack of them appeared off the ceiling and I was nearly bitten to death.

8. CROSSING THE BOSPORUS

A driving ban on heavy vehicles during the morning rush hours prevented us from leaving Londra Camp before 10:00 A.M. Almost immediately we became engulfed in a traffic jam that moved along the eight-lane beltway in spurts not exceeding ten miles per hour. A broken-down bus in the right-hand off-lane at Topkapi Gate was a contributing factor, but with no signs of the jam letting up before crossing the Golden Horn three miles away, we figured another obstacle lay ahead.

The slow pace was wearing for Graham as other drivers, with no respect for his size, kept on edging in on him, switching lanes, and jumping around. "Gaw on. Stay where you are!" he shouted at one idiot who kept dancing back and forth, looking for the breakaway. Each time the car moved in front of us, Graham had to regauge distances, check the mirrors, and maybe shift gears while allowing adequate braking time.

A juggernaut in Turkish traffic is not an easy beast to handle. But the slow-moving pace did give me time to reflect on the past grandeur and present realities of Istanbul. Its population of five million people made it Turkey's largest city. It advertised itself as the only metropolis in the world to lie in two continents. Two worlds really did meet here. We saw fair-haired women, dressed in European fashion, standing at a bus stop next to women in long Oriental robes and chadors. As we drove into Istanbul the day before we had noticed a painting on the side of a building of a bronzed beauty in a bikini, wearing sunglasses. She was a billboard-sized advertisement for Zeki Triko, makers of swimsuits and sunglasses. It was a pop-art masterpiece, really, except that

78

the radiant blonde had been splattered with gray paint, presumably by religious fundamentalists outraged by her show of near-nudity.

On our right were the still-intact walls of Constantinople, which had been built by Theodosius in the fifth century and which defied invaders for a thousand years. One hundred thirty feet high, they stretched for nearly five miles and looked as formidable to us now as they must have done to the Latin Crusaders who camped underneath them in the eleventh and twelfth centuries. The Crusaders, much like modern truckers, were forbidden entry into the city except in small numbers for fear they might rape and pillage.

"Gaw on, get out of the way!" Graham shouted, this time at a red pickup truck that cut across two lanes in front of us. He pulled the air horn, but the red menace showed no sign of having heard us, or for that matter of being aware that we were even there.

The first settler on the Bosporus, my guidebook said, was a Greek merchant-adventurer by the name of Byzas who in the seventh century B.C. founded a trading post on the Golden Horn and named it Byzantium. The town was prospering when Darius the Great arrived from Persia and became the first person to link both continents by a bridge. It was laid across one hundred galleys that had been lashed together and permitted his army of seventy thousand to cross from Asia to Europe without major mishap. Darius was defeated at the Battle of Marathon in 490 B.C., but his son Xerxes returned ten years later to force the pass at Thermopylae and sack Athens before returning to Asia Minor.

After the Greeks and the Persians came the Romans. As Rome concentrated on containing the Parthians in the East and was unable to push beyond the Danube in the North, the empire suffered a series of crises that in the third century led to the ruin of the western provinces without seriously affecting the prosperity of the eastern ones. This brought about a shift in the center of the empire to the east, and Constantine, the native son of Nis, made Byzantium the new capital of the empire.

The city, renamed Constantinople, rapidly became the wealthiest, most beautiful, and most civilized city in the world. "From every province of Asia and Europe rivulets of gold and silver discharged into the Imperial reservoir in a copious and perennial stream," wrote Edward Gibbon.

Constantinople was ideally placed as the capital of a great empire, lying both on the main overland trade route between Europe and Asia and at the narrowest point on the straits that joined the Black Sea with the Aegean and Mediterranean seas. A medieval traveler approaching the city by ship would have seen a skyline dominated by the domes of five hundred churches, for Constantine also made Christianity the state religion. Over them all rose Hagia Sophia, once the most important edifice in Christendom. Today, as we crossed the Golden Horn, we saw a skyline dominated by the domes of five hundred mosques, splendid and mysterious with their slender minarets pointing skyward like the lances of Islam waiting to be carried into battle.

Justinian, it is said, contributed 320,000 pounds of gold and the labors of ten thousand men to build Hagia Sophia. We may doubt the figures concerning the quantity of gold—at today's bullion prices it would be equivalent to two billion dollars—but whatever the amount, we can be relatively certain he had wrung it from the people in increased taxation. No dome of such proportions and grandeur had been built before. No other, owing to the technical problems and the cost involved, would be built there for a thousand years.

In the city's markets and bazaars, merchants and shopkeepers, beggars and visitors of every race and creed crowded and jostled. Visiting traders had their own quarters, like the Russ merchants, and their privileges were carefully specified by treaty. The local merchants and tradesmen, such as bakers, silk merchants, fishmongers, and perfumers, were organized into guilds. Imports and exports were strictly controlled. Customs duties formed an important source of imperial revenue.

With the incursions of the Bulgars, the pressures of the Turks, and the rise of the Saracens, the empire of the East was soon restricted to the Bosporus, the Dardanelles, and both coasts of the Sea of Marmara. The Venetians had stolen most of the Aegean, and Constantinople was increasingly bypassed by shifting trade routes.

The city fell in 1204 not to the Turks but to Norman, Flemish, and Venetian knights of the Fourth Crusade who, in the name of God and the Virgin Mary, took advantage of the absent Byzantine army to storm and sack it, raping most of its women and carrying off every bit of its nine hundred years of accumulated treasure. The part of the booty captured by the French knights, Gibbon tells us, amounted to seven times the annual revenue of the Kingdom of England. It has been described as one of the most shameful sackings of all time. Among the treasures were the four bronze horses that today adorn St. Mark's Cathedral in Venice. Jerusalem was forgotten by the Crusaders, who proceeded to divide the Eastern Empire among themselves.

For the next two hundred years, Venice, at the head of the Adriatic, became the mistress of eastern trade. Because of Venice's grip on Levantine commerce, the Latin Empire of Constantinople was never a viable trading enterprise and therefore was doomed from the start. Emperor Baldwin, then thirty-two, a descendant of Charlemagne and cousin of the King of France, was captured by the Bulgars at Adrianople in 1205 and died in captivity. His brother Henry came to the throne. His reign lasted ten years. He died in the defense of Salonika. With the first two Latin emperors of Constantinople, the male line of the counts of Flanders became extinct.

Constantinople as the seat of an enfeebled empire lingered behind its virtually impregnable walls until 1453. By then the city's population had dwindled through plague and decadence from over a million to under fifty thousand, and its territory was reduced to the limits of its walls. The final siege was conducted by Mehmet the Conqueror, then only twenty-one, and it lasted forty days. The access of his fleet to the Golden Horn was denied by a mighty chain. He drew his army of 150,000 men into battle lines in front of the land walls defended by eight thousand Greek and English mercenaries. He had brought with him the heaviest cannon the world had yet seen to pound the walls into rubble. But his master stratagem was to drag a portion of his fleet some ten miles across land to the inner harbor of the Golden Horn in a single night. Unable to cope with a double offensive, the exhausted defenders were soon overwhelmed, and the course of history reached another turn in the road.

We crossed the Golden Horn Bridge, and below us was the five-mile stretch of murky water that no longer served as a port. On our right we came abreast of a terrible wreck. A tonka, or small Turkish truck, was the apparent cause of the traffic jam. A police wrecker had dragged what remained of the vehicle to the side of the road. Traffic loosened, and the mad Turkish driver of the red pickup truck weaved in front of us again.

"Gaw on, beat it, you twit!" Graham yelled at the little red truck, which by then had zipped between two more cars and was speeding away from us. Graham was nervous because he had a blind spot down the left side of the cab where the mirrors didn't reach, and a car was stubbornly hanging in there. At times our left front wheel was only inches away from it, and I was sure our wheels would kiss until the erratic sod drifted aft of the trailer again.

We came over a rise and saw the 540-foot towers of the Bosporus

Bridge, then the main span itself. On the far side of the blue waterway
was Asia. My heart pounded with excitement as ahead of us lay the
cradles of not one but five of the greatest civilizations the world has
ever known. And with Asia in sight I felt confident that our descent
into the Arabian desert was now assured. We were heading for the
center of the mosaic that during millenniums running had brought
prosperity and war in alternating cycles to most of mankind.

On the Asian side we paid twenty-eight-pound toll; no toll charge
is levied on the return. Behind us a dozen ships were making their way
up the Bosporus from the Sea of Marmara. Soon we were steaming
along the E5 motorway, which runs the length of the Bay of Izmit.
After Gebze, where the ashes of Hannibal are buried, we passed an
Astran truck driven by Dick Snow coming the other way. The dean of
the route waved to us. We noticed he had a passenger with him.

At midday we stopped at Tukla TIR *kontrol*. While Graham and
Steve took their tacho disks and police forms into the office of the *trafik
polisi,* I entertained a track-suit merchant who wanted to sell his
counterfeit Adidas wares for fifty deutsche marks per set. "*Kollegen*
said to buy one each for them," he assured me and tried to throw the
suits into the cab. I batted them back at him. He was not offended. He
wanted to know if any more British trucks were coming down the road.
None, I said. He asked about Austrian, Dutch, French, or German
trucks. Maybe some Iranians, I told him.

After Tukla, the coast was as beautiful as the Côte d'Azur, without
the yachts, only a Turkish frigate anchored in a cove. The expressway
ended at Izmit, and the countryside became flat and fertile between two
mountain ranges. As we entered the town of Adapazari, people were
covering the body of a boy with a sheet. He had been knocked off his
bicycle by a runaway tonka, which had overturned in the field to our
right.

British drivers refer to the small Turkish trucks as tonkas because
they resemble the miniature ones made by Tonka Toys, a division of
Tonka Corporation of Mound, Minnesota. The people from Mound
advertise their products as being Tonka-tough. The real-life Turkish
tonkas are certainly tough: they are five-tonners with extra back axles,
painted with pastoral scenes, and have fancy trim. Their drivers are
perhaps the most fearless in the world. Tonkas are always overloaded,
carrying up to thirty tons, with inadequate brakes, sometimes no lights,
and nearly bald tires. They go everywhere, carry everything, and are
frequently encountered on the side of the road, hood up, the driver

bending over pieces of motor he has spread on the ground. But when they go, they go like mad.

Another distinctive feature of the tonkas is that they have *Masaallah* (Allah be with me) or *Allah Korushun* (Allah protect me) painted on them. Because of the way they drive, some need Allah sitting in the cab with them.

"We're getting farther away from civilization," Graham remarked as we approached the foothills of the Köroğlu Mountains to the east of Adapazari. On either side of the road were substantial two-story farmhouses covered in white stucco. They were surrounded by fields of corn, cabbage, and tobacco as well as vineyards and orchards. Roadside vendors had a patchwork of fruit and vegetables displayed in front of their stands: boxes of red apples and green pears, yellow peaches and purple grapes; pleated red onions hung from the roofs, pyramids of green melons and orange pumpkins were piled beside them. The fields were separated by copses of poplars. Flocks of white geese and brown chickens patrolled the edges of streams and reminded me of scenes from Flemish paintings.

In another village a tanker had collided with a bus, and the wreckage was so macabre it sent twinges through my stomach.

"Crazy drivers," Graham said, and I could only agree. Fortunately, the farther east we progressed the better the weather became. At 2:30 P.M. we entered the town of Düzce, a city of many mosques, and stopped to buy two loaves of *ikmek* for lunch at the next TIR *kontrol,* a mile down the road. When we pulled into the TIR parking it was empty—only one Austrian, one F-Troop, and six Wombles. Last year when we stopped here more than a hundred trucks were parked in the lot, and it was only half full.

The *trafik polisi* require drivers to rest one hour at Düzce before crossing Bolu Pass, so we cooked lunch of fried eggs, bacon, and mushrooms. Afterward I walked over and said hello to the Austrian. "Look at this place. It's empty," he said. "Trucking is finished, my friend." He was going to bed down for an hour before setting out on the road to Ankara.

At 4:00 P.M. we started our motors and, after building up air pressure, inched toward the gate. The gatekeeper asked us for our police paper, which had already been stamped. Graham gave it to him. He walked around the truck, checked the license plates, and came back, shaking his head. "No good," he said.

"What's no good?" Graham asked.

"Problem."

"What problem?"

"No trailer number."

"You don't need a trailer number, you silly twit. 'Ere, give me back that paper and open the bloody gate."

"No Marlboro, no go."

Graham was mad, but rather than argue he handed down a pack of cigarettes, got the TIR *kontrol* paper back, and raced out as soon as the gate was opened.

Steve roared through behind us without stopping. The gatekeeper, furious, picked up a rock on the wall beside the gate and heaved it at Steve's trailer. There was a bang as it rebounded off the side panels.

"Nasty blighter," said Graham.

A road sign indicated 140 miles to Ankara. Graham started moving down the transmission as we began to climb. The tonka traffic was one tenth of last year's flow. Toward the top we were in fifth gear and stayed there. The climb was only 2,970 vertical feet, but it was crowded into three miles of road. As Steve's Volvo was more powerful, he soon steamed by us. The Volvo whistled when Steve shifted gears. *Old Girl* wheezed.

In the last sweeping hairpin a bus had been sideswiped by a tonka, and a horse, hit by one of the vehicles, lay dead in the parking lot in front of a roadside bistro. The descent on the other side of the pass was nowhere near as difficult or as vertiginous, as we were entering a wooded upland similar, in parts, to the Swiss and French Jura.

"You come down a hill in the same gear you come up it," Graham said, sticking in fifth for the first few bends. The farther east we went, the more sparsely wooded the upland became until we reached the edge of the Anatolian Plateau. After Bolu it seemed like there were miles and miles of empty space, a few stands of poplars and pines, and a handful of villages with houses of whitewashed clay and wood. For a while I was spellbound by the harsh beauty of the landscape. It took me a long time to figure out why it looked so different. There were no fences; just wide-open spaces, like West Texas. Horses ran wild; small, dark cattle were watched by lone herders. Sheep and goats rambled across never-ending meadows; the grass was eaten to the soil. A few potato fields were being harvested by women with skirts down to their ankles and shawls over their heads. Some waved as we passed.

Another sixty miles and there were only scrub pines and sinister karstic rock formations. We had reached the beginning of the descent into Death Valley, picking up on the way a bit of tanker traffic. After a brilliant sunset, dusk drew around us. Skid marks disappeared over the edge of the road into a ravine. I craned out the window for a view of the wreck but could see nothing.

Death Valley is much feared by drivers. Its long descent looks deceptively gentle but is treacherously wearing as it swallows air pressure and overheats brakes. Before the road was improved, six British drivers lost their lives at the bottom of Death Valley due to brake failure. We crept down in fifth.

At the bottom of the first stage the road became an expressway again. It only lasted for a few dozen miles and had but recently been opened.

It was dark when we reached the tollgate. On our right was the wreck of an Iranian Volvo F85. We got out to look at it. The driver had been pushed through the roof, and his seat and steering column were still suspended above the cab. There was an acrid smell of diesel, motor oil, and death.

"Poor bugger," Steve murmured.

The last hour down to Ankara was easy enough, though Graham was worn out, trying to get through the remaining few miles without falling asleep. "It's a long and lonely road," he said.

We pulled into the Telex Motel TIR Park on the outskirts of Ankara at 8:00 P.M. Only three other trucks were there when we arrived, but as we were getting out of our cabs a pair of Prior refrigerator trucks steamed in. Robin Fraser and Bob Mattingly, two of Charlie Leadham's Chocolate Cowboys, were on their way home from Kuwait, where they had delivered twenty tons each of Mars Bars.

"Time for an *Efes kontrol*," Steve said. Upstairs we asked for Cairo, the night manager. Aytekin Atik, his assistant, said that Cairo had left that morning for Istanbul with Dick Snow. Cairo had a week's vacation and had gone to visit a girlfriend. Sitting in front of the TV over the fireplace, at one end of the dining room, was Leslie Massey. He was glad to see us. He had been at the Telex for three days, waiting for a certificate of origin to arrive from London. He was carrying a load of wood paneling to Kuwait. To transit Iraq he needed a notarized manifest in Arabic stating that the paneling was of British origin. We ordered dinner of chicken kebab and french fries. The chicken, as usual, was undercooked. We sent it back for an extra turn on the grill.

While we were eating, a Danish driver came in. We didn't know him, but he would later impress us as a walking encyclopedia on vintage British warplanes. He said that a German driver who had been following us had an accident in Death Valley. He was overtaking the Austrian we had met at Düzce and collided head on with a motorist. Nothing was left of the Turkish car or its occupants. Both the Austrian and the German had been arrested and taken to jail.

9. TELEX MOTEL, ANKARA

ALONG the route to the Middle East there are communications points where long-distance truckers can pick up messages or contact their operations managers back home. National Hotel in Belgrade, Londra Camp in Istanbul, and Telex Motel at Ankara fulfill this role. Other substations exist, such as Oryx's Garage at Adana or Hotel Wien in Budapest, but the National, Londra, and Telex are the main ones.

Truckers prefer telexing as a form of communications. From distant places where no direct telephone dialing exists it is quicker, and they are left with a written confirmation. On outgoing trips, Ankara is the last capital before entering Iran or the Arab world. Consequently Telex Motel has become a communications focal point. We had to stop at Ankara for two reasons: to obtain my Iraqi transit visa, and to pick up an Arabic translation of our manifest, in notarized form, to certify the origin of the goods. This "certificate of origin" supposedly ensured that no goods made in Israel or by firms blacklisted for trading with Israel crept into the Arab dominions.

One of the first things we did upon arriving at Telex was check the notice board. The largest message pinned to the board concerned Iraq, our next destination.

Attn. All Drivers Going to Iraq

All cargo to Iraq or for transit through Iraq must be accompanied by a manifest from country of origin. Arabic manifests acquired in Turkey are no longer acceptable. Many trucks have been refused entry. Don't be one of them.

87

We had already contacted Cengiz Ozdil, the Whittle agent in Ankara, to find out whether our Arabic manifest had arrived from London. His brother, Fatih, who was standing beside me, had a telex for Steve from Leon Ashworth; it had just arrived. It said our Arabic manifest had been skypacked to Ankara and that a legalized inventory of the personal effects for Roger Hayes, the Saudi Conduit general manager—Steve was carrying the effects in his trailer—was also on its way.

"When do you think the documents will arrive?" I asked Fatih.

"Maybe tomorrow," he said. "Your visa will be ready tonight."

A helicopter whirled overhead. There was a military airfield two miles down the road. Today they were practicing left turns, using the motel as a marker. Every five minutes another helicopter swooped in, a constant reminder that Turkey has one of NATO's largest and best-trained armies.

To "us" truckers it was entirely evident that Turkey's stability was crucial to the Western Alliance. Overland trade routes were just as strategic in time of war as air or sea lanes. Because of Turkey's long border with the Soviet Union, it was, as former U.S. Secretary of State Alexander Haig had pointed out, "an irreplaceable strategic asset not only for NATO but for the whole Western world." As far as we knew, Haig had never traveled in a juggernaut. We joked, however, that Maggie Thatcher and François Mitterand should ride with us once— just once—to find out what it was really like on the road. We were sure it would give them a different geopolitical perspective.

U.S. military aid to Turkey is about eight hundred million dollars a year. The country is the third-largest recipient of U.S. aid after Israel and Egypt. There are fifteen U.S. military bases in Turkey. A part of the foreign aid, as well as the chilled meat carried by Grangers, Prior, and others, and certain other supplies for the post exchanges (PX's) on those U.S. bases, came by road. Driving all that distance from Dover, we appreciated even better than General Haig that Turkey was the eastern hinge of the Atlantic Alliance, the wedge between the Soviets and the Arab world. Throughout history it has been the transfer point between East and West, North and South, between Hittite sophistry and Assyrian might, between the Persians and Greeks, the Parthians and Rome.

Fatih and his brother Cengiz (pronounced Ghengiz) ran Transcar, which they described as an international TIR assistance service. Every British driver carries one of their calling cards in case of emergency. On it is written: "In case you run into any problems in connection with your vehicle, yourself, or your company, please have the first Turkish official you meet read the entry on the back of this card.''

The notice on the back of the card explained in Turkish that its holder was represented in Turkey by Transcar, and in the event of a problem the official concerned should contact the Transcar agency so that assistance could be provided.

In addition to Transcar, the Ozdil brothers owned a textile business. But long-distance trucking and the merchant-adventurers who drove the juggernauts fascinated them. In many cases the drivers became their friends. Some were invited home for dinner. Fatih was telling me that Cengiz had the widow and daughter of an Austrian driver staying with him at the moment. The driver had been killed five years before by Afghan rebels who mistook him for a Russian.

"You know Alex Downie?" Fatih asked.

I had met Alex, another Falcongate driver, at Telex Motel the year before, when he was waiting for papers that would permit him to drive into Iran. "Sure, I know Alex."

"Big problem at Zahko."

Zahko was the Iraqi frontier point through which most TIR traffic going to the Arab world went. "What's the matter?"

"He got his certificate of origin at the border from Young Turk. The Iraqis won't accept it. He's been there a week, bouncing back and forth between Habur and Zahko."

The Iraqis and Saudis had for a number of years insisted on dual-purpose manifests written in Arabic and attesting to the origin of the goods. To save time and money, British freight forwarders used to telex their agents in Ankara or Habur and have them issue an Arabic manifest. The driver would then pick it up on his way through. Young Turk at Habur became very proficient at issuing Arabic certificates of origin for British cargoes. He had all the right rubber stamps. It made life much easier. But Iraqi Customs finally cottoned on to this little commerce. From the beginning of the Muslim New Year, Iraq disallowed Turkish-issued certificates of origin for foreign trucks, whether British, French, Dutch, or German.

"Here," Fatih said, "read this," pointing to another telex on the board.

Attn. Falcongate Driver Mr. R. Anderson, Truck B942

Bob, Alex Downie contacted us yesterday afternoon from Habur. He has been issued with another manifest by Young

Turk that shows place of origin as Yugoslavia. He was quite
confident he would obtain entry with this manifest. He was to
go through last night and would telex or phone as soon as he
could to inform us whether successful. We are still waiting to
hear from Alex and as soon as we do will let you know how to
proceed.

Regards, Barrie

So Young Turk was still in the game. "Good for him," I thought.
"Did Alex get through?" I asked Fatih.

"We haven't heard yet. He must get to Baghdad before he can
telex."

We had coffee before Fatih drove back into Ankara, five miles
away, to process my visa request. Victor the Kermit and Richie Thorne
had arrived during the night. Kermit was returning from Kuwait,
where he had unloaded a shipment of building materials for the new
conference center that was hurriedly being completed to hold the
Islamic summit conference in January 1987.

Kermit and Leslie were having breakfast while the mechanics
worked on Kermit's tattered blue Volvo. Richie, who was on his way
home from Basra, was talking to Steve on the sofa in front of the TV.

Steve called me over. "You got to meet Richie. He's Mr. Trucker
on the Middle East run."

Young Steve held Richie in some awe. Thorne was in his early
forties and was one of the veterans of intercontinental trucking. He had
suffered a good deal from the heat and the tension in southern Iraq and
looked worn. The Iraqis had made him wait a week in the desert before
escorting him to the bridge site where he was to unload. He had scabs
on his head and face, and although he had showered and changed still
looked like he could do with a good hot-tub soaking. Richie had tattoos
on his arms, hands, and chest. They expressed in words and imagery
the love-hate theme favored by many drivers. The Telex staff regarded
him as the No. 1 fighter, a title that showed their respect. One evening,
Aytekin told me Richie had brought a girlfriend to the Telex. A
Swedish driver eyed her a little too covetously. Richie got up and
slugged the Swedish driver clean through the door. One hour later,
they were drinking buddies.

Nobody seemed quite sure how Kermit got his name. He was of
medium height, had a paunch, rounded shoulders, and protruding
eyes. In fact, he was Kermit II. The first Kermit no longer drove, as

he had tried to blow his wife away with a shotgun and was now serving time. Victor was a battle-scarred veteran of the Middle East route. He had even worked "internal" Saudi for eighteen months and smuggled himself out of the country in someone else's food box. He was a prolific teller of war stories.

Leslie Massey was mad at Victor. He accused him of giving British truckers a bad name. The game used to be to buy black-market "red" diesel in Hungary. It sold at about a third of the regular diesel price. Red diesel is subsidized fuel that in theory is sold only to farmers. Most European countries provide their farmers with subsidized diesel, dyed red to distinguish it from regular diesel. In every country where red diesel is sold it is an offense to use it in vehicles other than farm tractors.

Near Kecskemét a service station attendant used to sell red diesel for hard currency. British trucks would roll up to the pump and the drivers would fill their own tanks, then go into the office to pay the attendant "under the table." The attendant trusted British drivers to tell him exactly how much diesel they had taken; then he would negotiate the price. Sneaky Kermit habitually told the blackmarketeer only a third of what he had actually pumped. One day, however, the attendant discovered that Kermit had been taking him for a ride. He threatened to shoot Kermit if ever he came back.

"Silly twat. Had it comin' to him, didn't he," Kermit told Leslie, laughing.

This was not the first time Kermit had resorted to such antics. He seemed almost pathological about it. When he described each adventure he made it sound like an amusing challenge. He remembered meeting a driver called Peanut one day on a services area near Amberg in West Germany. As Kermit told the story, Peanut wanted to sell some diesel he had left over in his belly tank at a cut-rate price to raise beer money. Kermit offered to take a full running tank, about ninety gallons.

"I stuck his hose into my running tank and then said, 'Wait a minute, Peanut. Before you start blowing her through, I'll make sure the belly-tank valve is shut.' " And he went around to the far side of the trailer and opened it full cock.

"Okay, Peanut, let 'er flow," he said back at the running tank.

When Peanut had blown through about four hundred liters, he started to wonder how long it could possibly take to fill up Kermit's ninety-gallon tank. "Almost done, Peanut. Give her a bit more,"

Kermit told him. And when he figured Peanut had actually pumped in close to 180 gallons, he said, "Whoa, old man, she's about full." Kermit paid Peanut for ninety gallons.

Kermit used to stop regularly at Oryx's in Adana on his way to Baghdad and Saudi Arabia. He didn't any longer, though. He'd met a local girl there whose father owned a trucking company. Kermit used to see her every trip down and in his own words got to like her "quite a bit."

As Kermit's wife was threatening divorce, he asked his Adana mistress if she would ride back home with him. She was a widow with two young children. She liked the idea of going to the United Kingdom, but said she had to present Kermit to her father. The father wanted to do what was best for his daughter, who had a local suitor as well. So he convoked Kermit and the local suitor to the house together and sat them down at his table to size them up. After talking to both men, and consulting in the back room with his daughter, the father informed the local suitor he had chosen the Englishman. The rejected Turk actually wept, Kermit said.

True to his word, Kermit took his mistress home to England, and they lived together for three months. By this time his wife had decided she no longer wanted a divorce and started making life impossible for Kermit. Finally he suggested to his mistress that she return to Adana to see her children. He arranged for one of his friends to drive her back home and said he would join her in a few weeks. Well, he didn't, did he?

For a while he stopped running beyond Istanbul. When he started going to Baghdad again, he drove through Adana with some trepidation. It took him a few more Baghdads before he had the courage to stop at Oryx's. His photo had been on the wall, the manager said, and the father-in-law had left standing instructions to call should Kermit reappear. Her brothers used to come by from time to time to ask if Kermit had been there. Kermit left right away. In the future, whenever he stopped at Oryx's he had other trucks shield him from the road.

For some reason this set Les thinking about driver solidarity, which was one of his favorite themes. He told about stopping at the Hotel Wien in Budapest on his way home from the Middle East, with literally only fifty deutsche marks left in his pocket. A Danish driver whom Les knew as Ulf bought him dinner in the downstairs restaurant, then suggested a final nightcap at the disco on the top floor. "What the hell," thought Les, "I can afford a round of beer and then call it quits.'' In the elevator he felt his accordion wallet being lifted from his back pocket, and he turned to find Ulf inspecting it.

"What do you mean, you've only got fifty deutsche marks? There's more in here than that," the Dane said.

Ulf had slipped a one-hundred-deutsche-mark note into one of the folds.

"Why do you do it, Ulf?" Les asked.

"Because whenever we're stuck on the side of the road with a problem, the first to stop and give us a hand are you Brits. You'll pay me back when you can. I know you. Besides, it's the only way we can show some appreciation.''

"British drivers are known by the Continentals as scroungers," Victor said.

"We never have any money," he continued, explaining that he only had seventy pounds left to get home with. "In Greece a couple of months ago I was out of money. I walked into this place, straight up to a table where a couple of lads were sitting. I said, 'Okay, I'll have a beer then. Anybody going to buy me a beer? I'll have one. I'm broke.'

"This guy next to me says, 'I suppose you're English, aren't you?'

"I said, 'I thought you were.'

" 'No, we're Danes. You're broke, are you?'

" 'Oh, fuck it,' I said. 'I'll have a beer, if you don't mind. Get you one back tomorrow when I get some money.'

" 'Typical English,' he said. 'Why is it all English drivers have no money? You do your trip. You get to your destination. No money!'

" 'Because in the past there's been too much fiddling going on and the foreman won't give us no more.' You don't tend to waste it if you don't have it.''

The Danes bought Kermit not one but several beers. He never saw them again.

The conversation changed to Andrew Wilson Young, whom Les described as "a legend in his own time." Andrew drives for Astran. He is acknowledged as the fastest man on the Middle East run. He can do a Muscat in eighteen days, or a Baghdad in twelve—there and back! He doesn't have a cooker and never stops for a hot meal. He lives on yogurt and canned foods—his favorite is canned rice pudding—and he sleeps slumped over the wheel.

Les had seen Andrew's Mercedes—Andrew calls her *Priscilla*—parked on Dover Docks on the way out. He knew it was Andrew's because the trailer had ANDREW WILSON YOUNG painted across the tarpaulins in big red letters. Apparently *Priscilla* had met a telegraph pole on the last trip home, for the front was bent in and the windshield was broken.

"Andrew must have fallen asleep at the wheel again," Kermit said. "You know, the only original piece left on that truck is the dashboard."

"Anybody who has been doing the Middle East for some time has a story to tell about Andrew. God forbid that we lose anybody on this trip, you know, but when Andrew goes, then we're going to lose one of the true characters, if you like, of the Middle East run. He's a true patriot. He tends to fly the flag so much it's unbelievable," Les continued.

"He's so well liked by everyone," Kermit added with uncharacteristic charity.

Andrew, Les explained, owned two pairs of boots—green for summer and black for winter. In the summer he wore white tennis shorts, a T-shirt, and the green boots, nothing else. In the winter his wife, Olive, made him dress properly. Last year, when Graham and I were on our way back from Baghdad, we had heard that Andrew had been stuck for several days on the Syria-Jordan frontier. As he had promised to take Olive to the Arc de Triomphe horse racing classic in Paris on the weekend, and realizing he couldn't make it through Syria in time, he parked his truck and flew from Amman to Paris, picking up Olive in London on the way. He returned to Amman on Monday and got his truck back into line, waiting to clear Customs.

One of Andrew's tricks was to walk to the front of any Customs line, holding his passport in the air and saying, " 'Scuse me, chaps, I'm British," and drivers who had seen it happen said it always worked. Only Andrew could get away with it, though. No one else dared. The Customs officials, even the Saudis, got to know him and condoned his eccentricities.

When a driver transits Kuwait, unless he's pulling a refrigerator truck, in which case he gets cleared right away, the authorities hold the truck in Customs overnight and require that the driver sleep in a hotel. Andrew refused to go to a hotel when the measure was first introduced and bivouacked for the night on the lawn of the British embassy. "I'm British and this is British territory," he told the policeman sent to dislodge him.

The embassy staff brought him tea in the morning. The Kuwaitis were so embarrassed that in the future they cleared Andrew's truck as soon as he appeared at the border.

Andrew's father owned a large estate in the Lake District, where he had been a private practitioner. His mother was a titled lady who allegedly had appeared in the *Guinness Book of World Records* for owning a hen that laid some incredible number of eggs. She was a noted horsewoman and was said to have competed in carriage driving events against Prince Philip. Andrew was a public-school boy and gentleman farmer. It was a common belief among the fraternity that he didn't need to drive for the money it brought him.

"I don't know what motivates the bloke to keep on doing it, you know. Adventure, of course. Every trip is a challenge. Although it's the same sort of trip, the problems are different every time," Kermit said, summing up not only Andrew's motivation but also probably the motivation of nine tenths of all truckers on the Middle East run.

"Like I said, every trip is a challenge," he repeated to make sure I had heard him. "Baghdad—wherever you go—every time you get there, something's changed; there's another new problem. The biggest problem on a Middle East trip is controlling your nerves. Most drivers, wherever they go, when they hear the words 'Problem, mister,' start paying out. That's wrong. If you tell them right back, 'There's no problem,' you don't pay nothing."

As an example, Kermit launched into a rambling tale of going through Turkish Customs at Kapikule on the Bulgarian frontier with a Turkish road permit, issued in the United Kingdom in the name of the vehicle owner—say, J. J. Smith—and a triptych, or Customs bond for the trailer, in the name of the freight forwarder—say, Transleam.

"There was a new copper on at Kapik when I came through last time, looking for anything he could get. He looks at my permit and then asks for triptychs.

" 'Problem, mister. Name on permit and name on triptych not the same. Triptych Transleam, permit Smith.'

"I say, 'So what?'

" 'Problem.'

"I say, 'No problem.'

"So he picks up the next file in the pile, which is for a Schenker driver, and, pointing to the names on both the permit and triptych, says 'Same-same.'

" 'But he's not an owner-driver. He works for the company he hauls for,' I tell him.

"He shrugs and puts the papers aside and starts doing someone else's while thinking about this. Finally he tells me, 'Two hours, come back.'

"I'm not bothered. I go brew some tea, have a nap, and come back. He gives me back my papers and says, 'Go, mister.' "

Kermit left for Istanbul after lunch. Later in the afternoon, Bob Anderson arrived. Two more blowouts had kept him at Kavala. He thought the wheels on his trailer were out of line. If that proved to be the case, he was going to have a difficult journey through the desert. Of course, he had no certificate of origin for his split Baghdad–Qatar load. Falcongate had originally told him to get one in Turkey, but now the office suggested he break the seals, offload the Baghdad portion, and have it transshipped by a Turkish firm, then carry on with the rest through Syria and Jordan.

"This is illegal," Fatih told him. "The goods are in bond and can't be offloaded unless you want to forfeit the bond and pay Turkish import duties."

Bob telexed Falcongate, asking for new instructions.

Terry Grant also had come in from Izmir. He had a quick nap, loaded more meat at the American PX in Ankara, then left for Adana, intending to be back at Telex Motel by Thursday.

Early in the afternoon, Alfie Jones arrived with his yellow-and-red Ford Transcon, returning from Baghdad. His truck wasn't hard to distinguish from other Fords because he had reversed the "F" and the "D" on the grille so that it read Dorf. A rotund, elflike man, about five feet five and with a grayish, full beard, Alfie was calm and unflappable, a person every driver respected. He went over and sat down with Robin Fraser and Bob Mattingly. The two of them had spent the day working on Bob's three-and-a-half-year-old DAF.

"She's been burning oil and not pulling," said Bob. "At the DAF agency up the road they told me the compressor was shot."

"But really the motor's fucked," Robin said. "Charlie doesn't service his trucks, does he? She burned twenty-five liters of oil going down to Kuwait, fully loaded. So far coming back she's burned fifteen liters."

Robin's Scania had burned only two liters since leaving Dover.

Robin was still shaken by his run of the day before. After crossing Tarsus he was booming down the long, straight stretch before reaching Aksaray. "Bob was running in front, blowing off steam, trying to clean out the compressor," Robin said. Robin, one of the steadiest drivers on the Middle East run, was traveling at more than a hundred kilometers per hour (62.5 miles per hour), trying to keep up with Bob. Robin was forced to slow down at a crossroads when a taxi pulled out in front of him, but he was picking up speed again when two old codgers on a motorbike cut left in front of him without warning. He jammed on the brakes, jackknifed, and slithered across the road onto the apron of a service station. As the cab swung back onto the side of the trailer, the second drive axle caught the motorbike and sent the two codgers flying.

Fortunately, only one of them was cut up, and the bike had no apparent damage. Robin got out his first-aid kit as a crowd started to gather and cleaned the old fellow's cuts. He offered to drive him to the nearest hospital, which was at Konya, thirty miles away, but the old boy refused. Half the bystanders by then were telling Robin to move off before the *trafik polisi* came.

"So I gave the bloke enough money to take a taxi to the hospital and left. It was a close call and could have had serious consequences. I was lucky, that's all."

Alfie, who had lit up his pipe, eyes twinkling, agreed. "The cops would have arrested you, for sure," he nodded.

With all their problems, Robin and Bob had run out of money, so they sent a telex to Gary Leadham, Charlie's son and operations manager at Prior's headquarters in a converted schoolhouse at Acrise, near Folkestone. It read:

> Pls don't shout now—later OK—but we need 600 DM from Belgrade to buy enough cheap derv in Hungary to get us home because of derv problem Iraq. Sorry about all this but it's out of our hands.

> GARY replied: OK, sorry, but no one on way down till Friday week. Can't get you money in Hotel National. Impossible, so you have to try and sort something out.

> ROBIN: OK, but I don't know how. But will try.

> GARY: Ask Cengiz if it is possible for him to advance you money now and I repay immediately on bank transfer. And also ask him to send telex on permit costs (3 permits) and I will include this.

> ROBIN: OK, and bye 4 now.

"What happened in Iraq?" I asked.

"They stole our derv," Robin replied. "We had filled the belly tanks with cheap Kuwaiti derv. But the Iraqis won't let you exit the country with more than a hundred liters each. We had more than two thousand. Normally you can fix it with a bottle of whiskey or some filthy magazines. But this time the chief dipper wouldn't take *baksheesh*. Said the derv was needed for the war effort. They took the whole bloody lot, didn't they?"

Richie Thorne had been intending to drive on to "Instanbull" late in the afternoon, after completing repairs to his trailer. But when he saw Alfie arrive, he said, "Cancel today. I've decided to stay." With so many friends at Telex, the prospects were excellent for a good piss-up that evening. He wasn't to be disappointed.

10. PEANUT GETS BUSTED

ONE message on the Telex notice board intrigued me more than the others. It read:

> *ATTENTION!!*
>
> I, Les Wren (Peanut), English ex-TIR driver, would appreciate any driver or my friends to give me a lift back to England. Can help with food and driving. If you can help, my telephone number is Ankara 47.47.34.

"What's this?" I asked Aytekin.

"You don't know Peanut?" he replied. "He got a ride home last week. I should take it down."

Peanut was one of those fearless juggernaut drivers in his late thirties who had been everywhere and done everything. Until a month ago, Aytekin said, Peanut had been one of Charlie's Chocolate Cowboys, running regularly to Jordan and Kuwait, his refrigerator truck filled with Mars Bars. He had a steady job. The work was interesting. No worries. Then three or four trips back he met a sixteen-year-old Turkish girl at Oryx's in Adana. Her name was Guller. Peanut took a liking to her. But Guller wanted to see a bit more of the world and asked Peanut to take her to England. On his next trip to Kuwait, Peanut made arrangements for Guller to wait for him at Telex Motel on his way home.

Without telling her parents, Guller got a bus to Ankara, using her older sister's ID card. She arrived at Telex Motel with a small cardboard suitcase. No Peanut. Gary had instructed him to return via Syria and Jordan, which was cheaper on derv. Unfortunately, though, Peanut had not counted on the Islamic New Year. He was held up at Saudi Customs because of it, and then was further delayed in the backlog of traffic waiting to clear Customs at the Jordanian and Syrian frontiers. Ten days in all.

This didn't bother Guller. Aytekin gave her a room on Peanut's credit but noted that she knew most of the drivers by their first names, which gave him the impression that she had been hanging around Oryx's for quite some time before Peanut met her. She was good-looking, but nothing extraordinary.

"A kid who hung around truckers. How do you say? A groupie," Aytekin concluded.

When Peanut made it back to Telex Motel he parked at the back of the lot, and Guller, taking her little suitcase, moved in with him. Peanut began openly discussing with his colleagues around the bar the best way to smuggle her out of the country. She was underage and had no passport, let alone the exit visa that all Turks traveling abroad must obtain. He thought of telephoning Guller's cousin in London—she was a naturalized British citizen—to ask if she could lend Guller her passport.

While Peanut was busily and openly conspiring to remove Guller from the country, Gary sent instructions to backload from Izmir on the very next day. When Gary tells you to move, you move. So Peanut prepared to leave early in the morning. That night the police drove into the Telex yard and went directly to Peanut's truck. Someone had tipped them off, Aytekin supposed.

"A hundred pairs of ears were listening to Peanut plan his coup," he said. "What do you think? Of course somebody told the police. Probably a jealous Turk who thought it was his duty to defend Turkish honor." He shrugged, as if to say that's the way it is around here.

The police knocked on the door of Peanut's cab. When Peanut poked his head out to ask what the problem might be, the police saw Guller cowering in the farthest corner. The police told both of them to get dressed, and they were taken to the local station.

Peanut was charged with statutory rape and sent to the holding cells. He was looking at ten years—the minimum for sleeping with a minor. Guller's father was contacted and came to Ankara to get her. To gain his freedom, Peanut offered to marry Guller. In Turkey, custom demands that if a man sleeps with an unattached woman he must do the proper thing and marry her. The British embassy was requested to find out whether Peanut already had a wife. Left to diplomatic channels, confirmation of his bachelor status took over a month to reach Istanbul.

Charlie Leadham was furious when he found out. His cab and refrigerator truck had been temporarily impounded, and it took some fancy stepping by Cengiz to have them released. Charlie, who is short on patience when a driver puts one of his trucks in jeopardy, promptly fired Peanut.

Peanut, without a job and no money, was finally released from prison and the same day married Guller. By then she had received her own passport. He scrounged enough cash from friends to buy her an air ticket to London. Finally, Astran's Mike Walker took pity and offered Peanut a ride home.

11. SING ALONG WITH ALFIE

RICHIE Thorne was scared, and trying his best not to show it. He could still crack a man's ribs with his fist. But he was engaged in another sort of battle: one for his own financial survival. He wasn't used to such anxiety. It was sapping his self-confidence and his desire to get on with the job. For one thing, he was heading home and didn't know how long it might be before another haulage job would come his way. Also, he had lost his lust for going to Saudi Arabia. He owned two trucks, which he had acquired and paid for through sheer hard work. It had meant backbreaking hours at the wheel and the worries of financing their purchase. His brother, Sammy, drove the second truck, but Sammy was in the hospital recovering from a motorcycle accident. Now Richie was facing the prospect of having to sell the trucks to meet the tax claims against him.

Richie hadn't wanted to go to Basra on this trip. He had felt uneasy about it, like some disaster was going to happen. He had been given the job by Leon Ashworth. Leon and Richie knew each other well, though not much love was lost between them. The contract was to deliver bridge sections to a Cleveland Bridge Company site near Basra. The Iraqi army was bridging a new access route through the marshes to the besieged city. After six years of war between the two Islamic neighbors, Basra was almost encircled by Iranian troops and could fall at any time.

Going out to Basra, Richie had dragged ass all the way. He stayed a day more than he should have at Londra Camp, then moved on to Telex, where he had hung around for a few more days on the flimsiest of excuses until Alfie Jones arrived on his way down to Baghdad. Alfie

102

kicked Richie's ass to get him going again. But when they stopped at Fallujah, outside Baghdad, the same thing happened. Kermit came along, so Richie ran south to Basra with Kermit, not somebody he really liked to drive with. He unloaded his shipment at the site, then was picked up again by Kermit, on his way back from Kuwait.

"We all go through moments like that. Your nerves wear thin," Alfie explained.

Alfie's nerves had almost popped on his first trip through Ar'ar, the Saudi Customs post where we were headed, a third of the way down the Tapline. He was carrying paint primer for Riyadh, and the Customs inspector assigned to clear the load couldn't find *primer* in his Arabic-English dictionary. The inspector was suspicious that primer was some sort of English trick to smuggle whiskey into the kingdom. He had his staff open half the cans—there were more than six thousand of them—and stir to see if any solid objects, like bottles or flasks, were hidden inside them. Alfie could not get the inspector to assimilate *primer* with *primary* (which was in the dictionary), as in a first coat of paint. Finally, after immobilizing Alfie for fifteen days, the inspector ruled that the paint was mislabeled and required payment of an additional twenty thousand pounds in unspecified duties, almost as much as the cargo was worth.

The importer paid but wasn't happy. And the trip took Alfie seventy-four days to complete. He came home exhausted.

On Richie's last trip to Saudi Arabia, four months before, he had led a convoy of three trucks. The other two were driven by Fred Williamson of Peter Forde Transport and an owner-driver named Mick. They were hired by Whittle to transport a computerized communications system to Riyadh for the Saudi National Guard. Richie had two twenty-foot containers on a standard forty-foot flatbed trailer. Each of the others had one container and two large packing cases. The containers were encased in plywood sheets, sealed, and padlocked. Leon had taken Richie aside and said: "Richard, I count on you to make sure that no one opens this load. It has top-security clearance."

When they got to Ar'ar, the Customs inspector in a flowing white jellaba came over to Richie and said, "Now, Mr. Richard, open the containers, please." He suspected they might be hiding whiskey or other contraband between the outer plywood sheets and the metal sides of the container.

"No way, mister," Richie told him.

Unbelieving, the inspector gathered in his robes and went back to the office. Two hours later he returned. "Mr. Richard, you go straight to Riyadh Customs. You take police officer with you."

"Not the fat, smelly one," Richie pleaded.

The inspector, pretending not to understand, went away to find a suitable candidate for the assignment.

During his fifteen years of coping with unusual situations, Richie had become a grass-roots psychologist. He knew exactly with whom he could be overbearing and with whom he could not. He had learned to use his considerable power of intimidation to good effect. He played games with it. For example, Mehmet, the bar manager at Telex, was scared of him. If Richie said he had consumed only ten beers when Mehmet had counted fifteen, Mehmet wouldn't dare contradict him. If Richie told Mehmet that ten was six, Mehmet would agree. To avoid such problems, Mehmet placed an empty beer case beside the British drinkers, and every bottle ordered during the session was, once consumed, laid to rest in the case and the number of empties counted, agreed upon, and paid for at the end of the evening.

One of Richie's ploys was to turn the tables on the bureaucrats who seemed to get such pleasure from harassing the public at large and truckers in particular. His game worked as follows. In the Middle East, should you have something that a functionary or official covets, he will ask you how much it costs and then will try to bargain for it. If ever you let him hold it in his own hands, you might have a tough time getting it back.

Richie would play exactly the same game. "Oh, I like your watch," he might say, even though he really didn't like it at all. "May I see it?" The official would be proud that the Inglyse driver liked his watch. He would take it off and offer it for inspection. Richie would pay him a dozen compliments on the beauty and quality of the timepiece and then ask if he might try it on. The other, beaming, would almost certainly agree, in which case Richie would try it on, admire it, and announce: "I like it. You, Ahmed, my friend. I keep it okay? Very good. Thank you." And he would walk off. Ahmed would be dumbfounded. Such a thing had never happened to him before. Usually it worked the other way around for Ahmed.

Richie had no intention of keeping the watch. Ten minutes later he would return and hand it back to the relieved official, who suddenly would be amused by it all. Thereafter he would think Richie a prince of a fellow.

I watched Richie practice his act on Fatih. It was truly remarkable.

First, I should report that Fatih always jokes with the drivers, who in turn play pranks on him, like stealing his car, hiding his office keys, or chasing him around the yard with a bucket of water. We were standing by the telex machine when Richie started admiring Fatih's watch. It was Swiss-made. Finally he asked Fatih if he could try it on. Fatih, suspicious because he knew the kind of tricks Richie could get up to, nevertheless did not hesitate to unstrap and offer the watch to him.

"I like it. You, Fatih, my friend. I keep it, okay?" Richie said.

Fatih was unconcerned. "Sure, Richie," he replied and turned to dictate a telex to Aytekin. Richie wandered into the bar, had a beer, then returned to see if he had received an answer to a telex he had sent earlier. Richie had a wad of Turkish lire in his shirt pocket.

Unexpectedly, Fatih picked the wad from Richie's pocket. "Richie, you're my friend. I need fifty thousand lire, okay?" And he peeled five bills off the wad and returned the remainder to the pocket. Everybody watched for Richie's reaction. He smiled, shrugged, then clapped Fatih on the shoulder. "You're a good friend, Fatih." And he handed back the watch.

After supper, Richie hounded Alfie until he consented to sing. A Welshman from Trethomas in Gwent, near Caerphilly, Alfie had a beautiful, self-trained voice whose timbre sounded of the Welsh hills.

"Sing us that one about Gallipoli," Richie prodded.

Alfie was trying to recall the words to another song, but Richie pressed him. "Go on, Alf. Sing us that one you know really well."

"Songs are awkward to place. I'm trying to remember the words to a ballad called 'The Green Fields of France.' It was written by an Englishman," Alf said.

"Well, if you can't remember, then sing the Gallipoli one. You know that the best of all," Richie insisted.

"That's a song written by an Aussie named Eric Bogle," Alfie started to explain to the rest of us. "He wrote it about World War One, when the Aussies got a bollocking in Gallipoli."

"Well, sing us 'Waltzing Matilda,' then," Richie interrupted.

"That's what I'm trying to do," Alfie said, almost losing his patience with Richie. "But you need to explain it first; otherwise some of the others might not understand." A Dane, a Geordie, a Canadian, two Blackpudlians, and Mehmet the Turk were in Alfie's near presence. A handful of other Turks and some German drivers were seated at more distant tables, not paying much attention.

"You sing that one best of all," Richie insisted. " 'Waltzing

Matilda' tells everything. We had twenty people in the room one night down in Instanbul, listening to Alfie sing it. Not even a Turk said a word. They understand the song, as well. They might not understand the words, but they know what it's all about. It was a magic time, wasn't it, Alf?''

Alfie sighed. ''It's called 'The Band Played ''Waltzing Matilda,'' ' '' he said. He leaned back in his chair, pushed out his stomach, and started to sing, unaccompanied except by Richie's humming. Richie was now relaxed.

> When I was a young man I carried my pack,
> And I lived the free life of the rover,
> From the Murray's green banks to the dusty outback
> I waltzed Matilda all over.
> Then in 1915 my country said Son,
> It's time to stop rambling,
> There's work to be done.
> So they gave me a tin hat,
> And they gave me a gun,
> And they sent me away to the war.

And the band played ''Waltzing Matilda''
As the ship pulled away from the quay,
And amid all the tears, flag-waving, and cheers,
We sailed off for Gallipoli.

> How I remember that terrible day,
> When our blood stained the sand and the water.
> And how in that hell that they call Suvla Bay,
> We were butchered like lambs at the slaughter.
> Johnny Turk he was ready, he primed himself so well,
> He rained us with bullets and he showered us with shell,
> And in five minutes flat we were all blown to hell.
> He nearly blew us back home to Australia.

And the band played ''Waltzing Matilda''
As we stopped to bury our slain.
Now we buried ours and the Turks buried theirs,
And it started all over again.

> Now those who were living just tried to survive,
> In that mad world of blood, death, and fire.

And for ten weary weeks I kept myself alive,
While around me the corpses piled higher.
Then a big Turkish shell knocked me ass over head,
And when I awoke in my hospital bed,
And saw what it had done I wished I were dead.
Never knew there were worse things than dying.

For no more I'll go waltzing Matilda,
All around the green bush wild and free,
For to hump tent and pegs a man needs both legs,
No more waltzing Matilda for me.

Now they collected the wounded, the crippled, the maimed,
And they shipped us back home to Australia:
The armless, the legless, the blind, the insane,
Those proud, wounded heroes of Suvla.
And when the ship pulled into Circular Quay,
I looked at the place where my legs used to be,
And thank Christ there was no one there waiting for me,
To watch and to mourn and to pity.

And the band played "Waltzing Matilda"
As they carried us down the gangway.
But nobody cheered: they just stood there and stared,
Then they turned all their faces away. . . .

By the time Alfie finished, there wasn't a sound in the room. I looked over at the terror of barrooms from Dover to Dubai, and by God, there were tears in his eyes. Richie, for all his aggressiveness, was a romantic after all.

Alfie sang without letup—Richie wouldn't allow him to let up—for nearly three hours, during which time he held his audience of ruffian truckers and uncomprehending Turks spellbound and silent.

Alfie's voice finally gave out well after midnight. But no one, except Robin and Bob Mattingly, who had left directly after dinner, wanted to hit the sack. In the absence of further singing, Richie dominated a discussion that quickly focused on the evils of *cabotage*. Traditionally this French word was used to describe the practice of coasters steaming from port to port to pick up or discharge cargo. It has come to have an accepted usage in the trucking industry, referring to trucks registered in one country picking up loads in another and discharging them in a third. British long-distance truckers believe that *cabotage* practiced by East European and Turkish firms was denying them a proper livelihood. *Cabotage* is forbidden among Common Market members when practiced by EEC-domiciled trucking firms.

The Dane had discovered before leaving Copenhagen that the other part of the load he was taking to Iran was being carried by a Bulgarian truck.

"How can a Bulgarian truck come to Denmark and take a load from Denmark to Iran?" Richie wanted to know.

"I'm asking myself the same question," the Dane replied.

"This is *cabotage*. You must speak to your government. We must speak to our government. This must stop," Richie said very seriously.

"Yes, sure," the Dane said, not yet certain where Richie was leading him.

"It's not right. It's fuckin' crazy, I'll tell you, mate. I'm going fuckin' bankrupt for the likes of those bastards. I'm going to kick up holy fuckin' stink when I get home this time."

The Dane didn't realize it, but he had touched upon the sorest point in Richie's very sore mind. Richie had also discovered that the other part of the load he carried to Basra had been given to a Turk. "When I found out that the Turk had unloaded in Basra and had lost twenty-six drums of paint, I said to myself, 'He sold the fuckin' things in Turkey.' How can he go from England and fuckin' unload in Basra? He can't, Bob, can he? It's impossible."

"By the rules, it's impossible," Anderson agreed.

"If you take your truck and you go over to France and you stop in France, right, then you get a trailer come over, you can't pick up that trailer to deliver it. 'Whoa, whoa,' they say. 'That's *cabotage*.' Then how the hell can that Turk come and unload in England and load for a third country? I don't know the laws, but definitely as soon as I get home I'm going to phone the Road Haulers' Association and I'm going to say, 'Can you define to me the correct procedures for *cabotage*?' "

The Dane was also an owner-driver. He said that over the past two years East German truckers had stolen almost all the haulage trade between Denmark and Austria by undercutting Danish truckers. The shortest route for Danish truckers to the Middle East was through East Germany. "Every time I go through their fucking country I have to listen to their propaganda on the radio telling how the workers in the West are without jobs. But they don't care about taking my job away."

"They don't care about taking his job, or taking my job, or anybody else's," Richie affirmed. "The only way we can possibly do anything about it is to get all the owners to join together and do something.''

''My foreman won't,'' Steve said.

''Well, he'll fuckin' have to,'' Richie came back. ''I'm here doing the same jobs as you lads all the time, right? Okay, I got two trucks. I wish to fuck I didn't. I'd be better off working for someone the same as you lads. You see, I can't get out. I can't afford to get out. I'd have to pay some asshole to wind up my company. I'm losing money, but I can't get out. So what have I fuckin' got? Those trucks are mine now. I own the blasted things. But I have to fuckin' fight to have the right to work with them. Mark my words, if I go bankrupt I'm going to go around to all those fuckin' Bulgarian trailers and Turkish trucks parked up in England waiting for a backload and I'm going to bust them to bits. It's fuckin' wrong.''

Richie banged the table with his bottle of beer, and no one spoke. Finally he said, ''I'm going to tell Leon Ashworth, 'Leon, you made a fuckup. You loaded a Turk.'

''I've already spoken to Cleveland Bridge. I've got a backload on for Cleveland Bridge as a favor, right, which I hope will put me in good stead with the fuckin' management of the company in England. And I'm going to say, 'I brought your fuckin' pipes home for fifty dollars. No problem. But Leon has just loaded a Turk. He's got there and he's twenty-six drums of paint short.'

''And Mike [the Cleveland Bridge manager in Basra] said to me, 'What do you reckon, Richie?' I said, 'I know exactly what happened. The cunt sold them in Turkey.' Mike signed his manifest but not his CMR. Mike then went into Basra on business, and the Turk was told by Mike's staff to wait till the manager came back to have his CMR endorsed. No way. The Turk's gone. He doesn't want the CMR to show he's twenty-six drums short. So who's it down to, then? Who'll pay for the loss? Movex, or Whittle?''

''The Turkish firm will cover that,'' Graham volunteered.

''They won't get paid nothing. If I know Whittle, and I think I do, Whittle will not pay that Turkish company one fuckin' cent. They [Whittle] will make forty-eight hundred pounds at least,'' Richie ventured. What he was otherwise saying was that Whittle would get paid by Cleveland, in spite of the missing freight, but would claim damages against the Turkish trucking company and refuse to pay them because they were unable to produce a signed CMR for satisfactory delivery of the merchandise.

It seemed to me that they were missing the point. Whittle boasted in promotional material that it concentrated on delivering British exports to the Middle East with British freight systems, but in particular with British trucks. This was Michael Whittle's stated policy, just as "Keep Moving" had been his grandfather's motto, and there was no scarcity of British truckers to carry British goods.

The Whittle brochure for clients pointed out: "Cowboy operations have given the whole industry a bad name, but if you entrust your cargo to Whittle you can be confident that it will arrive at its destination in good time and in good condition. . . . Operational control is the key to successful international haulage and we monitor the progress of each consignment right through to destination. Throughout each journey, drivers are in planned regular contact with our offices en route so that we can monitor progress daily. . . . Usually traveling in convoy, the drivers are mature, experienced, and British, and feel personally responsible for the safety of your cargo."

According to Richie, Whittle was employing "cowboy" operators; they weren't British and they did not feel personally restrained from pirating part of the cargo. But this wasn't all that was bothering Richie. "My rate for going down there was forty-eight hundred pounds. I got forty-one hundred pounds. They took seven hundred pounds off the top. How the fuckin' hell can you take seven hundred pounds just for giving somebody a load? That's robbery."

"If you don't do the job, somebody else will," Graham pointed out.

"No, no, that shouldn't be," Richie came back.

"The Bulgarians will," Steve told him.

"The Bulgarians shouldn't be allowed to come to Britain," Richie insisted.

The intellectual level of the discussion was declining. The argument was starting to turn in a circle.

"No circle. I call it tunnel vision. It's trucks, trucks, trucks all the time. It's like being stuck on the same trolley line and never getting off it," said Leslie, who had been silent during most of the evening. It was 3:00 A.M. and he announced he was going to bed.

12. PIG ALLEY

ROBIN Fraser and Bob Mattingly worked all Wednesday on the Mattingly DAF, trying to sort out its problems sufficiently for it to last the remainder of the journey home. Bob was having a run of bad luck. On his way back from Kuwait in June the DAF threw a "con rod"— the arm that connects the piston to the crankshaft—ten miles south of Nassariah, in Iraq.

"It was a Sunday morning. I'll never forget it," Bob said. "It went clatter, clatter, bang, and shot straight through the side of the engine."

Bob stands about six feet two and is lanky, with a receding hairline that makes him look more pensive than he really is. His manner is retiring, but underneath his quietness he is droll and warm. Fortunately, when the con rod went, he was running with Dickie Lewis, also off Prior's. Bob parked in the desert and drove back to Baghdad with Dickie to get a towline and an extra length of air hose, first removing everything of value from the cab.

When they got back to the truck the next day it had been broken into and all the bedding removed. Unable to use his motor, Bob could not build up air pressure to operate the brakes. So they ran an eighty-foot air line from Dick's compressor into Bob's compressor, and now he had brakes. They towed it back to Baghdad, where a towbar was being made, and had a towpin welded to the front bumper. That same day, a Wednesday, they left Baghdad. The two vehicles joined together, with their refrigerator-trailers, measured an illegal 115 feet. It was a long, long vehicle. Three-axled refrigerator-trailers weigh ten tons each, empty, so it also was a heavy, heavy vehicle,

111

given the slender air line and single compressor upon which the brakes relied.

Going up Zahko Mountain, which is a series of ascending hairpins on a disappearing road surface, the pin broke and the towbar dropped. "I could see my lifeline getting longer and longer, until it snapped. No more brakes. 'Oh, fuck,' I thought. 'I'm on my own now,' " Bob said. He jammed on the deadman. They had to drop the legs on both trailers, tow the unit up the remainder of the mountain using the tow cable, then return for Bob's refrigerator-trailer.

"We couldn't get up Cizre Hill, either," Bob continued. Same procedure. Drop legs, tow the unit up first. While the trailers were standing unattended, someone nicked one of the tow cables.

They got to Adana on Monday, five days after leaving Baghdad, having crossed the full length of southern Turkey. "The first three days was fucking harrowing. At the end it was still nerve-racking, but I had gotten more used to it."

Coming down Tarsus, they were stopped for speeding. The copper wanted to cite them for overlength, but they talked him out of it. Dickie had no brake lights either, so Bob could never tell when he was braking. He was also being towed at an angle, with right-hand drive, as close to the shoulder as possible in order to see what was ahead.

From Adana they got to Istanbul in two days, and they reached Salonika the following Friday: nine days on a towbar and 2,017 miles later. Bob stayed eleven days in Salonika having a rebuilt engine installed. The whole trip had taken him sixty-two days.

Richie said good-bye at midday Wednesday and left for "Instanbul." He seemed in better spirits. Terry returned from Adana late that afternoon. Fatih assured Les, Steve, Graham, and me that our papers would be there tomorrow. Les was going to run with us as far as Baghdad. With nothing to do, we decided to visit Pig Alley. After pressuring Fatih, he agreed to drive us into town in his Fiat and act as our guide.

Ankara had been a stopping place on both the Persian Royal Road from the Aegean to southern Iraq and the Roman Via Regalis. But long before Cyrus the Great or Julius Caesar passed that way, the Hittites had occupied the Hisar, Ankara's imposing citadel. We parked and made our way to a large green gate that pierced a twenty-foot wall under the citadel hill. The way it was guarded by a phalanx of Turkish youth made it appear at first glance to be a gateway to the citadel itself. But no, these young men with dark eyes and furtive looks, dressed in ill-fitting suits, were the prospective clients of the women within. Apparently the young men were summoning their courage to pass the single policeman with a two-foot billy club who was the sole guardian stationed *inside* the gate. In fact, there was a police post just inside the gate, which might have contained other officers, but this fellow, his fly undone, was the only one in evidence. It was unclear to me whether he was there to check the identity of those who entered the forbidden precinct or to ensure that the residents did not escape.

Pig Alley consisted of three small streets lined on both sides by dilapidated two- and three-story houses, some gaudily painted, most brightly lit from within, and all with a crowd of gawking men without. The houses—some of them, at least—looked like the sturdy burghers' homes in Swiss villages, with thick walls, high, sloping roofs, and projecting eaves, though they were seedily maintained. They gave the impression of having been there for quite some time, perhaps since Tamerlane. Others were modern and more functional.

As the precinct was on the flank of the citadel hill, the streets rose sharply to the farthest wall. They had been laid out in the shape of a lopsided three-branched candelabrum, joining at the bottom to pass through the single gate. It was already dark and they were festooned with garlands of multicolored lights. By a rough count, there were easily five thousand sweating men milling around in these confines, vying for the services of the three hundred overworked residents who sat coyly in their parlors, like spider ladies at the center of a web. It was only 7:00 P.M., which meant there were still four more hours to go, for the gate closed at 11:00 P.M. Any outsider caught within after that hour risked a severe beating from the ill-tempered copper.

Every Turkish city of any size, I am told, has its Pig Alley. The one in Istanbul is said to be especially colorful. While a few single ladies worked out of bedrooms, most of the merchandise—for that is finally what it comes down to—was gathered in parlors with open doors so the panting males could look in. Each parlor is supervised by a whoremaster licensed by the state, as are the women themselves. They are subject to monthly medical visits. The whoremaster shares the nightly take with each of his wards.

The gawkers were encouraged to come in and examine the merchandise more closely. The basic fee was a thousand Turkish lire (one pound), imposed by the state, for even the world's oldest profession is subject to price controls in Turkey. But if a client expected anything more than a peek and a caress, he had to pay a minimum of five thousand lire on top of the first thousand. Theoretically a woman can buy her freedom from the parlormaster—the price was said to be exaggeratedly high; two million lire was the figure quoted to me—but in the end few do, possibly because the degree of degradation to which they are subject soon desensitizes them to any other way of life.

A few of the parlors were particularly filthy. None was what you might term "clean." Of the more than one hundred women we saw that night, only three or four were appealing, young, or pretty. A few appeared to be well into their sixties, and they sat in their parlors with their pendulous breasts exposed, with soiled miniskirts and laddered stockings, their legs "invitingly" apart. One was strikingly pretty, with reddish hair and in her early twenties if not late teens. She seemed to enjoy her rating as the Princess of Pig Alley. The crowd of gawkers around her parlor was dense.

The women who ply their trade in these places, several friends assured us, were for the most part adulteresses who had not been forgiven by their husbands. There were other categories as well: those who had been sentenced for some petty crime like stealing and could earn a reduction of their prison terms by serving in a brothel, or those who were working off a family debt. It seemed doubtful to me that this could be entirely true. But the notion that in most cases these were supposedly fallen women who were being punished by society fascinated all of us. The idea of women held in perfectly degrading bondage seemed to unleash all sorts of male chauvinist fantasies. At first we were curious to see how this bondage worked. But the sordidness soon made us feel uneasy. Steve tried to hide his revulsion by joking about the appearances of the inmates or the squalor of the dens in which they sat. But you could tell his heart wasn't in it.

In a passageway a score of young men were standing around the doorway of a woman in a bedroom. Their mouths were agog as they waited. The door opened and a tired-looking, once-attractive, thirty-year-old blonde dressed in a short baby-doll negligee let out a client, still buttoning up his trousers, then motioned to another young buck among those waiting; once he had crossed the threshold, the door shut again. The audience was silent, sheepishly regarding each figure who slunk through the door almost as if he were a hero, for most of them were only gawkers, there for the looks, because either they dared not be or had not the money to be next in line.

Outside in the street, the Turkish equivalent of a carnie operator offered to guess the weight and age of any comer, then would try to sell him some aphrodisiacal potion. Business was brisk. For those who didn't want to take their refreshments inside, street kiosks sold hot dogs and soft drinks.

My curiosity quenched, and feeling somewhat soiled for having witnessed such degradation, both of the inmates and the gawkers, and above all wanting to rid myself of the odor of stale sex that hung in the streets, I suggested to Fatih that we leave. He seemed even more ill at ease than I and attempted to apologize. The reaction of the three others was mixed: Graham was noncommittal, which meant nonapproving; Steve thought it a poor joke; while Leslie was mesmerized by the bondage of the young princess.

The price of a trick in Pig Alley represented 15 percent of the minimum monthly wage approved by the Turkish government, which may sound like a meaningless statistic. But when you consider that government economists have calculated that 45 percent of the monthly wage is consumed in the purchase of food, any worker on the minimum-wage scale who saves up to relieve his frustrations in Pig Alley will have only the equivalent of seventeen pounds left to cover the rent and spend on other items that month. The average bureaucrat, of which there are a fair number in Turkey, earns only twice the minimum wage and therefore is not much better off.

For contrast, Fatih took us into the center of the city to a pedestrian promenade that was lined with pleasant sidewalk cafes, each one specializing in a different dish—kebab, pizza, grilled chicken, shashlik. We stopped at one that sold only fish and had Carlsberg on tap. We ordered sardines baked in tinfoil that were a welcome change from the undercooked chicken at Telex Motel.

Over dinner we learned from Fatih that earlier in the week the Iranian government had closed its borders to Turkish trucks. Turkish cargoes going to Iran had to be transshipped at the border onto Iranian vehicles. Similar restrictions were already in force for West European trucks (although certain exceptions existed) but not as far as we knew for East European vehicles. Entry into Iran was becoming increasingly difficult. A three-month delay for transit visas had just about stopped all overland traffic to Pakistan, though the magic buses were still getting through. They carried two drivers who took turns at the wheel, driving nonstop with the side curtains drawn from Baluchistan in the South to the Turkish border.

Relations between Turkey and Iran were not good. A few weeks before, Ayatollah Khomeini had announced from Qom that the greatest disaster to befall the Turks was a man named Mustafa Kemal, otherwise known as Ataturk. He had come to power in 1923, declared Turkey a republic, and, by way of modernization, closed down all religious schools, dissolved the dervish orders, and introduced the European alphabet and the Swiss civil code. He secularized Turkey, something for which Khomeini could never forgive him. No love was lost between the Turkish leaders and Ayatollah Khomeini, whom they accused of financing Turkey's increasingly vocal Islamic fundamentalists. The movement was making significant inroads with students by financing their tuition, their textbooks, and providing them with hostels in which to eat and sleep.

With the zippering up of the Iranian frontier, we speculated that the final onslaught against Iraq by Khomeini's Revolutionary Guards was not far off. We hoped that we would not be caught in Iraq when it happened.

We decided to make it an early night, and we returned to Telex Motel for a last *Efes kontrol*.

13. CICILIAN GATES

THURSDAY, September 25. Steve, Bob Anderson, and Leslie relaxed all morning in front of the TV watching *Life of Brian* and *The Assassination of Heydrich*. Other favorites in the Telex Motel's video library included *Convoy, Rambo, Smokey and the Bandit,* and *Vanishing Point*. Graham spent the time fixing his exhauster brake and tidying up the cab. Bob Mattingly and Robin Fraser had left at dawn. Alfie Jones was planning to check out at midmorning. He took me over to see the sound system he had installed in the cab of his Dorf. Fitted into each corner was a seventy-five-watt speaker, and he had upholstered the roof and back panel with leather padding. He had transformed his Dorf into a sound studio on wheels. He kept it spotless. And while he owned a house in Trethomas, the Dorf was really his home—a little bit of Wales on the road. An artist he knew had painted the Welsh coat of arms on the side of his unit, and he had a big steel smokestack at the back of the cab that the Saudis require for trucks entering the port of Jeddah.

"A lot of love has gone into this machine," I told him.

"It helps make the hours go faster," he said. The road was his life, the Middle East truckers his family, the Dorf and folk music his two loves. Alfie was a self-contained diesel gypsy, and yet the faraway look in his slate-colored eyes and that eagerness to assist others said he was tired of being alone, that even he wanted to settle down. A last cup of tea, and then with a rhythmic vroom-vroom puffing exhaust from the big pipe at the back, he wheeled his Caerphilly juggernaut out of Telex Mo-camp onto the road for the lonesome eight-hour shift down to Istanbul.

The morning dragged on. Everyone was restless. Departure time was approaching, but there was little talk and no joking. Aytekin invited me to partake of a staff lunch. We sat at a table by the window, looking out onto Route 8. The helicopters were practicing right turns that morning. Over lentil soup and stewed lamb with eggplant he told me some of the tales that had marked the year since we last met.

Aytekin was in his late twenties. The son of a Turkish diplomat, he had received his education at French *lycées* in Stockholm, Bonn, Warsaw, and Paris. We spoke, therefore, in French, which pleased him. Telex Motel was owned by a syndicate of businessmen headed by a local senator, Cerdet Karagülle, and his son. Their main trade came from the TIR drivers who treated the place as their club. This was encouraged by the staff. In a large frame behind the bar was a rogues' gallery of more than two hundred passport portraits of the drivers who at one time or another had formed the motel's regular clientele. Some had since been killed, others no longer drove the route, but each face had a story and memories attached to it in the minds of the Telex staff.

For the staff, every nationality has its own personality. The British are regarded as fighters, the French as chauvinists, the Danes and Swedes as drinkers, and the Germans as cold as refrigerators. The Greeks are mistrusted. Senator Karagülle had loaned one or two of them money and hadn't been repaid.

The drivers, for their part, appreciated having the run of the motel. Their antics, however, were not always viewed in the best light by the local clientele. The Turks were astonished—indeed, mesmerized, but infrequently amused—by the crudeness of the British drivers.

One evening, Aytekin recalled, some Turkish guests were quietly eating dinner, half fascinated by the raucous British drivers seated on the sofa watching the TV. One of the older drivers had fallen asleep with his head tilted backward and mouth open. When he started snoring, John Bruce off Astran got onto the sofa, lowered his pants, and placed his bare ass over the sleeping driver's face. He woke up quickly enough, but rather than yelling blue murder, bit into John's private parts. Squeals of pain from John brought peals of laughter from the other drivers, who thought this was hilarious. The Turks were not amused but fascinated by the vulgarity, and they talked about the incident for weeks.

Drivers might argue with Mehmet that they had been charged for more beers than they consumed, but none feared being robbed. Ali Baba guarded the entrance to the TIR parking lot at night with a

1910-model shotgun. On one occasion, after an *Efes kontrol,* two Swedes and a Brit stumbled into the parking lot, where words were exchanged. Words led to fisticuffs. One of the Swedes was carrying a briefcase full of his running money. It burst open; the money spilled out and scattered across the yard. While the fight continued, Mehmet and Ali Baba scurried around, picking up the papers and banknotes. The drivers finally got tired of the fight and stumbled off to bed, forgetting the briefcase. Next morning its owner was in a panic. He burst into the restaurant. Before he could say a word, Mehmet put up his hands and said, ''Moment.'' He went behind the bar and produced the missing briefcase. The Swede immediately checked, and to his astonishment he was not a deutsche mark or Turkish lira short.

As departure time crept up on us, we avoided mention of the Iraqi-Iranian war, even though it was ever-present in our minds. Two German drivers returning from Baghdad the week before had reported they were robbed of twelve hundred deutsche marks and all their food by drug-crazed cops. Brian Moody wouldn't run beyond Ankara any longer because the year before he and Geoff Frost had been held up by army deserters south of Baghdad. With Kalashnikovs pointed at their heads they were relieved of eighteen hundred pounds between them. Black Billy Hall, returning from Kuwait one night, ran a gauntlet of fire after refusing to stop at a deserters' roadblock.

We had heard of another British driver, whose name we didn't know, being nearly beaten to death earlier that month by Iraqi Customs police. He had been kept at Zahko for five days because his manifest and certificate of origin allegedly were not in order. On the sixth day he was told he could go. As he was about to climb into the cab, one of the border guards jabbed him in the kidney with a billy club. He turned to protest and was hit with a blackjack behind the ear by a second soldier, sending him to the ground. The two then started kicking and beating him. Several Turkish drivers intervened. They probably saved his life. They dragged off the soldiers and boosted the British driver into his cab. As soon as he had regained consciousness, but still groggy, they told him for his own safety he should leave the compound immediately.

The situation was getting meaner by the day as the Iraqis, with no taste for war, smelled defeat.

Fatih appeared with our papers at the end of the afternoon. Bob Anderson was still waiting instructions from his office. Alex Downie had apparently gotten through, so Bob was hoping to get a Yugoslav manifest at Habur from Young Turk. But he was in no hurry to leave. We had a final drink with Fatih before climbing into our cabs. Ali Baba looked sorry to see us leave. In the yard, which was large enough to hold two hundred trucks, only three were left: the Falcongate rig, a Turk, and an Austrian pulling a Maltese trailer. It was deadsville.

We kept on the outer ring road, turning south on a dual highway, past a *trafik polisi* checkpoint. Leslie, in a Volvo F12 pulling a blue step-frame box trailer known as a Super Cube, was in front. We noticed that Steve, who was behind us, had been stopped. Later we asked him what it was about.

"Nothing," he said. "The copper only wanted to practice his English. He asked me where we were going, what my name was, whether I was married—things like that—then waved me out."

As soon as we drove over Gölbasi Hill, the weather became warmer. It was dark, and the night sky was bright. By 8:00 P.M. we were running along the shore of the Great Salt Lake on the edge of the Anatolian plain. We were on the old two-lane highway now, broken by miles of intermittent pick-and-shovel. Sheet lightning lit the eastern sky, and after a while we could make out the silhouette of the Hasan Dagi Volcano, which announced we were nearing Aksaray, where we would spend the night.

The Aksaray TIR park contained two Austrian trucks, about a dozen Wombles, some F-troop, and two Russians who were having dinner together. We brewed a pot of tea and listened to the BBC World Service. The Iranians had bombed Baghdad, the announcer said, and were shelling Basra in retaliation for yesterday's air raid by Iraqi jets against Iranian civilian targets.

We were on the road again by 8:00 A.M. the next morning, heading for the Cilician Gates. The day started brightly, with wind from the south. We were driving through country in which man's oldest settlements had been found, notably the ruins at Catal Hüyük, near Konya, a town that apparently had prospered as the Stone Age turned to Bronze. Recent archaeological digs indicated that the craft of metallurgy was born here, as well as stock-breeding and agriculture. *Hüyük* is Turkish for mound, or tumulus, and we noticed scores of them across the broad ocher plain stretching 150 miles from the mountains to the west to Cappadocia on our left.

After having already supported a civilization for four thousand years, in about 2000 B.C. the Anatolian Plateau was overrun by the Hittites, an Aryan race from Europe. A military society, much like the later Spartans, they imposed political unity on the peoples of Anatolia, and probably because of the area's newly discovered mineral wealth they struck up a thriving trade with the Assyrians and Egyptians. Merchants from both foreign lands established trading communities in Hittite country, from where they exported local ores, grains, textiles, implements, and pottery.

We stopped at a garage and carpet shop not far from the 10,735-foot Hasan Dagi, where a blacksmith made metal lockers and iceboxes for tractor-trailers. Graham wanted a locker fitted to the back of his wagon. The smith took the measurements and told us to stop by on our return trip. At 9:00 A.M. we were under way again. Hasan Dagi was now directly in front of us, imposing with clouds around its crown. On our left were four flocks of maybe a thousand sheep each.

In another hour we reached the foothills of the Toros Mountains, which form a natural barrier between central and southern Turkey. They rise like blue and purple ramparts to almost twelve thousand feet. It looked as if there would be no way through them until, rounding a corner, we saw that the road disappeared into a narrow gorge with weirdly shaped walls of volcanic rock on either side. We had arrived at the Cilician Gates. In places no more than one hundred yards wide, they command the northern approach to Tarsus Pass. For centuries they marked the limit of European penetration into western Asia.

The Hittites first cut a path through the Cilician Gates wide enough for a cart to pass. Cyrus, when he marched north in 516 B.C. to defeat the Lydians, found the gates barely wide enough for a chariot; Alexander managed to march four lightly armed soldiers abreast through them in 333 B.C. The Arabs were able to squeeze through with loaded camels, but only in single file. That juggernauts could now wheel through them was due in large measure to the Egyptian general Ibrahim Pasha, who in 1838 blasted a road to carry his artillery onto the Anatolian Plateau. He hoped to make himself master of the Sublime Porte, but British and French intervention caused him to withdraw. Ibrahim Pasha was followed seventy years later by German engineers, who carved a series of tunnels and galleries out of the Cilician rock for the track of the Baghdad Railway.

Once through the gates, but before beginning our ascent to Tarsus Pass, we pulled onto a services area and brewed a pot of tea. The clouds around the summit of the pass were thicker now, and light showers made the road slippery. Graham almost jackknifed as he pulled in.

Over tea, Leslie made the point that a Middle East driver probably notches more mileage in a single trip to Muscat than the average domestic driver does in a year. What makes it totally unlike driving at home, he said, was that "once you leave Dover you're on your own, and when you leave the Common Market you're not only alone but also out on a limb."

"Now, if I were driving over Tarsus and broke down, what would I do if we drivers didn't help each other out?"

A police car passed and gave us the sign to get moving or risk a fine. We drove through Pozanti, a garrison town at the foot of the pass. Bits of the old Roman road were discernible now and then, and near where we had stopped a magnificent Ottoman bridge arched over a tributary of the Cydnus River, which runs through the gates.

For the run over Tarsus, I had moved up front with Leslie. He had been driving the road for seven years and knew it well. Before that he had been a brewery truck driver, but he found it boring. As a former HGV instructor, he handled his machine with nimbleness, always alert, always watching what the tonkas, kamikaze buses, and tankers were up to. Leslie was a reflective man in his midforties. He avoided hassles and took administrative functions like clearing Customs and dealing with bent coppers with patience, trying to understand their motivation and the source of their greed. It was only when behind the wheel that he became a demon.

Tarsus Pass was one of the most critical parts of our journey. In Turkish it is called Gülek Bogaz, a name derived from the castle of Gülek, which dominates its crest. The Turks have a saying "Whoever does not dread the Gülek Bogaz does not fear God." Now a four-lane expressway takes traffic to the top, where we were stopped by two policemen who asked what our problem was—a new approach. "No problem," Leslie said.

"What about Marlboro?" they asked.

We obliged and they thanked us politely.

The road leveled for a while. Untethered donkeys stood warming themselves on the asphalt, and herds of black goats, cows, and a few horses wandered across the upland meadows. Mount Taurus, dark and foreboding, rose on our right to a height of 11,850 feet. A road sign said that the top of the pass was at an altitude of 4,521 feet.

Coming around a corner on a sharp uphill gradient, we almost collided with a tonka immobilized in the right-hand lane. The driver had placed some rocks in the road to warn of the hazard and all but disappeared under his truck. We swung by him, narrowly missing an oncoming bus. On our way down the pass an empty tanker overtook us, misjudged his speed and the distance to the next bend, and as he swung back in, hit a patch of dirt that caused him to slither onto the shoulder, beyond which was a two-hundred-foot drop into a ravine. He was at the limit of his adherence and fishtailed a moment as another bus sped toward us. He managed to regain control, and off he went at the same fast clip, skirting disaster.

We reached the city of Tarsus at about 1:00 P.M. In the days of Julius Caesar, travelers took thirty days to reach Tarsus from Rome. It had taken us the better part of two weeks to drive there from Blackpool. The roads were better than in Roman times and we had more horsepower, but otherwise nothing of any overbearing importance seemed to have changed. Cypress and cedars stood in neat rows between the fields. Donkeys pulled outsized two-wheeled carts that designwise had not changed an iota from the Roman *cisium*. St. Paul, though a citizen of Rome, was born at Tarsus when it was one of Asia Minor's richest cities. Alexander and Augustus passed through on their way east; Antony met Cleopatra here; and Julian the Apostate was buried at the city's gates. For a time Tarsus was governed by Baldwin of Boulogne, and then by Harun-al-Rashid, greatest of the caliphs. Tarsus's fortunes, it is true, had declined. Today the city has been supplanted as the capital of Cilicia by Adana, a textile and carpetmaking center forty-five miles to the east.

Adana was on the right bank of the Ceyhan River, where Hadrian spanned it with a curiously lopsided bridge that counted more than twenty arches. The bridge was still in use eighteen hundred years later. Now, that was engineering designed to last. We did not take Hadrian's bridge, however, because to get to it you had to drive through the narrow streets of Adana's old town. Instead we stayed on the four-lane expressway to the north, sighting our first Kurdish encampment in the plain after Adana. A few miles farther Leslie noticed three brightly robed Gypsy women running across the fields toward us. They flagged us down. Curious, Leslie stopped to see what they wanted. The one with the brass dentures opened Leslie's door and climbed onto the running board. "Fickie-fickie?" she asked, grabbing his crotch.

"Get away, you witch!" he shouted at her. But she wouldn't get down. He started to roll forward until finally she jumped. We were heading for Osmaniye, an easy fifty-mile run to the east. We planned to stop for the night at a bazaar and service station there known as Ali

Baba's. A towering fortress stands on a prominent rock outcrop over the town of Ceyhan, halfway to Osmaniye. It is known as Yilanli Castle. *Yilanli* in Turkish means snakes. In 1097 the Crusader princes installed a garrison of knights here on their way to Antioch, eighty-five miles to the south. But the castle predated them by a few hundred years. The ruins, I remarked to Leslie, were imposing. Most of the ramparts still appeared intact.

"What ruins?" he asked.

"There," I said, pointing. "Yilanli Castle."

"Oh," he said, astonished. "I never noticed it before."

"In this job," he explained, "you don't have time to take your eyes off the road. You've got to be looking in front, behind, checking your mirrors, judging your distances, watching the shoulder, concentrating all the time. In this country, they come at you from every direction. You have to be alert."

He shot another glance at Yilanli. "Hey, that really is beautiful," he said. "It makes you wonder, though, doesn't it? You think of all the trouble we've had getting this far. How the hell did the Crusaders do it? On horseback, three thousand miles from home, hostile country, fighting every inch of the way."

The sky in the northeast was dark, with the first autumn storms sweeping down off the Taurus barrier. The light was mystical, silhouetting lemony yellow minarets against a charcoal background. The fields were golden, the mountains copper and purple. At the turn-off to Iskenderun and Antakya, which is modern-day Antioch, the even larger castle of Toprakkale sat atop its own plateau, guarding the crossroads. The origins of the two castles are uncertain. Toprakkale was probably Byzantine. Some English drivers believe it once belonged to Richard Coeur de Lion. Mad Mick Moody assured me it was called Richard's Folly. French drivers are convinced it was built by Godfrey of Bouillon, Duke of Lorraine, or perhaps his brother Baldwin of Boulogne, who became the first Latin king of Jerusalem.

When we arrived at Ali Baba's, Steve hurried to the barber shop for a ritual shave and haircut. Three French trucks were already parked in the yard, which was covered with water, as we had just missed a torrential downpour. Two of the Frenchmen were on their way home from Baghdad. The third driver, Jean-Louis Gautier, off Iochum Transports of Marseilles, was going to Baghdad with a load of French telephone equipment.

Jean-Pierre, one of the homeward-bound Frenchmen, reported that the situation in Iraq was extremely unpleasant. "You can feel the decay," he said as we sipped raki on the terrace beside the barber shop. "People have less and less to eat. They steal more—anything they can lay their hands on. Be careful."

"When they do cabin control at Zahko, the border guards lift whatever pleases them, especially at night, when they are even less inhibited," the other added. Jean-Pierre had seen the crater left by a Scud missile the Iranians had launched against Baghdad two weeks before. "Tehran said it hit the army headquarters. I can tell you, it landed just beside the Novotel. It blew out all the windows in a half-mile radius. The Iraqis admitted it killed twenty-one people, but probably it was more."

The ironic thing, he added, was that the missile had been captured by the Iranians when they overran Iraqi positions near Basra. How he knew that I don't know, and he didn't say.

The French contingent had parked because of the rain. The storm had transformed the layers of rubber laid down on the road surface during the hot summer into a ribbon of greased slate. A tonka tanker had gone off the road at the bottom of the second mountain coming from Gaziantep and spilled its load of crude into the road. The passing traffic had spread it three miles in either direction. Six other vehicles had skidded into the ditches. The *trafik polisi* were slowing traffic to five miles per hour.

Jean-Pierre and his running mate wanted to make Aksaray by midnight, so after another raki they set off again. I went for a shower, and Jean-Louis joined Steve, Graham, Leslie, and myself at Ali Baba's bistro for dinner. The weather had turned balmy following the rain. But with the heat came the mosquitoes, and they were ferocious. We asked Jean-Louis if he wanted to run with us. He was pleased because he didn't relish driving to Baghdad alone. We went early to bed, I on a sofa in Ali Baba's office, for an intended 5:00 A.M. departure.

14. PROBLEM, MEESTER

THE night on Ali Baba's sofa was the worst of the trip. The office was infested with mosquitoes of a type that made those at Londra Camp seem like tiny tigers. There was no evading the Osmaniye bombers. I tried wearing my knitted hat and burying myself at the bottom of my sleeping bag, all zippered up. But it was hot and humid outside, more humid still inside the down bag, and soon I had to come up for air, so drenched in sweat that next morning I literally had to wring the moisture out of the sleeping bag.

Five o'clock the next morning came like a deliverance. I admired my swollen face in the mirror, then awakened the others. We made haste to leave, and by 5:50 A.M. we were on the road. It was Saturday, our thirteenth day out, and we had a long, hot journey ahead of us, across the upper Mesopotamian plain.

We passed an overturned tanker on the left side of the road. Toward the top of the first plateau, a second tanker had gone straight over the edge in a sweeping curve. Its cabin was sticking up in the air like a fist on the end of a mechanical arm.

"They certainly have a knack for that sort of thing," Graham commented.

Running through the uplands we noticed a mile-long stretch of Roman aqueduct descending from the hills to the south, reminding us that this was once a heavily fortified Roman military road to the eastern frontier with Parthia.

Traffic began building up as we neared the top of the first pass. In addition to the tankers, a lot of the trucks were carrying large-bore steel pipes made in Japan. They were being hauled overland from the port of Iskenderun to Mosul on large flatbeds and were destined for the new pipeline under construction from Baiji, in central Iraq, to the Turkish port of Mersin, on the Mediterranean coast, eighteen miles west of Tarsus. The pipes were tied onto the flatbeds by a pair of cargo straps, one forward and the other aft, and looked frighteningly insecure. As Iraq owed Japan 280 million dollars on this project, there was some doubt whether it would be completed. But for the moment, work was continuing as fast as the Turkish trucks could deliver the pipes.

Iraq had two other pipelines to Mersin. One was the traditional large-bore kind and went underground; the other was rolling along the road with us. It consisted of the thousands of Turkish tanker-trucks that ran to and from Baiji day and night, carrying crude and naphtha. The tankers were mostly twenty-five tonners and had *Dikkat! Tehlikeli Madde* (Danger! Explosive Material) written on them. As the tankers had a high degree of leakage, it was not the most economical of pipelines. But war was war, and Iraq needed to maintain its oil exports at a minimum of 1.5 million barrels a day to pay the high costs of Saddam Hussein's disastrous military adventure. Some experts estimated that the war was costing Iraq seven hundred million dollars a month. Meanwhile, the rolling pipeline was another hazard we had to contend with, and it made us more vigilant than usual.

We stopped for tea in the first rays of sunshine atop the pass. Before long a police car drove up and instructed us to move on. We shrugged our shoulders, and Steve told the two officers we were unable to comply. "Problem, *chef*," he said. "Trucks must drink *chai*." They laughed and left us alone. The first units of a large military convoy heading west were parked a bit farther along, on the far side of the road. The Turkish soldiers standing around the armored personnel carriers and jeeps looked tough and battle-weary. Their vehicles were covered with dust, and we wondered whether they were returning from a policing operation against the Kurds. Earlier that month, quoting Kurdish rebel sources, the British press had reported that Turkish forces had stepped up their incursions into northern Iraq, attacking Kurdish *peshmarga* strongholds.

Climbing the second pass, we noticed a solitary Turk sitting in the road surrounded by plastic roadwork cones and tinkering with a differential.

"Did you see that?" Graham asked in a fit of laughter.

"Yeah," I said. "But where's the vehicle?"

"Beats me. Can't see one anywhere."

In another two hours we were on the outskirts of Gaziantep, the first large city of southeastern Turkey, but had come to a standstill in a mile-long queue of vehicles. Military police had stopped the traffic while another convoy of howitzers drawn by five-ton trucks and jeeps with mounted cannons crossed the main highway to their hilltop barracks on our left.

Gaziantep, at the gateway to Kurdistan, is a large garrison city. We took the modern diversionary road around the north of the city, dodging kamikaze buses, lunatic tonkas, and an occasional horse-drawn cart. The soil under the pistachio trees that spread out in neat rows across the countryside was rose-colored. This area is the center of pistachio nut cultivation, but the largest cash crop of the Kurdish hill people has always been the opium poppy. It grows wild in these parts. According to official statistics, opium cultivation remains the main occupation of two hundred thousand Turkish farmers, and in 1985 they produced thirty-five hundred tons of opium resin.

Some Kurdish opium is shipped abroad as contraband on Turkish trucks and, according to Interpol, roughly 20 percent of all opium-based drugs seized in Western Europe are of Turkish origin. The opium route runs through Sofia and is said by the U.S. State Department to be tolerated by the Bulgarian secret police, who have a stake in the traffic.

We continued rolling along an increasingly eroded road, descending toward the bridge over the yellow waters of the Euphrates and the hot white cliffs of Birecik on the far side.

Birecik means ''little fortress'' in Turkish. Although the Euphrates is broad here, it has always been a fording place, and at one time was a Customs post on the frontier between Rome and Parthia. Today the bridge is guarded by two mosques, the one on the western side still under construction, and a smaller, more elegant Ottoman one at the far end of the bridge. Aside from the Byzantine fortress and the limestone cliffs with a foul-smelling tunnel through them leading onto the Mesopotamian Plateau, Birecik, a city of thirty thousand, has little to boast for itself. To the south, near the border with Syria, lie the ruins of Carchemish, a Hittite city that once controlled the flow of trade between Mesopotamia and the Mediterranean. T. E. Lawrence worked as an archaeologist at the digs in Carchemish between 1911 and 1914. In these yellow sands, beside the Baghdad Railway and a bridge the Germans were building over the Euphrates. He got his first taste for espionage. Of the fortress at Birecik, Lawrence wrote: ''[It] would be typically Byzantine if the Arabs under Malek-es-Zahir had not rebuilt the high towers looking southward.'' We saw the fortress to our left, but not the towers.

After climbing onto the plateau east of Birecik, we could see in places bits of Roman viaducts and stone culverts. We drove around Urfa, one of civilization's oldest cities. A Roman emperor with an army of seventy thousand disappeared here somewhere around mid-summer in A.D. 260. When Baldwin arrived in February 1098, the city was ruled by a despot who adopted the French knight as his son and made him coregent. A month later a revolt broke out against the despot, and an angry mob tore him limb from limb. Next day the people invited Baldwin to become their king. The city, which had converted to Christianity 170 years after the death of Christ, had a great cathedral with vaulted ceilings that was rated among the seven wonders of the world, and more than three hundred churches. Today none remains.

We continued to Viranşehir, on the edge of the Syrian desert. For miles and miles that afternoon we crept over a broken road surface at twenty miles per hour with a long line of Turkish tonkas and tankers in front and heavy traffic coming against us.

"The roads are getting worse and the sun is getting hotter," Graham said with a sigh.

The arc of the Taurus Mountains reappeared on our left; Syria was on our right. We were beginning to encounter Kurdish change experts along the roadside, but we had been warned that some of them were offering counterfeit Iraqi dinars, so we took no notice and kept rolling along the arrow-straight road.

At 5:30 P.M. we pulled off at an unofficial TIR park west of Kiziltepe. A police car roared in behind us and wanted us to move on. We refused; words were exchanged and a pack of Marlboros was given. The *polisi* moved off. The owner of the TIR park and restaurant was a "friend." Business was slow—"No *kamyon*, no *kamyon*," he kept on saying with a moan, and he wanted us to stay the night. We told him we were behind schedule and had to move on, though his kebab was said to be one of the best along the route. We had some *chai* and, because he was known to be an honest dealer, changed some Deutschmarks for dinars before leaving.

A riot had almost broken out there before Christmas. Leslie told us that a group of British drivers were having an *Efes kontrol* and some Turks were seated at the next table watching them. One of the British drivers got up to go for a piss and, without noticing, dropped his wallet on the floor. A Turk saw the wallet fall. He slyly picked it up and started to leave. But Peter the Plater, another British driver, had seen everything and grabbed the Turk, demanding the wallet's return. It was Gallipoli all over again. The owner came out with his largest kitchen knife and tried to intervene. He was knocked flying. He then announced he was calling the police. Peter said, "If you call the coppers, make sure they send big ones, because we're going to tear this fuckin' place apart."

Five minutes later a riot wagon drew up, and out tumbled a squad of police with machine guns. Order was restored and the wallet returned.

Kiziltepe means "red hill" and as a town it has existed since at least the sixth century B.C. We know this because it was on the Royal Road that Persian engineers had graded and paved during the reign of Cyrus the Great. Cyrus, who defeated the Assyrians, ruled the whole of western Asia. His road, which we were now bouncing along, but in a later edition, ran from Sardis, the capital of Lydia, not far from modern-day Izmir, to Susa in southern Iraq. In Cyrus's time caravans took three months to travel its sixteen hundred miles. According to Herodotus, the average traveler could cover seventeen and a half miles a day and rest each night at one of the post offices Cyrus had built along the road. A Persian dispatch carrier, riding posthaste, could cover the distance in seven days. Kiziltepe was the site of one of these post offices.

The Persian Royal Road was history's first paved trade route, and the volume of commerce that flowed along it surpassed anything previously known. In addition to luxury goods, which until then had accounted for most of the world's exports, the traffic also included manufactured products such as household items and cheap clothing. These were carried to and from countries that previously had not traded with each other—for example, between Babylon and Greece. Industries such as the manufacture of tunics, footwear, furniture, and cosmetics were beginning to develop in towns. The first private banks were established in Babylon to help finance the expansion of trade, and the Persians seized control of the Pontic wheat trade, which directly threatened the Greek city-states that depended on imported cereals. Patterns set then were still more or less intact. The fact that we were rolling along a route that Cyrus had mapped out, carrying with us French telephone equipment for Baghdad, Scottish wood paneling for Kuwait, and a British-designed industrial oven for Al Khobar was proof that the essential dynamics had not greatly changed, only the volume and bulk of the cargoes, their sophistication, and the ease with which they were handled.

Then as now, Kiziltepe was a violent place. At the beginning of September, three weeks before we passed through the town, the mayor had been shot in a family vendetta, and a curfew was imposed to prevent the city's two major clans from tearing each other apart. One side of the dual highway through the center of town had been asphalted that afternoon, and the tonka jockeys were having a ball. The other side was blocked by road-building machines, so all traffic was channeled into the two left lanes: horse-drawn carts, kamikaze buses, tonkas, lunatic tankers, and us. Traffic continued to whiz by in spite of a head-on collision between two junior tankers. The police were trying to sort it out, and a wrecker had just arrived to pull the tankers apart.

"Oh, it's such a lovely mess," said Graham, chuckling. "Just how do they do it? Can you tell me that?"

What had become evident to us was the heavy investment the Turks were making in their overland transportation network. The *Turkish Daily News,* published in Ankara, reported that 1.6 billion dollars had been budgeted to build 660 miles of new expressway by 1988. By then they hoped to have converted the southern TIR route into a full-length expressway connecting the north–south Trans-European Expressway with the Trans-Asian Expressway at Gürbulak on the Iranian frontier and Habur on the Iraqi frontier.

I was now riding with Jean-Louis. We were rumbling alongside the Syrian frontier. The border was fenced and guarded, much like the border between Eastern and Western Europe. On the Turkish side there were towers and machine-gun nests, concrete bunkers and fortifications that normally one would not expect to find between friendly neighbors. But Diocletian had first fortified this same frontier seventeen hundred years before. It was a tempestuous corner of the world that in all of man's existence had rarely known peace.

The wire fence was floodlit on the Turkish side and looked like a necklace of light extending for miles and miles into the night. Every once in a while we were swept by a probing searchlight.

Jean-Louis, thirty-two, had been driving the Middle East run for six years. He was as timid as a church mouse. A body-repair mechanic by training, he had given it up to become a diesel gypsy after his girlfriend of six years' standing left him for another man. He also made two trips a year across the Sahara to Niger.

"Now, that's driving," he said. "No roads for the last third of the way. The 120-degree heat will kill you, but the people—the few you see—are nice."

He was placid-looking for a Frenchman. Perhaps it was his almost dreamy eyes. He spent his time in his air-conditioned cab thinking about the road ahead, worrying about the danger of accidents and about getting back home safely to see his parents and sister. His Volvo was a year old; he looked after it as if it were a prized Citroën CX and drove it with approximately the same ease. He was a most competent driver.

Strange, I thought, that the British regard their trucks as something feminine, but not the French. A truck is *macho*. When French women find a man handsome, they say he is *beau comme un camion* (good-looking like a truck). No wonder these two nations have trouble understanding each other.

Jean-Louis had installed an extra set of headlights on his roof rack to highlight the sand ripples in the Sahara—a telltale sign of soft terrain and therefore trouble. When an oncoming tonka didn't get over well enough or dim its lights, Jean-Louis would flick on the overhead set. They were so bright you could distinguish the brand of the cigarettes on the Turkish truck's dashboard. When overtaking, if the truck ahead showed the slightest reluctance to make way, Jean-Louis flicked them on again and you could see the face of the driver ahead reflected in his wing mirror.

We had been hoping to make Cizre, near the Iraqi border, but by 7:30 P.M. we were too exhausted to continue and pulled into a TIR parking lot and caravansary at Girimira, fifty miles short of our destination. We showered the dust off us, had kebab and red wine in the caravansary, and headed back to the trucks.

"You're going to break me by insisting we eat in these high-class places," Graham complained. He was goading me lightheartedly, and I didn't answer. It was already an achievement to get him to eat local fare, and in a Kurdish caravansary to boot. That was progress. I gave the parking lot attendant a pack of Marlboros and showed him where I intended to bed down for the night, under a palm tree in front of Steve's cab. I didn't want to be disturbed. He got the message, and not even a mosquito bothered me.

We left at 5:30 A.M. We wanted to reach Habur before the tonka traffic built up. Graham was having alternator problems, and the refrigerator had stopped working. Obviously it was not Graham's day. His speedometer cable broke thirty-six miles from Cizre, in the barren uplands sprinkled with nodding-donkey oil pumps. Strong winds rose with the sun out of the east and we were able to appreciate for the first time the barrenness of the country we were driving through. As the Romans had pushed east, this broad expanse between the Tigris and Euphrates became a virtual no-man's-land, constantly changing hands between Rome and Parthia. The armies of both empires marched back and forth across it, devastating crops and burning villages.

Freya Stark, in her book *Rome on the Euphrates,* described it so well. In A.D. 362 the Parthians advanced north to the Tigris, crossed it, and began making for the Euphrates. This marked "the opening of a war that outlasted the reigns both of Constantius and Julian, and wasted the frontiers of Mesopotamia to their familiar desolation." The Romans withdrew, burning crops after them. The historian Ammianus Marcellinus provides us with an eyewitness account in which he reports that "the violence of the [fire] so completely destroyed all the corn, which was just beginning to swell and turn yellow, and all the young herbage, that from the Euphrates to the Tigris nothing green was to be seen. And many wild beasts were burned, and especially lions, who wander in countless droves among the beds of rushes along the banks of the rivers in Mesopotamia."

Nothing but wasteland remained; the countryside never recovered, as the desolation we encountered on our approach to the Tigris testified. We noticed countless humps rising from the plain with a collection of mud-brick houses atop them, perhaps the site of settlements that predated even Cyrus and his corps of engineers. After each invasion the farmers would rebuild their village on the rubble of the old, so that gradually their settlements rose above the floor of the plain.

"There's one that didn't make it," Graham suddenly said, pointing to a wrecked tanker with two men in long overcoats guarding it. Kids suddenly appeared from nowhere with melons to sell. We started descending Cizre Hill into the Tigris Valley.

Going down the hill minutes ahead of us that morning, a tonka livestock transporter had lost three sheep off the top deck. A Kurdish family tending their own sheep on the hillside had come running down and butchered the crippled animals. When we passed, two were already skinned and quartered. Women were carrying the meat up the hill to their black-goat-hair tents, while two men dismembered the third animal.

"Fresh meat," Graham said.

Farther down the road, two more sheep lay on the roadside, half dead and bleeding.

"A real massacre," he observed.

The old town of Cizre was ahead of us, on the right bank of the Tigris. We crossed the river on a heavily guarded bridge, turned south, and climbed into the sunlight to reach the bluffs overlooking the Tigris, from where we noticed a line of military observation posts and gun emplacements. The countryside was golden, with a green band running along either bank of the river shaded by strands of poplars and tamarisks. I found it among the most beautiful scenery of the trip.

"We're lucky. There're only twenty trucks ahead of us," I said when we reached the lineup to enter Habur Customs.

Before Graham had time to respond, swarms of money changers and truck washers were climbing over us.

"You're standing on me bloody mudguard. Get off with you! Gaw on, get off!"

Most of them were kids. They used to throw rocks at you, demand cigarettes, or, if your window was open, try to toss a viper into the cab. Now they only want to change money or wash your truck. That was progress.

Young Turk walked down the line to collect our papers and clear us through Customs. He also offered to sell us some Saudi riyals, but his rate was way off. He got mad when we told him this. He was offering 150 riyals for 100 deutsche marks, when the bank rate was around 182 riyals for 100 deutsche marks.

"Your rate is no good," I insisted.

He protested. "Best rate around. Where you get better?"

"At bank."

"You see bank here? In Baghdad, no one sell you riyals. How much you got?"

He had a point. We didn't have any, and because of Iraqi exchange controls we would not be able to buy any in Iraq. Tony Medding, who knows the code of the Middle East route better than almost anyone, had warned us always to change a bit of money with Young Turk or else he would drag ass with our papers. So we gave him 100 deutsche marks. This cheered him. It should have: He was making 20 percent on the exchange rate.

"It's some game," Graham said, repeating his favorite phrase.

Young Turk shrugged. "Mister, on the road if you have money, you have friends. If you have no money, no friends. Simple." Both of us thought about this for a moment and came to the same conclusion. Once you got this far from home, it became the abiding philosophy of the route. None other counted. Meanwhile, Young Turk had walked away, leaving us to the tigers who were out for whatever they could steal: diesel tank caps, wing mirrors, the long-vehicle sign at the back of the load, running lights, a Whittle badge.

While only twenty trucks were waiting to be admitted to the Customs compound, at least 120 were already inside. They squeezed, bumped, inched, jerked, and bullied their way forward in five, then six, and finally eight lines abreast. Tonkas carrying fence posts, pipe-joining material, and Finnish newsprint. Tonkas with lists due to shifted cargoes and lopsided weight distribution, others with bales of wool piled twice as high as the vehicle and tied down with slender ropes. One tonka driver was upset because he was carrying sixteen tons. Normally, he said, he carried twenty-four tons—as much as a juggernaut. His axles were almost bent under the weight he had, but he insisted he was light.

Most of the trucks were empty tankers heading for Baiji to pick up loads of crude. They were directed into separate lines and let out of the compound in groups of twenty. When every twenty minutes or so the signal was given to roll, the tanker drivers jumped into their cabs, opened their engines to full revs, and began jockeying to overtake each other before clearing the gate. Their engines gave off throaty roars, as they had cut their exhaust pipes off behind the front axle and put on short silencers, which they imagined gave them extra power. The din was something akin to a Le Mans start amplified tenfold.

Young Turk returned and told Steve his tractor triptych had expired since entering the country and he would have to pay for a one-time extension. This made no sense. He was on his way out of Turkey, and the triptych rules stated that as long as the document was valid upon entering the country the Customs bond remained in force until it left again. Steve didn't question Young Turk's statement and handed over twenty pounds.

Young Turk told Jean-Louis he was overweight and would have to pay an excess charge. Jean-Louis protested. "No way," he said. His manifest showed a gross weight of thirty-eight tons. They had put him on a weighbridge at Ipsala, and without Jean-Louis noticing it the Customs inspector had written in the wrong numbers on his transit paper.

"No pay, you must weigh, mister," a Customs officer insisted. To go back to the weighbridge at the entrance to the compound would mean in this chaos losing a full day. With that alternative, he said to hell with it and paid the equivalent of thirty pounds.

"Oh, aye, it's quite a game," Graham repeated.

It took us five hours to leave Turkey. And before we were finished we had to pay fifteen pounds each in overtime charges, as it was Sunday. We crossed the milky-green Habur River, a tributary of the Tigris, into Iraq. Behind us Turkish gun emplacements nestled under camouflage netting, and on the south bank of the river three Iraqis in long white underwear were bathing.

As we entered Iraq, the first thing we heard was a Customs guard telling us, "Problem, meester."

"What, already?" asked Graham. "We hardly got here."

15. MOSUL

WE remained seven and a half hours at Zahko Customs. A new Customs terminal was under construction. Already partly in use, it dwarfed all others we had so far passed through. The provisional parking area for TIR trucks was half a mile from the half-finished complex. We gathered our papers and steeled ourselves for the *baksheesh* derby. We had filled our pockets with packs of cigarettes, throwaway lighters, ballpoint pens, and vials of supermarket perfume.

The procedure was complex. First we had to go to the border police in the old compound and get our passports stamped. Then we had to find the future restaurant, temporarily being used as an office, to have our transport documents registered. After that we were required to take out Iraqi insurance and pay the road tax in another building. Last, we had to have our transit documents stamped in a fourth building. At every turn we were pinched and patted, cajoled and insulted, threatened and then punished by being ignored for lengthy periods.

While our manifest was checked, the Customs inspectors asked for cigarettes, toilet water, pipe tobacco, camera films, pocket calculators, fashion catalogs—in short, anything they could get. The chief inspector told Jean-Louis that his Baghdad freight agent had been expelled from the country two weeks before.

"Problem, meester. You have to go back," he said.

Jean-Louis realized this was the beginning of a shakedown. He asked to see written confirmation that the agent had been expelled. The inspector rummaged around his desk for a paper—any one would do—with Arabic script. He picked one up. "Ah, here, my friend—it's written here.'' Some Arabic squibbles adorned the paper, nothing we could read.

"Okay, I go back. I don't care,'' Jean-Louis said. The communications equipment he was carrying had been ordered by the government. The last thing the chief wanted was to see Jean-Louis walk out the door. He was going to take great care to see that it didn't happen. This meant opening negotiations, which he did instantly.

"We'll see what can be done,'' he said with a sigh, shooing away a fly. "But it would help if you could provide us with a carton of Rothmans.''

"Sorry, but I don't smoke,'' Jean-Louis lied.

A carton? This guy was really up front. Most limited their scrounging to a pack at a time. Also, it was curious how he specified Rothmans. The Iraqis preferred the distinguished Rothman taste to the cowboy image of Marlboros. Maybe they thought it made them more upmarket. They all asked for Rothmans.

"How about a cigarette lighter?'' Jean-Louis proposed. "Very sexy.'' It had a blonde in a bikini on it.

This interested the chief. "Let's see,'' he said. Once in his paw he turned it over, looked at the bathing beauty, flicked it to make sure it worked. "Why she not naked?'' he asked.

"Oh, no, chef, that would be sleazy,'' Jean-Louis said. He was doing fine, holding his own in English, albeit with a heavy French accent that seemed to appeal to the chief.

"Any magazines? We can't get European magazines.''

I had a copy of *Time,* which I contributed to the cause. This was like handing the chief the deed to a gold mine. He immediately placed it in his desk drawer and locked it. The last prize was a squirt bottle of French deodorant, and the problem evaporated. Jean-Louis was processed through like greased lightning. Unfortunately, this was not the case with us.

They toyed with us as a cat might toy with a family of mice. And we felt like mice. Powerless. We couldn't complain. There was nobody to whom we might complain. We couldn't argue, because either they would put our papers at the bottom of the pile, throw them across the room, or, worse, call the border police to have us evicted. We couldn't go forward, because we needed their visa to leave, and we couldn't go back, because there was no other Iraqi Customs post in a thousand miles. We were stuck. And we had to eat humble pie. Graham was very calm about all this; he hung back, observing, letting events unravel at their own speed, in their own time. Never a sign of impatience, never a word more than was needed. Steve was more pushy and breezy. He adopted the jocular approach, but it advanced neither him nor us any faster.

Once we thought we had bought our way around every obstacle raised by the chief and his crew, who by then had become rather well disposed toward us, there was a shift change. In the meantime, some of us had been offered chairs. Leslie made the mistake—who could have guessed it was a *faux pas?*—of crossing his legs, thereby exposing the sole of one sandal to the head of the new shift seated across the room from him. The official considered this a mark of disrespect and, yelling insults in Arabic, had all of us ejected from the room. We were made to wait outside in the 105-degree heat. For further punishment, a dozen Turkish drivers were processed ahead of us.

We were allowed back in, finally, one by one. A Chaldean Christian woman registered the manifests in a large ledger. She was our last hurdle but one. She was dressed in European-style clothes and asked whether we had brought any mail-order catalogs. Women in these parts collect them. They are highly prized because the local ladies copy the latest Paris and London fashions out of them. We had not brought any. She was a sturdy woman of indeterminate age. On her fingers were rings of turquoise set in silver that looked like they might have been fashioned around the time of Jesus, small treasures that no doubt had been handed down from mother to daughter for more than a thousand years. She placed our manifest at the bottom of the pile. "Next!" she called out. She looked up at us and said, "You can go back outside and wait. Next time you remember to bring catalogs."

When you thought about what the quality of her life must be like, and the example set by others on her shift, who could blame her, really? A catalog costs nothing at home. It's not a filthy magazine. It doesn't pollute. And it brings real pleasure to these people. So why not indulge in a little harmless corruption? It was better than being sent back out to the stifling heat.

Her Arab boss, sitting across the room, said nothing. He was smoking a cheroot and inspecting his fingernails, unconcerned. He could have been a million miles away, and at that moment he probably was. We went back outside as we were told, such good little mice. Another member of her shift, also a Chaldean Christian, seeing an opportunity for profit, intervened at once. He would see that our manifests got replaced at the top of the pile quickly. Meanwhile, we

were sent back to the trucks for additional documents, duplicates of
documents, more cigarettes, and more cheap perfume. Our friend
professed to be embarrassed by the treatment we had received, blaming
it on his Arab superiors, whom he clearly despised. "The situation is
very bad. We live from day to day. We never know if tomorrow the
government will fall," he confided.

He had raised a pertinent point. Saddam Hussein's government
was indeed in a most precarious situation, and this due to its own
incompetence. Let's not talk about the colossal miscalculation of
beginning a war he was unable to finish. But since Iraq happened to be
in a state of war, a war it was losing, it stood to reason that it needed
smooth-functioning supply lines. Now they had only three, all overland, as the enemy had already reduced Iraq's two ports to rubble. The
three overland routes still open were the road from the north, through
Zahko; the Jordan road from the west; and the Saudi road from Ar'ar.
A fourth, from Kuwait, had become increasingly iffy as the enemy
drew the ring around Basra ever tighter.

As Iraq was self-sufficient only in crude oil and dates, it needed to
keep supply lines wide open and well oiled or face strangulation. But
while this seemed so self-evident, drivers like Jean-Louis bringing vital
supplies into the country faced incredible viciousness and venality, not
to mention delay. We didn't count, as we were only transiting this
madcap place, but we did pay a rather hefty transit tax, bought their
Mickey Mouse insurance, and brought in revenue. If we didn't count,
the Turkish tanker drivers who carried Iraqi crude to world markets
certainly should have. They were especially important to the war effort,
and yet they were treated like dirt. The fact that Saddam Hussein and his
henchmen didn't understand this situation indicated how incompetent
the Iraqi junta really was. "Unfit to govern," one Turkish driver told us,
expressing a sentiment that even the Iraqis were beginning to believe.
And yet "smart" Western bankers had lent this pompous madman fifty
billion dollars so he might wage his war.

The Customs compound was heavily ringed with antiaircraft gun
and rocket batteries. The border with Iran was in the mountains, about
150 miles to the east. If ever the Iranians or their Kurdish allies cut the
road at Zahko—and the only reason they had not must have been fear
of Turkish intervention—they could shut down the Iraqi economy,
such as it is, within weeks. There had been continuous Turkish air
strikes into northern Iraq against Kurdish *peshmarga* bases.

Once cleared, you are not allowed to dawdle in the Customs

compound. You must move out. So Jean-Louis was forced to leave us to our fate and roll on alone toward Mosul. He gave us a rendezvous at the gates of an abandoned French construction project north of Mosul and said he would have dinner waiting. We returned to our trucks at 8:00 P.M. to find we were surrounded by open sheep transporters bearing tortured animals emitting a foul stench and covered by clouds of flies. To get more space, or simply to better their balance, some sheep had pushed their legs through the wooden slats on the side of the transporters and, caught, were trying to wrench them free. A few had become panicky and hurt their legs; one may even have broken a hind shank. Steve became upset, and climbed the sides of two of the trucks to calm the animals and help them get their legs back under them. He was really concerned.

Now came the difficult part. We had to obtain a green slip of paper to exit from the compound, and to get the slip we were required to pass a particularly vicious cabin control unless we handed over girlie magazines, cigarettes, toilet water, or whatever else we had left.

The cabin controllers worked in pairs. A khaki-uniformed guard was sent to soften us up, demanding *baksheesh* for himself and his supervisor. When this was paid he got the supervisor who, depending on the tribute received, would let you go with a superficial control or turn your gear upside down until you consented to improve the ante.

"These are the biggest scroungers of the lot," Graham said contemptuously.

"It's for my father," one of the guards had the audacity to claim as he took a second pack of the despised Marlboros.

Leslie gave his cabin controller a girlie magazine, which brought sighs of delight, a rolling of eyes, and the gesture of an ape masturbating. This got us all waved out of the compound without further hassle. More than five hundred trucks were parked in the compound, but that was nothing compared to the numbers we now passed on the northbound side of the road, waiting to get into the compound. It was an unbroken chain of tonkas, tankers, empty sheep transporters, and an occasional tractor-trailer waiting to exit Iraq. The line stretched back more than twenty miles, all the way through the town of Zahko and down the hairpin bends of Zahko Mountain. At the top we passed a police station with a policeman in a black-and-white uniform sitting on the porch in a wicker chair, its back tilted against the wall.

While trying to see what the policeman was up to, we were almost cut off by a tanker in its haste to overtake us. It was dark and we were

crawling down the incline which, because of oil spills, was treacherously slippery. The smell of crude filled our nostrils. Graham was
nervous. The place was a deathtrap. Steve was in front, Leslie behind.
Going down the hairpins we encountered pick-and-shovel barriers and
asphalting plants that we could avoid only by drifting to the left.
Without warning, the road became a dual highway, and we were on the
wrong side. At the bottom of the first steep descent two policemen
barred our way. They signaled us to stop by waving flashlights. We
saw one of them get into Steve's truck. The other came running up to
us and pulled open my door. We had lost sight of Leslie.

"Passports," he demanded gruffly, like he meant business. He
was out of breath. But of course! It was the slob in the wicker chair.
He had coming running all the way down the first three hairpins to nick
us. "Beeg problem, meester."

While we were looking for our passports, he climbed into the cab
and instructed me to move over. He smelled awful, like his last shower
had been the month before. Steve was already under way again. He
steered his truck over the unfinished meridian onto the newly surfaced
right side of the highway. There was no place for me to sit on the
engine cowling as the refrigerator was there, so I slid onto the dashboard, back to the windshield. The policeman now had the passports
and was leafing through them.

"Fifty-dinar fine, meester," he said, waving the passports. So that
was the game. Damn, we should never have given them to him. I was
wondering how nasty he intended to be and how I could get them back.
For the moment they were being held for a fifty-dinar ransom, and our
wild-eyed policeman was armed with a revolver in a holster on his hip.
Fifty dinars at the official exchange rate was worth almost two hundred
dollars, a small fortune. *"Yallah! Yallah!"* he ordered. "Go! Go!"
Meanwhile, he was looking around, familiarizing himself with the
interior of the cab. We were listening to the BBC World Service. He
poked at the radio. Graham found a pack of Marlboros and put it on top
of the refrigerator.

"No cigarettes, meester. You have beeg problem."

I figured he was going to take us to the police station at Dohuk,
twenty miles away, for a more fitting shakedown. Graham was
descending the hill very slowly. The road, again two lanes, was torn
up and dangerous. Along the left-hand shoulder was the unending line
of immobilized trucks. At one pothole Graham braked hard and I slid
into the windshield, cracking it.

"That's going to cost me a hundred pounds," Graham said. He was by now in a foul temper. Then he yelled at the policeman: "Look what you did, you damn silly twit!"

The copper didn't understand, but Graham's temper seemed to make him less sure of himself. "What means tweet?" he asked.

"Give back passports," I said, trying to take them from him.

"No! *Yallah! Yallah!*"

"This bloody trip is going to bankrupt me," Graham said again.

We were reaching the bottom, where we could see a third policeman. He was supposed to be regulating the flow of trucks waiting to go up the hill, but he signaled Steve to stop. Our policeman ordered us to pull in behind Steve. He then started rooting through the cab. He poked at the radio as if he might try to remove it, then spotted Graham's cassette case, which Graham slammed shut on his fingers. Next he spied a plastic bottle of Mazola oil tucked behind the right-hand seat.

"Whiskey," he announced triumphantly.

"No whiskey," Graham replied.

"Champagne?" he asked hopefully.

"Cooking oil," Graham said.

"No, whiskey," he insisted.

"Here, you can have it," Graham told him, handing over the bottle of oil.

He smelled it and put it down, disappointed.

He found two cans of tuna fish in one of the boxes and was examining them.

"No good," I said. "Pork."

His eyes lit up. "Ah, very good," he contradicted me and pocketed them.

"Fickie-fickie magazines?"

"No magazines," Graham said firmly.

"Yes," he insisted, pointing at my open briefcase. Going into Czechoslovakia I had picked up a Czech national tourist office catalog with a girl in a bikini on the cover. I handed it to him. He leafed through it and threw it back. We had an old *London Observer* color magazine. He flicked through it but found no naked ladies. Finally he settled for two packs of Marlboros and climbed down.

Steve was having a more difficult time. The policeman with him had asked for his passport, too, but Steve, smarter than us, had said, "No, you can't have passport."

"Okay, you go back Zahko," the cop had ordered.

Steve said okay, he'd go back to Zahko. The cop said nothing, and Steve continued down the hill. Steve doesn't smoke and carried no cigarettes with him. The copper wanted perfume. Steve had none. The copper was high on something, probably kef. He kept giggling; his eyes were wild and rolled. Every time they rolled, he turned nasty. He wanted Steve's radio and was about to rip it out. Steve lost his temper. "No, you fuckin' scrounger, you're not having that!"

He grabbed Steve's Instamatic camera.

"It's just a wee camera," Steve said.

The policeman pocketed it, left Steve in the hands of his two colleagues, then came running over to us. The one who had ridden with us must have told his companion that we had cigarettes. We gave him the last of our *baksheesh* Marlboros.

Satisfied that they had picked us clean, they waved us out. They appeared delighted with themselves.

"Where's Leslie?" I asked.

"Dunno," Graham replied. He was fuming.

We were almost out of the hills, and the sky was clear. A searchlight swept the countryside to our left. It was an armored patrol, reminding us that Iraq was not only at war with its neighbor Iran, but also with its own Kurdish nationals, whose irregular forces, the *peshmarga* (literally, "those who face death"), were tying down an estimated 160,000 troops in the North of the country. They were fighting for their own autonomous region and claimed to have "liberated" considerable tracts of territory in the Northeast, along the Iranian and Turkish frontiers.

On the last bend at the foot of Zahko Mountain an accident two months before had killed five drivers and critically injured a sixth. A tanker had lost its brakes and come screaming down the hill. Unable to gear down, the driver sideswiped five trucks waiting in line to get up the hill. One of the waiting trucks was carrying naphtha. The whole lot burst into flames, including one Hungarocamion and a Jugtransport truck.

We passed a second military patrol: a Soviet-made armored vehicle with eight axles, an open truck with a searchlight, and a three-ton truck carrying soldiers in battle dress. The refinery at Dohuk was lit up like a Christmas tree and could be seen for miles away. We pulled into the diesel stop beside it. Even though it was after 9:30 P.M., a maze of tonkas and tankers was ahead of us, but the line moved quickly and the price was ten dinars for 150 liters, or roughly ten pence a gallon. There

Graham Davies behind the wheel of Old Girl. Below, Steve Walsh sitting by the roadside above the seaport of Kavala, northern Greece

Above, crossing the Euphrates River at Birecik, in southern Turkey. Below, Old Girl parked in front of the Davieses' home in Blackpool. Bottom, heading north to the plain of Konya and Aksaray, after crossing the Tarsus mountains from southern Turkey, with Hasan Daği, an extinct volcano, in background

An Austrian driver, who travels with his wife and child, working on his DAF turbo in the yard at Telex Motel, Ankara

Steve Walsh, Graham, and Falcongate driver Bob Anderson dig into some *camion* cuisine in the yard at Telex Motel.

The Saudi ''see-through box effect'' at Ar'ar Customs

Stopped for a ''TIR Control'' in Turkey. HGV drivers must carry a special police paper and have it signed and stamped seven times along the TIR route through Turkey. No deviations from the route are allowed. Below, overloaded Turkish tonkas at Ar'ar Customs. The grain they are carrying was refused because of alleged contamination from Chernobyl fallout.

Iraqi president Saddam Hussein's larger-than-life portrait at the entry to Karbala

Left, Steve's Volvo driving under the Ottoman aqueduct in the northern Greek seaport of Kavala. Below, Graham steams by a camel in the Saudi desert.

A wreck in the Iraqi desert

The "blue-bottle wreck" going over Tarsus Pass. The driver lost his brakes coming down the hill and crashed. He was carrying blue gas bottles. "They must have been empty," Graham said. "None exploded."

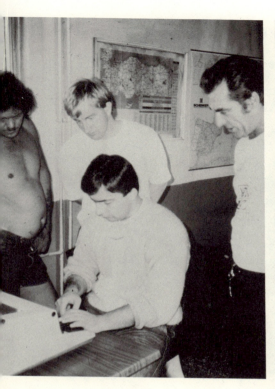

Left, British drivers around the Telex machine at the Telex Motel, on the outskirts of Ankara, waiting for instructions from their operations managers back home. Above right, the trucks lined up in the Telex TIR Park yard as Alfie Jones is checked out by the guard

Heavy traffic crossing Bolu Pass between Istanbul and Ankara

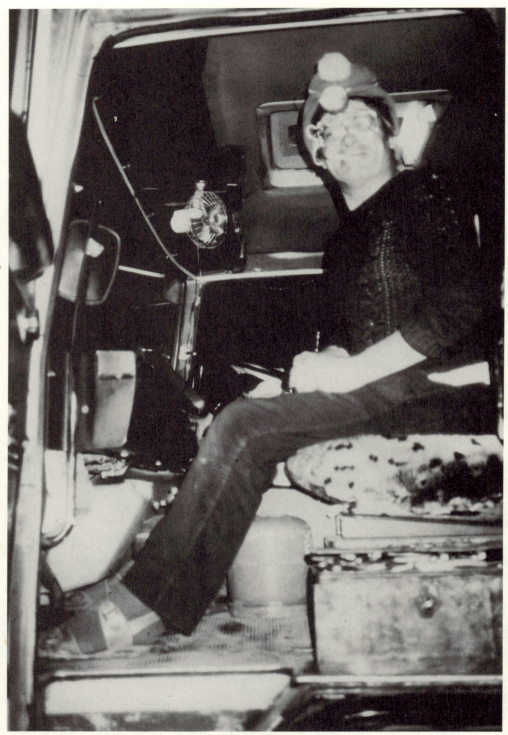

Graham celebrating our return to the National Hotel, Belgrade

were armed guards everywhere; the diesel pumps and fuel tanks were protected by walls of sandbags. The pumps were floodlit.

Turkish tonka drivers are paid by the trip, and they are paid peanuts. So for them it was always rush, rush, rush, and in situations like these, push, push, push. The more trips they make, the more money they earn. One bull of a man in a baby tanker cut deftly ahead of us and hurried up to the pump. Graham got out and gave him hell. Afterward the Turk came over to me and tried to make amends.

"Schnell, schnell, alles macht schnell," he said. He was pleasant enough, dressed in a T-shirt, baggy *cheroual* pantaloons, leather sandals, and covered with grime. I felt sorry for the poor slob. He said he carried whatever he could load, from crude to naphtha. Sometimes he had to wait in line three days at the pipehead in Baigi to be filled, and then it was a two-day delay in the lineup to get through Zahko Customs and a two-day drive to the dockside at Mersin or Iskenderun.

"Naphtha ten-ten is worst," he said, struggling with his few words of English. He shrugged, got back in his truck, and waved good-bye. His smile—or was it a look of fear?—etched itself on my mind as he disappeared into the night.

We made it out of Dohuk by 10:00 P.M. A black-and-white police car was parked at the roadside, the two coppers eyeing us. There was no sign of Leslie and forty miles to Mosul.

"If the Iranians wanted to hit Dohuk, at least they would have no trouble finding it," Graham said.

"It's a phony war," I ventured. If they were just a hairbreadth more competent than the Iraqis, they could have cut this road months ago and destroyed the Baigi refinery.

We passed a third military patrol and a few miles later a tonka-tanker overtook us on a bend. He blew his horn in desperation as he drew alongside us because he had seen what was coming around the bend toward us. Graham was having trouble distinguishing lights and judging distances on this bumpy two-lane stretch of road and took a moment to realize the danger, then braked to let the tanker move quickly in front of us in the nick of time.

"Look at the mother go," I said. No sooner had the Turk tucked himself in front of us and the danger passed than he scooted out again, apparently unconcerned, and on his way.

"Some crazy nuts on this road, all right. I'd rather be doing Greece anytime," Graham complained.

Wrecks, several of them the results of head-on collisions, littered the side of the road, "enough to make a happy man out of a scrap merchant," he observed.

"Hey, wasn't that Les's Volvo?" It was parked in front of a roadside bistro.

"Didn't see," Graham replied. His nerves, and mine, were on edge. We were rolling up to a police checkpoint. There was a stop sign and three ridges, which the French call sleeping *gendarmes,* across the roadway. Two policemen were seated on the curb, idly looking at us. Steve was behind.

"Keep rolling," I suggested. "Don't give them any encouragement to get up and inspect us." We crawled over the bumps without stopping. They showed no interest, so Graham put his foot to the floor and accelerated away.

Minutes after 11:00 P.M. we pulled into an empty parking area on the desert a few miles north of Mosul, where Jean-Louis's red Volvo was parked by the gates of an abandoned French construction site. He was still shaking from an encounter with the secret police. Two of them had watched him execute the same maneuver as ours at the checkpoint up the road, then jumped into their unmarked squad car and came roaring up behind him, siren blaring. One searched his cab, seized his passport, then sat himself down in the passenger seat and told him to follow the squad car to the central police station in Mosul, Iraq.

"No stop at control, meester. At station you have very much problem."

"Nom de bleu," said Jean-Louis, "I knew I was in for something unpleasant. Pissing in my pants, I was. But then I saw he was leading me away from the city onto the ring road, so I settled down."

They directed Jean-Louis to pull off the road, and then the real shakedown began. While one plainclothes officer stood him against the side of the truck with his revolver drawn, the other emptied everything out of his suitcase. Other than Jean-Louis's reserve of cigarettes, he could find nothing that interested him. Finally they demanded money. He gave them a hundred dinars and said he had no more. They accepted that and returned his passport. "I don't mind telling you I thanked *le Grand Chauffeur* upstairs for not being whiplashed." He drove to the chicken shop in town and bought two grilled chickens to go, then came back to the rendezvous to wait.

We broke out the last bottle of Côtes du Rhône we had hidden in the back of the lower bunk and drank to our safe passage into Iraq. Jean-Louis got a mechanic's lamp out and hung it on the front of the truck, then prepared a tomato salad. We were picking away at the chickens when a black car roared off the road and skidded to a stop in front of the trucks.

"Oh, shit, the special police," Steve said. "What the fuck do they want?"

Our nerves were ajangle. We hid the bottle of wine and watched as they wrote down the registration numbers of the trucks, then sped off again. We said nothing and were wondering who our next visitor would be when Leslie rolled in, followed by another French truck, pulling a refrigerated truck.

Steve's mouth fell open. "He's got a fuckin' copper in the truck with him!"

More trouble, we thought. But Leslie wandered over, smiling. "Who's the security riding with you?" Steve asked.

"Him? A soldier going on leave. He was hitchhiking at Zahko."

"Saved yourself a spot of bother, didn't you?"

"Nice kid," Leslie said.

The French driver whom Leslie had met at the roadside bistro was, by the strangest of coincidences, also called Jean-Louis Gautier. The two homonyms, however, were utterly different in personality and appearance. Our Jean-Louis was meticulously tidy. Gautier II was ragged and hippie-looking. He had shoulder-length hair, a beard, and earrings. Rare for a Frenchman, he didn't drink wine, but rolled his own cigarettes, which were not always straight. He got some bread out of his truck and came over and joined us for dinner.

Gautier II used to drive for Carry International, a Paris-based haulage firm that had gone bankrupt the year before. Carry trucks, painted red, had been a familiar sight on the Middle East route, which the French drivers call *la ligne*. They were known as *le brigade rouge*. Gautier II had had the misfortune to run over a farmer in Bulgaria and had spent the previous year in prison. It hadn't been his fault, he explained. The farmer had been drunk and was driving his tractor at night without lights. He turned left without warning, straight under the wheels of Gautier's truck.

When he called his wife to tell her that he had been arrested, she announced she was pregnant. Carry, meanwhile, went belly up and offered no help. The police acknowledged that it wasn't his fault—his tacho showed he had nudged over a forty-kilometer-per-hour speed limit in the sector—and were lenient with him. So, too, was the judge. But as Carry couldn't pay the fine, he was given a twelve-month sentence. His cell measured fifteen feet by seven. He shared it with seven other people.

Once sentenced, conditions improved. He was allowed to work in the prison workshop, making shoes for babies. "That preyed on my mind, I can tell you," he commented in French. But for every two days' work he earned one day's remission as well as the equivalent of a pack of cigarettes per day. Now he drives the touristic route through northern Greece. Gautier II didn't tell us what was in his refrigerated truck, but he was unloading at an airbase near Tikrit, halfway to Baghdad. We assumed that whatever he was carrying it wasn't edible and left it at that.

As we drank the last of the Côte du Rhône, a third French truck pulled in, driven by Pascal, also known as *le Berger* (the Shepherd). He had a full-grown beard and the singsong accent of the French Southwest. He was on his way to Kirkuk. Pascal was full of news. Within the past few weeks, he said, a member of Saddam Hussein's family had led a coup against the president but killed a bodyguard instead. He was hung within the day. Fifty-two Egyptian workers had been arrested for illegally exporting currency to their families back home. They were hung within the week.

Gautier II had a little brown chunk of contraband that after dinner he rolled into joints. Leslie and the Shepherd stayed, but Steve and Graham retired to bed, locking themselves into their cabs. The two Jean-Louis's, the Shepherd, and I sat back and relaxed in the cool night air, discussing road philosophy with Leslie. We were on a low, rolling knoll, and the desert drifted off to the southwest. On the left lay more desert, but the view was hidden by a couple of ridges. We could see a dark ribbon in the distance to our right, probably the Tigris snaking southward through the Mesopotamian plain, and a couple of fairly large mounds. Did they, I wondered, hide the ruins of Nineveh, the ancient Assyrian capital? Desert dogs barked and came nearer, drawn by the smell of the chicken carcasses.

At about 3:00 A.M. we were talked out of ideas and headed for bed. I rolled out my mattress and sleeping bag on the ground between Graham's and Jean-Louis's loads. Sleep was no problem, even with the wild dogs prowling nearby. I dreamed of Assyrian warriors and Babylonian princesses, and of the splendor of palaces belonging to Sennacherib and Sargon. They, too, had secret police and dissolute generals. The Assyrians, bless them, invented the secret police as a state institution.

16. THE ROAD TO FALLUJAH

THE road from Mosul to Fallujah is 245 miles long. Although expressway most of the way, it is treacherous. In the daytime the heat of the desert can pop tires like toy balloons, while at night there is danger of bandits.

We left at 9:00 A.M. and descended to the Tigris. From the roadside we could see no sign of the twin mounds of Kouyunjik and Nebi Yunis, on the east bank of the river, that hid the ruins of Nineveh and where also the prophet Jonah is said to be buried. But in fact we were disoriented and probably looking on the wrong side of the road.

Nineveh. Just the name conjures magic. Before Constantinople or Rome, Salonika or Tarsus, Athens or Antioch, Nineveh was a thriving metropolis, the grandest city of its day. According to Genesis, Nineveh was the capital of the first empire to rise after the Flood. Founded by Nimrod, a great-grandson of Noah, it was situated in the fertile plain between the two great rivers Tigris and Euphrates, a corridor barely one hundred miles wide and four hundred miles long. At its zenith, the Assyrian Empire stretched from Egypt to India, from the Caspian to the Arabian Sea, and across the Mediterranean to Cyprus.

For more than thirteen hundred years Assyrian monarchs ruled from Nineveh, attaining their greatest splendor in 700 B.C. during the reign of Sennacherib. According to Arnold Brackman in *The Luck of Nineveh,* he built a "palace without rival," so richly embellished with gold that "the whole city shone like the sun."

The Assyrians were counterbalanced in the North by the Hittites and possibly learned from them the art of smelting, which they added to their own skills of enameling and inlaying. Their libraries were filled

157

with works on mathematics, astronomy, and astrology. They established the world's first zoological gardens and maintained vast hunting reserves. They deported whole populations and practiced genocide as an instrument of state. To maintain their power, the Assyrians possessed a mighty military machine: 1.7 million foot soldiers, two hundred thousand horsemen, and sixteen thousand war chariots; they also had a sophisticated network of spies and secret police. Wherever the Assyrian armies trod, the Book of Isaiah lamented, there was "darkness and sorrow." Cities were "smashed like pods," and "the smoke of burning towns obscured the heavens."

During the days of Nimrod the Hunter and Sargon, wildlife abounded between the two great rivers. Lions, elephants, gazelles, wild asses, horses, porcupines, foxes, and camels roamed the riverbanks. Fowl of every description lived in the forests. Today there is no wildlife and there are no forests.

"I slaughtered the land," wrote the leader of the Babylonian rebels who sacked Nineveh in 612 B.C. "I turned the . . . land into heaps of ruin." The injury was total. What Nabopolassar left undone, the Romans and the Parthians took in hand. After them, the Arabs systematically annihilated what wildlife remained.

I looked across the dung-brown wasteland as we rolled toward Mosul that morning, hoping I would see a blade of grass, some scrub, a tree, or a herd of gazelles. The last of the gazelles had been hunted from moving cars in the 1930s. It had been great sport. Against the speed of the car and the deadliness of repeating rifles, the gazelles stood no chance. We saw only stray dogs and a few woebegone donkeys. It was an empty tribute to the total devastation man can bring to his environment.

We crossed the Tigris, with the ancient Abbasid fortifications of Mosul to our left, and drove through the city's outskirts. In a main square was a reminder of the country's military heritage: a MIG-17 on a crude cement pedestal, two howitzers, a tank, and giant portraits of Saddam Hussein in military uniform were on display. An octagonal Chaldean church stood alone on a nearby hilltop. Heading out of Mosul we passed an army barracks with hundreds of new conscripts lined up on drill squares in the early-morning sunlight. They looked to be in their late teens, future fodder for Hussein's folly and Khomeini's blood lust.

We slowed for a police checkpoint but avoided stopping. We were soon back in the desert, the kerosene trails of a jet fighter dissecting the sky. Easy Steve rolled past in his automatic-pilot mode, feet on the dashboard. As he drew alongside, he leaned out the window and said, "Good morning!" like it was a nice day for a drive. On the side of the road, among a constant line of wrecks, was the mangled product of a head-on collision between a junior and a senior tanker. Two live tonkas were in the desert, one backed against an embankment loading the other onto its back. We had seen quite a few tonkas being piggybacked home this way. We assumed it was to save diesel. Ahead, a convoy of a dozen Turkish sheep transporters carried their cargoes of misery to the slaughtering squares of Saudi Arabia.

We crossed the Tigris a second time later in the morning. Here the river had a green band on either side of it shaded by poplars, tamarisks, and ash. I tried to image how green the plain might have been in Assyrian times. But my thoughts were abruptly ended at the next checkpoint. A military policeman made me get out so he could climb into the cab and look around. He stole a pack of Graham's Rothmans.

North of Baigi, an oil-refining town, there was another checkpoint. By this time we had caught up with the pipeline being laid northward to Turkey at a cost of more than three hundred million dollars. Earthmoving equipment kicked up clouds of dust, scooping out the trench where the huge sections of Japanese pipe we had encountered on the road were being laid.

At Baigi we joined a line of three hundred trucks waiting to buy cheap diesel. "Looks a bit like Blackpool, this," Graham observed drily. A sixty-ton bulk tanker had jackknifed at the turnoff and the trailer was over on its side, dripping crude. Little brown men in pajamas and with rags around their heads drive these monsters— Jordanians, Kuwaitis, and a few Iraqis. The line moved quickly up to the four double pumps. We purchased 200 liters for 12 dinars. This worked out at 750 liters for 100 deutsche marks. In Hungary, the black-market price for red diesel used to be 200 liters for 100 deutsche marks. After a quick lunch in 105-degree heat, and with no air conditioning, only the open windows and air vents, we got back on the road.

At about 3:00 P.M. we saw Jean-Louis and Leslie parked in some shade beside a van having tea with two Turkish drivers. We pulled in and joined them. At a graveyard up the road, which we had passed the year before, we noticed a dozen new graves with Iraqi flags either draped over or painted on them. While we were stopped, several hopeful civilians in white cotton jellabas came over and asked if we had cigarettes or whiskey to sell. We told them the police had robbed us of everything we had. This didn't seem to surprise them. During this time, four taxis drove by with flag-draped coffins on their roofs and what we presumed were the next of kin sitting in the back. Until two years ago, Saddam Hussein used to give the families of soldiers killed in action a Volkswagen made in Brazil. Now he only gives them a taxi ride home.

Jean-Louis was anxious to get moving. He didn't want to drive the Fallujah road after sundown. Several European drivers had recently been held up along it; two had disappeared without trace. At Samarra, not far away, we turned off the main north–south expressway and took a narrow road across the desert to the west of Baghdad. The Customs administration for the governorate of Baghdad is at Fallujah. TIR trucks are not allowed to park overnight in the capital and may only transit it at certain hours. So when they get to Samarra long-distance truckers always make tracks for Fallujah.

We were driving along the canal that carries the Tigris floodwaters into the Thartar Depression. The canal had first been constructed in Assyrian times for irrigation purposes but now is used only for flood control. We decided to drive down to the water's edge for a swim. But the water was turgid, and fear of bilharzia kept me on shore, snapping pictures. The trucks spun their wheels going back up the incline to the road, which would carry us back to the Euphrates. Along the way the ragheaded driver of a Toyota pickup gave us a driving lesson when we tried to overtake him. There was another truck coming toward us in the faraway distance, but our friend in front decided it was unsafe for us to pass, so he stepped on the accelerator and stuck his hand out the window, squeezing the tips of his fingers together to tell us to slow down. We stayed on his tail. When he felt the time was proper to pass, he waved us on. Graham decided to return the lesson and almost drove up his ass.

"Just giving him back a little of his own," he said.

"Don't play around with these bastards, Graham," I warned him. "If anything happens, it'll be our ass as well. You don't know how he might react. Remember, they don't reason the same way we do."

I could see the raghead getting nervous with us about to swallow him. I was afraid he might panic and jam on the brakes. The heat was making me edgy.

For years British drivers had refused to park in the Fallujah Customs area, driving into the desert beyond it. They would rather park out there than in the overcrowded and filthy compound. For almost as many years, the Iraqi authorities had attempted to bully the British into abandoning their desert parking spot. This year they succeeded. We drove past the Customs area and tried to pull off into the desert but couldn't. The desert had been plowed into furrows that nothing short of a personnel carrier could get over, and this for a couple of square miles. We had no alternative but to go back to the hated Customs area.

The place was big enough to hold two thousand trucks, and indeed it seemed last year that there had been at least that many. But this year the huge asphalted compound was only a quarter full, another sign of the times. We drove twice around to make sure but found no other West European trucks. Scores of Turkish, Jordanian, and Kuwaiti trucks. A few Wombles. But that was it.

The Iraqi government had spent millions floodlighting and surfacing the place but had installed no running water, no toilet facilities, no telephones; above all, it was never swept clean. Carcasses of tires abounded by the hundreds, if not the thousands; garbage and little piles of human excrement lay everywhere. We parked beside four Turkish tractor-trailers. Two tonka drivers were engaged in a tire-changing exercise in front of us.

Jean-Louis told of being camped here one night about a year before when a lithe-looking lady appeared, knocked on a few doors, and offered her body for ten dinars a trick. She said her husband had been killed at the front and she needed the cash to live. She had done about four tricks and was inside a French truck, curtains pulled, with a gallery of Turks standing around the front of the cab, when the police arrived. Because of the gawkers the police knew exactly which truck they were looking for. They drove up and banged on the cab. When the driver opened the door, the police saw the woman on the bunk. Immediately they dragged her out, unbuckled their belts, and started whipping her. She ran into the desert, screaming. The French driver had been parked there for ten days waiting Customs clearance, and the police didn't bother him. Nobody knew what happened to the woman. She was never seen again.

Our Turkish neighbors invited us for a supper of soup, brown garlic rice, and green tea. They had delivered loads from Istanbul to England and were backloaded to Baghdad. It had taken them eighteen days to drive from London to Baghdad as against an average of fourteen days for British drivers. It had taken us sixteen, including our three-day wait in Ankara.

"First they take your work away and then they feed you," Graham grumbled on our way back to *Old Girl*.

Leslie was leaving for Kuwait at 3:00 A.M. and Jean-Louis hoped to unload in Baghdad in the morning. So we said good-bye and turned in early.

"A solid fellow," said Graham of Jean-Louis.

"Very quiet, very calm," I agreed.

The Turks provided me with a ladder so I could sleep on top of the load. It was dusty but cool up there, and as I gazed at the stars I could see bursts of light that resembled flashes of artillery fire in the mountains along the eastern horizon. The frontier with Iran was only a hundred miles away. Tomorrow we would find out whether the Saudis would allow a truck with two drivers to enter their country and whether we would be permitted to keep our belly tanks.

17. A DAY IN AR'AR

AT 6:00 A.M. I knocked on Steve's and Graham's doors. We had time for a cup of tea while we warmed up the motors, but no more than a cup, as we had to beat the 7:00 A.M. driving restriction for HGVs on the ring road around Baghdad. Leslie had already departed, and Jean-Louis was still asleep.

We drove into the sunrise until we reached the outskirts of Baghdad. The urban planner who designed the highway network leading into the capital was a genius. Between the pedestrian walkways and the main road he had installed children's playgrounds. At 6:45 A.M. the traffic was already jammed in both directions. The pollution level was high, the noise factor debilitating, and it didn't seem surprising that under the circumstances these playgrounds, with their red and green swings and slides, had become garbage repositories. Moreover, pedestrian overpasses had been built at intervals along the highway. But these were not ordinary overpasses. In this desert environment, where the *khamseem* brings dust storms as dense as arctic blizzards, some enterprising fellow had convinced the ministry of public works to install automatic escalators instead of ordinary steps to gain access to or descend from the uncovered overpasses. Because of the dust and grit, not one of these escalators worked. I saw women in long robes lugging their children and shopping bags up the motionless steps. Such were the steps of progress around Baghdad.

We turned onto the main expressway to Hilla and Basra; the sun was an immense orange ball rising behind a green and gold mosque with its attendant minarets. South of Baghdad we ran into heavy industrial smog that reduced visibility to a few hundred yards. There

163

was not a hint of breeze, and the pall of factory smoke hung over the road in a thick yellow band, slowing traffic to fifteen miles per hour. In the midst of this chemical haze a road sign vaunted the delicious quality of Iraqi dates. Farther along, another billboard, whose blue paint was peeling, proclaimed: IRAQ: MOTHERLAND OF CIVILI-ZATIONS.

Palm trees were an increasing feature of the landscape. Sixty miles south of Baghdad, where we took the turnoff to the holy city of Karbala, we saw a forest of them bordering on an irrigation canal to our right. A road sign told us we had entered the governorate of Babylon.

"I thought Babylon was in the West Indies," Graham said.

"Whatever made you think that?"

"I dunno. That song by Boney M, maybe. What was it called? *By the Rivers of Babylon* . . ." He started to hum. But he was tense. All three of us were covering new territory, and although the unknown had our adrenaline running, we were concerned about the reception that awaited us at the Saudi frontier.

We crossed the Euphrates a final time at Musayab. The bridge was heavily guarded by antiaircraft batteries. On the west bank the road broadened into a dual highway, with large octagonal portraits of Saddam Hussein on every second lamppost. He was a man of many suits, Saddam Hussein. At the entrances to factories and office buildings, larger-than-life portraits showed him in well-tailored business suits. In front of military barracks the portraits were ten and twelve feet high. Sometimes he appeared in the uniform of an air force marshal, a tank corps general, or a commando in battle dress. Outside housing estates he also appeared in military dress this year.

Although Sunni Muslims ruled Iraq, at least for a while longer, the Shi'a Muslims made up a majority of the population. We were now in the heart of Shiite country, where Khomeini himself had spent the first few years of his exile from Qom. We entered the city of Karbala, whose central mosque is the holiest of Shiite shrines. For the devout Shiite, Karbala is the most important pilgrimage after Mecca. It was here that their holiest saint, the martyr Hussein, grandson of Mohammed, was killed by his Sunni rivals. Karbala, not Baghdad nor Basra, was the objective of the repeated Iranian offensives.

No pilgrims stared as the two yellow juggernauts rolled into town on this last day of September. The broad, palm-lined avenue that led toward the center was empty of traffic. At the first traffic circle there was a particularly imposing portrait of the leader in Bedouin dress. I looked quickly to see if anyone was watching, leaned out the window, and snapped a picture. Two coppers appeared from nowhere and started blowing their whistles for us to stop.

"You've done it now," Graham said. "Not only are they going to confiscate your two cameras, but mine as well."

"Try the first right," I suggested.

But we had already passed the first turn off from the traffic circle, and all others were marked "No Entry." As we looked for an exit, Steve overtook us and was pulled over by the policemen, who were by then standing in the middle of the road. They hadn't noticed the switch in positions. A yellow truck for them was a yellow truck, whether a Volvo or a Scania. We hung back and watched. They demanded his camera. "But I have no camera," Steve protested. They didn't press the matter but told him to move out of town on the same road we had used to enter it.

"Ar'ar?" Steve asked.

"First left," one of them said. "And no more cleek-cleek!"

Well, we got lost. We forked left, and then left again, and we rumbled back toward the center of the forbidden city. We were in a downtown street. At two supermarkets we noticed a line of people waiting to get in. But no food was displayed in the windows. Both stores appeared all but empty of merchandise. The women were mostly in long black dresses with chadors covering their heads. At the end of the street was the back entrance to a great blue mosque. Parts of it were under repair. The domes of the minarets were gilded; the courtyard seemed busy like a bazaar. We kept rolling, expecting to be whistled down by police for ignoring a ban on heavy-vehicle traffic.

We made it to the outskirts without further incident, then stopped to ask a baker for instructions. The man was a natural comic. He bounced up and down giving directions in Arabic and pantomiming them so he was sure we could understand. Finally, when we were good and confused, he asked: "Briteesh?"

Steve said yes. He smiled. "Okay, good, good." And he bid us good day.

We stopped at four more shops to try to buy a case of Coke for the lukewarm refrigerator. Nobody had any. At one I was offered cold water for a jug kept in a vintage icebox. It was only 9:30 A.M. but stifling hot, and we were about to set off across the Iraqi desert with our water containers practically empty. I drank without hesitation.

We later learned that no Coke existed in Iraq because an Iranian rocket had landed on the bottling factory in Baghdad. No Iraqi had wanted to tell us this, as if the hit had singed their national pride. The factory was now only a crater, and, without realizing it, the Iranians had done more damage to Iraqi morale with that particular Scud than had it landed on the army headquarters.

Heading out of town, we passed a Lunapark with fun rides and gaudy sideshow attractions, shut, we presumed, until nightfall. Lunaparks, so-named after the giant amusement park in Moscow, seem to capture the imagination and fantasies of Arabs everywhere, whether it be in Kuwait City, Dammam, or Merza Matruh. At its entrance stood another imposing portrait of Saddam Hussein in desert garb with crossed bandoliers. We joined Al-Hadj Road, which took eastern pilgrims to Mecca. A road sign told us we had 140 miles of desert driving before we reached the Saudi border.

An hour later on our right loomed the ruins of Ukheidir Palace, built in the eighth century by Harun-al-Rashid's father, Caliph Mahdi. The palace was immense. The walls were of orange sandstone blocks that rose two and three stories high. A vast cube in an otherwise empty desert, it stood unguarded, inviting for some, uninteresting for others.

After passing a police checkpoint, we pulled onto a paved shoulder and brewed tea with the last of our water. Two young men in a large American car drove up. They watched us for a moment, walked around the trucks, and then came over and asked if they could buy the Long Vehicle sign off the back of Steve's wagon. Steve said no. They thought it was his initial bargaining ploy and started to talk money— dinars, that is. Steve curtly told them to "piss off." They accepted that as the close of negotiations and departed.

Five minutes later a plump and happy-looking army sergeant wandered over and asked if we were going to Ar'ar. When we said we were, he wondered in the mildest manner if we could give him a lift down the road to his barracks. We had learned by then the benefits of carrying one's own military escort. Steve saluted. *"Chef,"* he said, "be my guest."

Once in the Volvo, the sergeant beamed with pride. He was living a real vroom-vroom experience. At midday we stopped at an oasis to fill our three water containers. The sergeant bought us countless glasses of *chai* in the little corrugated tin shed by the well. He beamed proudly at us as he described to the one-eyed *chai* man his ride in Steve's yellow wagon. Twenty minutes later we moved out again. We passed six

Turkish refrigerator trucks coming the other way and two dead camels on the side of the road. At night the camels come out of the desert and sleep on the warm asphalt. They are hard to see. It is not uncommon for trucks to run over them. It's a bit more serious if the camel's owner happens to be sleeping beside his beast, as occasionally occurs.

An hour later we dropped the sergeant in front of his desert barracks and watched him trip over the sand to the apparently unguarded gates. Every few steps he turned and waved at us.

"Now, how can you send a guy like that to war?" Steve asked. We had no answer, except perhaps that if war did reach into this far corner of Iraq he would not have far to run to the Saudi frontier.

The rest of the trip to Ar'ar was uneventful, except that *Old Girl* almost caught fire. For a while I had smelled the fumes but couldn't see any smoke. Then suddenly it started billowing out from behind the dashboard. Graham jammed on the brakes and pulled onto the shoulder. Steve went racing by, not realizing we had a problem. Graham pulled out the ashtray, behind which he kept a stash of money—"my strongbox," he always said. Thick smoke billowed out. "Oh, shit," I thought, "there goes five hundred pounds."

"Quick," he commanded. "After I've disconnected the battery, you throw water on the dash."

I did just that. The smoke cleared. Steve did a U-turn down the road and was returning. "What's it look like?" Graham asked.

"No more smoke. I think it's out."

He got in and felt for his cash. Miraculously it hadn't been touched. The refrigerator plug, though, was red hot. And the garbage he'd accumulated between the dashboard and the windshield was soggy and singed. He tossed it into the other garbage—the one outside the window.

"One of your cigarette butts, I suppose," I said, half joking.

"Naw. If it were a cigarette butt it would have gone behind, into the bunk."

From among the trash wedged between the dash and the windshield he produced a piece of broken mirror. "Haw," he said triumphantly. "That's it."

"That's what?"

"This—it's friggin' hot." He figured the sun reflecting off it had burned a hole in the plastic air vent. "There," he said jabbing at the charred vent set back from the windshield. "Now let's see if it's burned the wiring. I'll connect the battery; you start her up."

Magic. *Old Girl* kicked into life.

Iraqi Customs, when we arrived there at about 4:00 P.M., was an unimaginable shithole. Trash and abandoned tires were scattered over the compound, which was seasoned by a smell of urine and diesel. Desert dogs spotted with motor oil pawed the trash for fresh pickings. We parked in some crud—there was no other place. A group of waiting Turks told us that Customs was closed for another hour. The Customs office was a prefab unit, a series of trailer boxes strung together. Quarters for the Customs guards and officials—more trailer boxes— were off to the right of the office. Two had been gutted by fire, and only their skeletons remained. At the back of the box camp was a filthy shed that served as the communal toilets and showers. As disgusting as it was, I showered and changed clothes. The feeling of delight that followed made it worthwhile. But after checking the facilities, Steve and Graham decided not to risk it, not realizing that their next shower would be in two weeks.

In front of the Customs window, where drivers handed in their papers, was a carpet of cigarette butts about ten layers thick. After standing there for an hour, Steve and Graham succeeded in getting our papers processed, and as the sun set behind the dunes, we moved into no-man's-land.

"Stop worrying," Graham said as we approached the Saudi compound. "Just act normal—like you're one of us. You'll have no problem."

We had decided that, if challenged, I was a driver-mechanic transiting Saudi Arabia to recover an abandoned truck in Qatar. I had a provisional HGV license, which looked exactly like an ordinary one, and a multiple-entry three-month Saudi visa issued in London.

We rolled under the concrete canopy of the Saudi immigration port, parked in one of two truck lanes, got out, and stretched. Conditions on this side of the wire fence were dramatically different. It was clean, to begin with. And the Customs attendants were polite. We filled out the immigration forms and handed in our passports. The immigration officer stamped them. No problem. Cabin control was next. Now, that was a slightly different experience. It took three hours. Not only were there lots of chiefs, but lots of Indians, too. The Indians, however, were from Bangladesh. Some wore green overalls; others, red overalls. The chiefs were in the navy blue uniform of the kingdom's Customs authority. They were a mixture of Saudi, Malaysian, and Pakistani. Both chiefs and Indians now descended upon us.

We were not feeling very confident because we noticed that a Turkish truck next to us had been stripped to its chassis. Motor out, tires cut open, diesel tank removed, cargo offloaded. "Sex tablets," one of the chiefs told us. "Driver in calaboosh."

A team of Indians was brought over to help us empty *everything* from the cabs. They poked their way through our food, baggage, spare parts, tools, bedding, briefcases, camera equipment, books, cassette library. "Ah-hah," one of the chiefs said, his interest picking up at the sight of the cassettes, "you like Boy George?" No. "Prince?" No. "Good." Both singers are blacklisted in the kingdom.

We had one Saudi and two Malaysian chiefs supervising our operation. They wanted to know how long it had taken us to drive from Dover, where we were going, whether we were married, how many children, good mechanic, like whiskey? Don't drink. "Good." The Saudi chief, in his early twenties, had discovered one of Graham's country and western cassettes. He was a cowboy freak. "Please, can I buy it?" he asked. It was Graham's cassette; I graciously offered it to him. "No, no. Five riyals okay?" He stuffed the money into my hand.

After the cab was emptied, a dog called Sambo arrived. He was an Alsatian from northern Virginia. He jumped into Steve's cab and jumped out again. He was directed back into the cab and jumped out again.

"He doesn't like it in there, does he?" I commented to Steve. "Probably thinks you've got mange."

"I feel like I do for sure."

"What you got?" the Saudi said.

"Er, well, we said we hope the dog doesn't have mange."

"Mange. What is it?"

We tried to explain. Words didn't work. So we started scratching. "Dog?"

"Yes."

"Very clean dog," he said, upset. "No problem."

Arabs are brought up to believe that dogs are dirty animals. Almost as unclean as pigs. But Sambo was a clean dog. He had special status. He even had a medical certificate and, we were told, did not consort with those common desert dogs we could hear barking on the other side of the wall. His handler was now asking him to sniff the metal paneling behind the cab, then the tires and the diesel tank. Sambo was bored. Same procedure with *Old Girl*, after which he got a rolled towel to play with and we got our clearance out of immigration.

Finished? No—cargo inspection tomorrow. Upon leaving the immigration compound we had to surrender our passports to the gatekeeper. The exit gate opened and we entered limboland between the immigration and cargo compounds. "Welcome to Judaidat Ar'ar," the sign said. More than two hundred Turkish and Jordanian trucks were parked in this square mile of desert between the two compounds. We selected a spot on our own and maneuvered the trailers together so I could suspend a board to sleep on between their sideracks.

Al Jahany is the name of the Saudi Customs clearing agency that handles Whittle's work. The agency is headquartered in Dammam. The next morning Steve and Graham walked over to Al Jahany's local office to find that the manager, a Palestinian by the name of Mr. Yusef, was not there. Gone to Jordan for the day, somebody volunteered.

"Probably to buy himself another wife," Graham suggested.

Our first setback. Steve gave our cargo papers to another agent, Mr. Ibrahim, so he could submit them to the Customs director, who would then assign us an inspection berth inside the cargo compound. Having been forewarned about the slowness of Saudi administrative machinery, we supposed further movement for the day was out of the question but were hopeful that next morning—Thursday—we would be admitted to the cargo compound so we could be cleared before it closed that evening for the two-day Muslim weekend. Mr. Ibrahim did not share our optimism.

"Saturday," he said, *"Inchallah."* God willing. And God had not willed us to enter the cargo compound for quite some time.

The weather had turned muggy. Steve wanted to call King Leon in Preston and Roger Hayes, the factory manager in Al Khobar, to let them know that we had arrived, but he could not find any riyal coins to operate the pay phones. Graham and I explored the Customs village. The place was certainly large. In addition to the immigration and cargo compounds, both behind ten-foot-high walls, was a third walled compound in the distance, reserved for pilgrims. It was covered and included its own mosque. The Hadj attracts three million pilgrims to Mecca each year. But it had finished in mid-September and the pilgrim's compound was now closed.

When archaeologists of some future civilization stumble upon this compound, by then half buried in the sand, they might wonder what fabulous king lived in such a palace. Standing aloof from the immigration and cargo compounds, it looked no less impressive than the ruins of Ukheidir must have seemed to the hadjis of five hundred years ago.

The archaeologists might also discover that next to the Hadj palace was an attendant village with dwellings and offices. The main street was lined with saplings that were kept alive with water piped from 650 miles away, the distance by road from London to John O'Groats, a town on the northernmost tip of Scotland. Garbage cans, not a usual feature in Arab lands, were emptied every morning into a little white Daitshu garbage truck with two Thais clinging to the back—one of them with a broad-rimmed straw hat tied on with a pink scarf and as happy as a cootie in a haystack. And there were no abandoned tires.

Heading south along the right side of main street one passed a compound with offices for the Customs agents, two banks that refused to change money, a post office that had no coins, a mosque with a stubby minaret, a canteen that served no alcohol but had near-beer, and a Red Crescent first-aid station with an ambulance that had only flat tires. The left-hand side of the road, because of an administrative building and a National Guard center, was out of bounds.

The restaurant was run by a smart Filipino. He had a Saudi boss who checked the cash register every now and then but didn't want to soil his white jellaba with the day-to-day operations. The Filipino had learned that British drivers prefer soggy fried potatoes to "rice crap" with their fried chicken. The other dish on the menu was lamb stew with "rice crap", not a big favorite among the Blackpudlians but certainly not inedible.

It was a quiet little town. At noon the muezzin called "Allah Akhbar" from the minaret, summoning the faithful to worship. He did it five times a day and, boosted by amplifiers, his voice resounded around the compounds.

The *khamseen* struck at midafternoon. The wind rose gently at first, but then without further warning clouds of reddish dust burst upon us. Even inside the truck, with the windows rolled up and the roof vent shut, the dust infiltrated everywhere—between your teeth, up your nose, in your eyes and ears—and covered everything with a layer of grit. Our already familiar landscape—the Hadj palace to the north; two large, square water towers to the west; the cargo compound to the south; and the more than two hundred Turkish and Jordanian trucks parked around us—vanished as if obliterated by the swipe of a wet sponge. The *khamseen* lasted half an hour, and it was hell. Then the wind dropped, the air cleared, and it seemed lighter than before, like after a summer cloudburst in the Alps.

That evening, while Steve and Graham cooked *camion* stew, I wandered over to the cafe for some chicken and rice crap with a can of near-beer that made Efes Pilsen seem like champagne. The two Malaysian dog handlers were there and insisted that I join them. Norman Jayatilake and Thomas Ramakrishnan were on their second three-year contracts and longing to leave. "It's no life," said Thomas. "There's nothing in it." On his last home leave, he had married, and his wife was waiting in Kuala Lumpur. He and Norman had been sent to Virginia on the same three-month dog-handling course. They were copper-skinned and extremely well-spoken. On occasion, white people in Virginia had called them niggers, which surprised them somewhat. They said that most Americans they encountered, whether in shops or on the street, had made them feel unwanted.

They were being perfectly sincere when they stated that drugs were one of the greatest evils facing civilization. They were in favor of the death penalty for drug traffickers. They got large bonuses, paid in cash on the following day, for drug busts. Two seizures of Turkish drivers were made at Ar'ar the day before we arrived.

"How long have you been driving, Robert?" Norman asked.

"Just over a year," I lied. They looked surprised.

"What did you do before that?" was the next question.

"Oh, I worked in a bank," I lied again. My last book had been about banking.

"Have you ever written any books?" Norman wanted to know.

I liked these two. They had a directness about them and yet an innocence that was surprising. "Be careful of the *khamseen*," Norman warned. "It can swallow a truck in no time."

They were leaving for Al Haditha in the morning and wanted to be in bed early. We walked out of the restaurant together. They went their way, and I wandered back to the trucks. I found Graham in a state of agitation that was to become a nightly ritual. He had rolled up the windows, shut the roof hatch, and was filling the cab with Aroxol insecticide. He got out and smoked a cigarette while watching the mosquitoes and other flies flitter in front of the roof light. When satisfied that they had been exterminated, he climbed back into the cab, locked the doors, and went to bed without any ventilation in the night heat of the desert.

Friday is the Muslim holy day. Ar'ar was dead. Graham was at a loss for things to do. "If we're stuck another day here, I'll go bankrupt," he complained.

"Quite some game, isn't it?" I said.

"Oh, aye," he began, and then looked at me. "Are you kidding?"

"Me? Certainly not." But I was, gently. I wanted him to laugh.

Graham spent most of Friday writing a letter to his son, Martin, in New Zealand. Steve and I tried to converse with some of our Turkish colleagues. They were most hospitable. They told us they were on a protest strike and refused to move. Their trucks were laden with sacks of grain from the Gazientep area. The Saudis had refused the grain because they said it was radioactive, contaminated by the fallout from Chernobyl. One hundred grain trucks were parked in front of the cargo compound, their drivers seated cross-legged in front of them on carpets. Some had been there for two weeks. They had a problem: They had to reenter Iraq fully loaded but had no manifest to do so. And they had been unable to fill their tanks on cheap Saudi diesel to get them at least as far as Baiji.

The BBC World Service announced that evening that six Arab states had requested an emergency meeting of the U.N. Security Council to discuss the Gulf war and that Jordan had sent a military mission to Iraq to inspect the Basra defenses. Whenever the topic came up among people we met, there was increasing fear that the war was about to spill over into the neighboring Arab states.

After listening to the end of the newscast, Graham announced, "Well, everything must be all right with the missus."

"Why's that?" Steve asked.

"They would'ave said something about it on the news if it weren't."

"Did you hear that, Bob? Our friend's going crazy."

The evening call to prayer seemed full of nostalgia for the days of Mohammed when the supporters of Islam built an empire based upon the word of Allah, the sword, and control of international trade routes. Mohammed himself had been a wealthy merchant, and after he fled to Medina in 622 the first battles of Islam were fought for control of the caravan routes to Mecca.

While the muezzin chanted, the desert dogs that prowled the sands in opposing packs barked menacingly at each other, and in the immigration compound men in red overalls could be heard hammering away at suspect Turkish trucks.

On Saturday, our fourth day at Ar'ar and the first day of the Muslim workweek, Steve was waiting for Mr. Yusef, and Al Jahany manager, when he arrived at his office. Yusef was not hopeful. He said we would be cleared as soon as he received a telegram giving the value of the personal effects on Steve's trailer—a trunk of clothes for Roger Hayes' wife and two tea chests containing toys for Louise, the Hayes's four-year-old daughter.

Sunday, October 5. Still no progress. All day we fought a losing battle to keep out of the dust. Yusef said we would go into the cargo compound first thing Monday morning and that we should be out by noon. Attaining the interior of the cargo compound had become a fixation with us. It was a place full of promise, like Nirvana; you knew it was there but could not get to it unless you were very, very good.

Monday, October 6. Yusef informed Steve that the Customs inspector handling our file wanted a detailed cost breakdown of each of the thousand items we were carrying. On instructions from Roger Hayes, Al Jahany's head office in Damman had lodged a protest with the Customs authority. Yusef went to see the inspector. The inspector handed back the entire file and told him to translate it into Arabic. The inspector had a copy of our Iraqi transit manifest, already in Arabic, but said it was not detailed enough. Back at the trucks it was Spam and gloom for lunch. Spam is pork, and therefore forbidden in the kingdom. We were breaking the law and, like naughty kids, secretly felt good about it.

While negotiations continued, another sandstorm enveloped Ar'ar— so violent it seemed it would carry the trucks on rivers of sand some distance down the road. After the sandstorm passed, I spoke with the Jordanian driver of a Mercedes bulk carrier loaded with fifty tons of phosphates. His name was Hussein, and he was taking the phosphates from Iraq to a site north of Riyadh, but as the sacks did not have the the country of origin stamped on them he also had been denied access to the cargo compound.

Hussein spoke of the "border war" between Iran and Iraq with strong distaste, as if it were some sort of tribal conflict. The war was entering its most dangerous phase, he said, with a strong likelihood of it involving other countries within the year.

"Khomeini crazy," he added. "He wants to come to Jerusalem. This could overturn many tables."

What he meant, from later explanation, was that if Khomeini did trample Iraq it would completely change the power structure in the Middle East, overthrowing traditional alliances. Khomeini, he said, had announced that he wanted Jerusalem under Shiite control. Should Iran defeat Iraq, Jordan and Israel would be forced to join forces to block Iran and Syria.

"Yes, honestly. You wait, see," Hussein assured me.

That evening we noticed a black Cadillac with two antennae on its roof driving along the road among the three compounds. We had seen the Cadillac on previous evenings making a similar tour. This time it stopped above us—we were parked in a depression—and the driver, in a white nightshirt, black shoes, and red kaffiyeh, got out of his car and came down to speak with us. Immediately the fat police sergeant drove up in his Nissan patrol wagon.

"How long have you been sleeping here?" the man in the jellaba asked.

"Six days," Steve replied.

We told him that our Customs agent had gone to Jordan again and we were stuck without him. We realized by then that we were speaking to the *gumruk chef*. He turned and spoke in Arabic to the police sergeant.

"This is not good," he said to us. "In the morning you must have Mr. Yusef bring your papers to manager's office. If he not come, it's calaboosh for him, mister. Tomorrow, you go."

We were elated and could hardly believe our ears. The police sergeant, who had threatened to whack one of us the night before, now smiled benevolently.

"Why you have two trucks and three drivers?" the *gumruk chef* asked.

Before we could answer, the sergeant said, pointing at me, "He mechanic."

"Oh," said the *chef*. And departed.

Even the Turkish drivers were happy for us.

The record for being delayed at Ar'ar, Steve said, was seventeen days, held by another Whittle driver, Dave Cawtherly. Deaf in one ear, Cawtherly tended to shout without realizing it, especially when excited. He had been fouled up by Al Jahany, and he never could get a straight reply from Yusef about what the problem was. On the sixteenth day he stormed into the *chef*'s office and tried to explain his predicament. He was a bundle of nerves and about to go nuts.

The *gumruk chef* thought Dave was being disrespectful. He had him arrested and taken to the calaboosh in the Tapline Ar'ar, forty miles down the road. Dave was in a terrible state. He hadn't locked his cab, its windows were open, and all his cash and papers were in it. The police kept him overnight. The next morning they brought him to his truck and told him to proceed into the cargo compound. The truck's windows had been shut in his absence, but nothing had been touched. He was cleared out of Customs that afternoon.

Before the sun dipped under the horizon, a rainbow appeared in the northwest. We interpreted it as a good omen, but damned if it didn't rain during the night. I protected myself with sheets of cardboard but was soaked anyway, and the two warring dog clans barked till morning, fighting over the carcass of a sheep dumped by one of the Turkish transporters. Still, I dreamed of entering Nirvana.

18. THE CARGO COMPOUND

A day in Ar'ar had become a week, and in spite of the *gumruk chef*'s promises, our stay in this frontier spa was destined to drag on for some days longer. It was Tuesday, October 7, and the Arab weekend began on Wednesday afternoon. So I estimated we were looking at midday Saturday. *Inchallah.*

As instructed, Steve and Graham went to Mr. Yusef's office at 8:30 A.M. to find the agents' compound awash with activity. *Gumruk chef*'s intervention on our behalf had already become known to other agents, through which channels we knew not, and they were trying to locate Mr. Yusef by telephone in Tapline Ar'ar to tell him to get to Judaidat Ar'ar immediately.

At 11:00 A.M. two Customs clerks came onto the road above and gave us the signal to move. We circled onto the road and approached the north gate of the compound in low range. At the gate we were handed a Customs form admitting us for cargo inspection. At the bottom of the form it said: "This service is free of charge." The guard instructed us to proceed to the southwest corner for unloading.

Suddenly we had entered a new world. The compound covered maybe ten acres and was surfaced in concrete so that the sun heated it like an oven. It was enclosed by a ten-foot-high buff-colored wall that prevented us from seeing out. And although we were destined to drive no more than four hundred yards that day, our horizons completely changed. The compound, some 250 yards long, was not quite square. An island of covered unloading bays in the center divided the compound into two sections. We wheeled through the west section to our appointed corner and backed the trucks into a space bordered on

one side by an unused cold-storage warehouse and on the other by
administrative offices. Inside the north gate a fleet of forklift trucks
were lined up next to four mobile cranes.

The two square water towers were now to our north, and the
mosque was directly in front of us to the southeast. Also in the
southeast corner was a concrete cube that housed the compound's only
toilets and cold-water sinks. Opposite the cube was the Customs police
headquarters.

As soon as we were parked, three forklifts driven by red-overalled
workers raced over to us. The drivers were Bengalis. The foreman
sidled over to Steve and said, "For a hundred riyals we unload you
very fast."

"What if I don't pay?"

"We unload you slowly."

"One hundred riyals for two trucks?"

"Okay."

Suddenly a dozen smiling, red-suited workers were unsheeting our
loads and lowering the sidegates. Within an hour they had Steve's
shipment completely offloaded. It looked like a see-through box,
which is what the Saudi Customs inspectors wanted it to look like. In
another hour our shipment was emptied and the little red men left,
grumbling that the agreed-upon hundred riyals was not enough
baksheesh.

The Ar'ar customs community was a Muslim United Nations. The
imported labor needed to make the place work numbered some four
thousand Malaysians, Egyptians, Bengalis, Indians, Thais, Filipinos,
Pakistanis, and Yemenis. They were housed in a self-contained village
without bars, movies, or women about six miles down the road. It had
been built four years before at a cost of untold millions.

Once the shipments were unloaded, a Customs inspector in a white
nightshirt and black-spotted kaffiyeh came over to size up our loads.
He was accompanied by a crew of green-overalled workers equipped
with circular metal-cutting saws, drills, and crowbars. The words of
the Infrasystems engineer suddenly flashed through my mind: "Don't
worry, they'll never find the whiskey."

"Oh-oh, do you think that guy in Luton—"

"Quiet," Graham said sternly. "Say nothing, act dumb, and stay
out of the way."

The inspector, a short, lean-faced fellow in his early thirties with
black curly hair and a pointed goatee, had alert eyes and took his work

seriously but without apparent concern for the damage he wrought. He indicated to the green foreman, a Bengali, which pieces he wanted pierced, sliced open, or otherwise dismantled. Holes were drilled through galvanized panels, the control console was stripped of its sealing and opened, a part of one of the ovens was sawed off, vent ducts were unbolted and left hanging, and cans of retouching paint had their lids pried open and left standing.

"Did you see what that weasel did to Mrs. Hayes's trunk?" Steve asked.

Mr. Weasel, as such became his name, had opened it and tipped out the neatly folded contents, examining with special interest the lady's undergarments and some rather sexy evening wear. When finished, he motioned to one of the green men, who stuffed the clothes back into the trunk pell-mell so they no longer fit and the trunk could not be closed.

Across from us eight Jordanian-registered Mercedes bulk carriers loaded with cement and phosphates were parked facing the exit gate. Two of them were being offloaded by the mobile cranes. I walked over and started chatting with one of the drivers, whose name was Ibrahim. He was in a dirty white nightshirt, wore rimless glasses, and, about fifty years old, looked more like a schoolteacher than a truck driver.

"Problem," he said, laughing. "Phosphate comes from Iraq in half-ton sacks. Egyptian manager of bulk freight section is crazee. Says no stamp of origin on bags. Must get permission from Riyadh to clear us. Sleeping here eight days now. Wait maybe one week more. Mail very slow."

"What weight are you carrying?"

"Gross seventy tons; fifty-four payload." And all this on four axles! "How much you have?"

I told him Steve had six tons and we five tons.

"Oy-yoi-yoi," he said with a laugh. "Very heavy."

As we talked, Inspector Weasel strode across the compound to his office at the south end of the center island to resume the debate with Mr. Yusef about whether our freight should be considered as a single piece of machinery (albeit dismantled) or whether it should be imported as separate parts and taxed accordingly. Mr. Weasel was leaning toward the latter because the Customs duty on spare parts was three times higher. This argument continued for the rest of the afternoon, and by 5:00 P.M., when the work crews knocked off, we understood we would not be reloaded for at least another day.

Most trucks are cleared within a few hours of their entering the cargo compound. By the time the workmen leave at the end of the afternoon, between eighty and one hundred vehicles have been offloaded, inspected, and reloaded. Usually only one or two trucks are held over for administrative reasons or if a further search for contraband is thought necessary. That night there were eleven trucks— Ibrahim and his seven friends, a surly Turk, and ourselves. At 6:00 P.M., as we were preparing supper, *gumruk chef* drove by at the wheel of his Cadillac. We waved at him. He waved back.

"Friendly slob, isn't he," Graham said, stirring canned potatoes into the *camion* stew, which he was cooking on the cold-storage dock between two crates marked for a customer in Riyadh and an International Harvester engine block never expedited to its consignee.

For after-dinner tea we moved to the back of the loads, by the wall, where we could sit on some flat cargo. As we were talking a black cat strolled by, inspecting the dismantled oven and no doubt hoping for a lick of the stewpot.

"What's a nice cat like that doing in a place like this?" I asked.

Steve and Graham gazed at it for a moment. Then after a pause, Graham reflected, "My father used to have a cat like that. It would go anywhere."

He started telling us the story of this cat that would follow his father into the workshop and watch him tinker. One day his father was cleaning the jets of a carburetor with gasoline, which he poured into a saucer. When finished, he absentmindedly put the saucer on the floor. The next time he looked around, the cat was lapping up the gasoline. Suddenly it jerked upright and started running all over the place.

"Crazy it was. Up and down the workshop, all around, and then it just upped and stopped."

We waited for the rest of the story. When it didn't come, I asked, "Did it die?"

"No," Graham replied. "It ran out of gas."

The three of us burst into near-hysterical laughter and Steve and Graham rolled off the piece of machinery, pounding each other.

"Fucking hell," Steve said. "Any more like that and we'll send you home."

The desert heart was getting to us. Beyond the wall there was sheet lightning in the west. We listened to the BBC World Service. Her Majesty's government had obtained a high court injunction against the *New Statesman,* prohibiting it from publishing excerpts of a memo to the foreign secretary, Sir Geoffrey Howe, from the former British ambassador to Saudi Arabia, Sir James Craig. But the *Glasgow Herald* beat the injunction and published snippets from the memo that were said to jeopardize British-Saudi relations.

After the news, Graham prepared to turn in. It had been a long day's drive, he said, and he wanted to be in shape for tomorrow's grueling pace. He sprayed the cab with more Aroxol fly killer, smoked a cigarette while waiting for his victims to die, then climbed in and locked the doors. I got into the empty van and set up my office and parlor. I intended to spend an hour or so catching up with my notes before turning in.

It was almost imperceptible at first. A slight breeze rustled some loose metal sheeting on one of the oven parts a few feet from the trailer. And then it burst upon us in a fury, a sandstorm out of the desert, driven by gale-force winds.

Within minutes it had ripped the canvas off Steve's load and almost ripped ours off as well, collapsing part of the metal frame in the process. I managed to tie the rest down. At times visibility was zero and the sand was blinding. Then Steve's laundry blew away and I went after it, only to find when I returned that our kitchen utensils, which we had left on the cold-storage dock, were drifting across the compound. I finally abandoned the van because I feared it might be overturned by the wind.

Mrs. Hayes's trunk and the two tea-chests of toys were out in the open. The fat police sergeant drove up in his Nissan patrol wagon with four men, their heads covered in kaffiyehs. He asked if any of the cargo "feared water."

"You mean it's going to rain, too?"

He nodded yes.

I pointed to the personal effects, and the four men hopped out of the Nissan and dragged them to shelter. But nothing could be done for the machinery and the electric motors that drove the oven's beltline. I rescued the tube containing the plans and threw it into a corner of the van. Steve, incredibly, slept through the storm, but it woke Graham. Then it started to rain, and the sand was dampened down.

My eyes ached. But the sand didn't seem to bother the desert dogs. They wandered through the compound, checking out the situation. The storm stopped after midnight. A red film of sand was everywhere. It took an hour to clean out my bedding and then, feeling gritty and stiff, I rolled into the sack.

On Wednesday, October 8, the weather remained moody and heightened our gloom. The constant threat of a renewed sandstorm hung in the air; some rain fell, and it was muggy. More delays. Mr. Weasel brought his colleagues around to look at us. They included Mr. Pretty Pants, who had white pointed shoes to match his nightshirt; Mr. King Cockroach, long and tall; and Friar Tuck, who missed only the tonsure.

We had watched Mr. King Cockroach in action. A Turkish tonka carrying bolts of material was parked next to us. Mr. King Cockroach wanted to see what might be hidden inside a bolt of material, so he ordered one of the greenies to select two or three bolts at random and cut them open with a power saw. Fluff everywhere. He adopted the same procedure with a tonka carrying rolls of tissue paper. More fluff everywhere.

Mr. Weasel reappeared every twenty minutes, trying to match pieces of machinery to the names on the manifest: "Where is the dipcoater?" he asked. Steve fumbled around and found something he thought might fit the description. Satisfied, Mr. Weasel returned to his office, then came back almost immediately. "Postheat oven?" he asked. Another problem became apparent: The names on the manifest did not always match those on the CMR.

On his next trip across the compound, Mr. Weasel wanted to know where piece No. 007 was—the main function pump. Steve led him to it. Mr. Weasel made a note on his pad and returned to the office. Twenty minutes later he was back, asking for something else. Steve, unable to remember which pieces he had already shown him, made another stab in the dark. Finally Graham intervened.

"We're only truck drivers, you know, not bloody engineers."

Then Mr. Weasel discovered that two sets of plans were listed on the manifest, and he asked to see them. Steve dug them out. Where was the manual? In with the plans. Next he wanted a picture of the machine in its assembled state. This was no catalog item, we told him. That didn't matter. Fortunately, Richard Hayes had taken a picture of it at the factory in Luton. A request was made to have it sent from Al Khobar, 680 miles away.

Steve found enough coins to phone Roger Hayes at the factory. Hayes had Al Jalhany in his office with him. Al Jalhany said, "You've got a good inspector. He cuts only little holes."

On Wednesday, Mr. Weasel concentrated on probing the trucks for contraband. He instructed the green-suited mechanics to open "little" holes, about the size of picture postcards, in the belly tanks, the floors of each van above the fifth wheel where there is a hollow metal casing, in the back bumpers, and in the running tanks.

Every time Mr. Weasel gave instructions to cut another hole, Graham and Steve became tense. You could tell it was hurting them. Steve came very close to losing his cool but caught himself in time. For a young driver, he was remarkably agile as a diplomat, clown, and negotiator. He had several techniques for defusing situations. One was the hat trick. If a foreman, worker, or clerk was wearing a hat, Steve made conversation with him till he felt he knew the fellow well enough to lift the hat off his head and try it on. He would walk around with it, make faces, smile, get laughs from the others, then return it. It was a variation of the Richie Thorne technique, and usually at the end of it he had the hat's owner as a friend.

On Wednesday morning we were also visited by the radiation doctor, an Egyptian, with a Geiger counter. He quickly determined that our trucks were clean. He wore a white lab coat over a white suit. He asked which route we had taken. No, we had not driven through Chernobyl.

We asked if many trucks showed traces of radioactivity when they came through Ar'ar. "Oh, yes," he said. "Some Turkish trucks have 100 percent radiation." Sheep were not a problem, he said, but their feed often was. "Yesterday we turned back three sheep trucks because the feed was contaminated."

By midday we suspected we were stuck in Ar'ar for a second Muslim weekend, and our hearts sank. We had had enough and wanted out. When Mr. Weasel returned, we bitched at him. He said *gumruk chef* would come at 4:00 P.M. and decide whether we could leave. But no workers were left in the compound to reload us, and we still had open holes in our diesel tanks. Then at 4:30 P.M. Mr. Weasel returned to say we had been cleared and asked Steve to see *gumruk chef* with him.

Gumruk chef was still puzzling over how our paperwork had gotten into such a mess. Nevertheless he had stamped it all, and said we were cleared to go as soon as Mr. Yusef paid the ten thousand riyals in Customs duties. But Mr. Yusef had already left for the weekend. When *gumruk chef* heard this he became very angry. "That man must not leave before Customs closes. He is in serious trouble. Perhaps calaboosh."

Steve called Roger Hayes a second time. Hayes had given Al Jalhany, Yusef's boss, the ten thousand riyals that morning and told him to shift ass. Hayes was fed up with waiting, as he wanted his oven installed and working. Our papers were deposited with the Customs police. We went to get them. "No money, you stay," the fat sergeant told Steve.

We were depressed. Graham was worried because he had no more canned potatoes, no more bread for butties, and soon no more cigarettes. What were you going to do without canned potatoes? Our menu for supper that night was ersatz hamburgers, canned carrots, and Ryvita. "You can't make butties with Ryvita," Graham complained.

Before supper we paid a visit to Ibrahim and his friends Amal, Mustapha, and the other whose names I never got. They were Palestinians from Hebron, now in the Israeli-occupied territories, and they always ran together, transporting some of their village life with them. They hadn't been back to Hebron since 1967. They played dominoes and gin rummy to pass the time. They owned their own rigs and were in no hurry to leave Judaidat Ar'ar because their client was paying three hundred riyals in demurrage per day.* "Mercedes Hotel pretty good," Ibrahim said.

They had a hubbly-bubbly water pipe set up between two trucks, with collapsible chairs and a table for dominoes. They poured us sage-flavored tea and offered us dinner. We were too embarrassed to accept because we didn't have anything to offer in return.

Ibrahim said that Ar'ar was a bad Customs post because too many Turkish tonkas came through. "They do much smuggling. Bad boys. Six caught this week," he said, pointing to their confiscated vehicles lined up between the lavatory cube and the police headquarters. The smugglers stuff hashish in the double lining of their iceboxes, in their brake drums (no wonder some can't stop) and fuel tanks. In addition to the contraband, more than one million Turkish sheep come through Ar'ar each year. Other Turkish tonkas that we saw carried baled wool, bagged oats, furniture, hardware, and spools of yarn. Turkish refrigerator trucks brought foodstuffs. But foreign-registered refrigerator trucks are no longer allowed into the kingdom, except in transit. They are offloaded at the border and their cargoes put onto forty-foot Saudi refrigerator trucks.

Steve had spent most of the afternoon resheeting his tilt and tying the canvas down so it wouldn't blow away again in another sandstorm. He suggested that Graham do the same. Graham wasn't interested. I

---

* Demurrage is a penalty payable to the shipping company or vehicle owner by the consignee for failure to discharge within a contracted time or for loss of time due to abnormal Customs delays.

had become terrified of sandstorms and took refuge this night inside Steve's empty van. Sure enough, right on schedule, it swept it from the desert. The van creaked and shuddered. Graham's canvas sheeting flew off.

Next morning a skeleton crew appeared to load us. The machinery had suffered through two sandstorms, rain, and the attacks of Mr. Weasel. Thursday was clean-up day in the cargo compound. The toy garbage truck scooted around emptying bins, and a team of Thai workers swept out the unloading bays.

As soon as the trucks were reloaded, Steve's and Graham's humor improved. They started cleaning out their cabs. Steve emptied everything onto the cold-storage dock, dusted and shined the interior, then reloaded it back. "If you don't have a clean truck, you don't pick up nice girls," he said.

Where he was going to find nice girls, any girls, in Saudi Arabia I didn't have the heart to ask.

Friday was barnyard day. Thousands of sheep padded their way through on their last journey. Some had been so damaged in transport that they were hobbling on three feet. One was propelled like a wheelbarrow by a Turk holding its back legs. A couple of herds of black goats passed through as well, and dozens of poultry wagons. They parked at the unloading bays so that mobile cranes could lift off the cages, allowing inspectors to search underneath them for contraband.

That Friday we noticed trucks with sea containers coming north, heading into Iraq. A hundred of them, in groups of ten or twelve, went through Ar'ar without stopping. We asked Ibrahim what they were.

"Weapons for Saddam Hussein," he said. "Hussein is a madman, but Khomeini is crazee. Have your choice." He added that he was a supporter of Yasser Arafat.

The truck convoys, we later found out, came from the Kuwaiti port of Shuaiba and carried Soviet and French armaments.

On Saturday morning more sheep paraded through the compound. They came in flocks of two and three hundred. One panting creature tarried in the shade under Ibrahim's trailer. He and Mustapha collared it and marched it behind the truck, gave it water, and encouraged it to stay, which it did without much coaxing. The Turkish shepherd never missed it.

Ibrahim was pleased. "We have lamb stew tonight," he said, giggling.

Mr. Yusef was still arguing about the ten-thousand-riyal payment. Finally *gumruk chef* told him to pay or go to calaboosh. His decision was irreversible. At 1:00 P.M. we were given our exit tickets and our passports. We were back in business. Steve and Graham paid twenty riyals each in *baksheesh*—"This service is free"—to have their diesel tanks welded shut. The guard saluted as we left the compound. "I've forgotten how to drive," Steve said out of his window as we turned south, toward the Tapline.

19.
UNLOADING IN AL KHOBAR

"WELL, come on. Get in and let's get going," Graham called from inside the cab. I looked up and he was sitting in the passenger seat, waiting for me to take the wheel.

We had parked on the side of the road, a couple of hundred miles down the Tapline, to stretch our legs and drink diet Cokes from the refrigerator, which we had transferred to Steve's truck.

I climbed behind the wheel, started the motor, and made myself familiar with the transmission and instruments while waiting for the air pressure to build up in the master brake cylinder. *Old Girl*'s ten-speed transmission was a bit tricky because it wouldn't stay in fourth or ninth gears—evidently the gearpin was bent—so those gears couldn't be used. In front of me was the speedometer, but it didn't work, either, because the cable had snapped in southern Turkey. I had oil pressure, temperature, and fuel gauges around the speedometer clock. There was also an rpm meter to tell me how many revolutions per minute the motor was doing. It still worked and was the only instrument by which I could judge our speed. An air pressure gauge was off to the left. When the needle moved out of the red, I flicked the lights to signal Steve that I was ready; released the hand brake, which was a stubby lever to the left of the steering wheel; and felt with my left hand for the short gear lever, making sure the switch on the side of the lever was down, indicating that the transmission was in low range.

I put on the left indicator, got in first gear, checked both wing mirrors again, and gently started to roll. Halfway onto the road I shifted into second, then immediately into third, skipped fourth, and went into fifth. We were fully onto the road now. Although everything

187

so far had gone smoothly, I sensed that Graham, unused to being driven in his own truck, was about to have kittens. Now a tricky two-part shift: from fifth into neutral, flick the range-change switch into high range, and start at the bottom of the transmission again, going into sixth. As soon as we were in tenth, I relaxed. What a beautiful feeling sitting six feet above the road with 280 horsepower at the tip of your toes.

"Keep your line!" Graham shouted, bringing me back to the here and now. "Don't let those wheels drift over the center line like that!"

I hadn't appreciated how narrow the two-lane tapline was. I rolled the steering wheel right. It seemed to take forever to bring her back on course.

"She's got nice, direct steering, don't you think?" Graham said, looking at me for confirmation.

"Direct? Oh, yes," I said. But I didn't think so. It had taken a half turn of the wheel to edge her back, and then I found her almost impossible to hold on line because the road surface bounced us around like a Ping-Pong ball.

The Tapline is one of the most extraordinary stretches of highway anywhere in the world. It takes 663 miles to get from nowhere to nowhere through nothing but sand and lava, with scarcely a bend and no change in the scenery. A gray thirty-inch steel snake runs along the west side of the road. This is the famous Trans-Arabian Pipeline, which gives the highway its name. Completed in 1949 at a cost of two hundred million dollars, it connects the Persian Gulf oil fields with the Mediterranean port of Sidon—a distance of one thousand miles. But because of the vagaries of Middle East politics, the pipeline was closed in April 1975 and has never been reopened. The road has been poorly maintained ever since.

When several months later I flew over the Tapline in a British Airways jumbo, the road appeared even more excruciatingly narrow than I had remembered: a thin thread of charcoal extending through a dung-colored sea to infinity. From the air the desert resembled spun-cotton waves, but what a bitch it had been to drive across those ripples with twenty-six tons behind me.

I fought with the steering to make our right wheels hug the desert's edge. There was no hard shoulder. Sometimes the sand drifted in patches onto the roadway and tugged at the wheels. As *Old Girl* was a right-hooker, I had the impression that I was sitting over the edge of the road. Jolting along at about fifty miles per hour, though the exact speed was hard to judge, I recalled Gordon Durno's story of a driver who had let his truck wander off the paved surface. His wheels caught in a soft patch and the truck flipped over. Both driver and vehicle were wasted. I didn't enjoy the thought of that happening to us.

Spectacular car wrecks lined both sides of the highway: cars cut in two, cars stuck under the backs of trucks, cars bent in half, cars flattened like pancakes, and thousands of abandoned tires, but no wrecked trucks. The afternoon heat was grueling, and at every moment I had to keep an eye on the side of the road, as *Old Girl* had a tendency to wander. The sky was milky blue, the sand grayish brown, and the highway as straight as you could imagine over utterly barren country.

The road melded into a heat haze along the horizon. The rim of infinity was fuzzy. A spot appeared out of the haze and hung there. Was it moving? Or was it an illusion? Yes, it was another truck. Several of them. But they got no bigger. Maybe they were parked. Three in a line. No, they were moving: I could see a plume of dust curling off their roofs. Then they were upon us, giant tankers, steaming in from the gray. Suddenly my heart was in my throat. They were filling the whole damn road. Graham didn't say a word but was sizing them up as well. I had to hold my line and not wander out. Direct steering? It felt awfully loose to me—like there was an ocean of play. Only small corrections, fractions of an inch. Steady!

We closed on each other at a hundred miles an hour, or so it seemed. When only yards separated us I saw the first driver nod. Like me, he had both hands on the wheel and was watching his line, too. Paff! The compression of air between the two vehicles shook *Old Girl*. Paff! The second truck zoomed past, only a foot between wing mirrors. Can I hold her steady for the third one? Paff! again. They were gone. What relief.

Oh, shit! A truck was ahead of us. A slow-moving monster. I'd have to overtake it. I counted the minutes till I was behind it, then swung out to the left. Gently, gently. Keep those outside wheels off the sand. Don't waver. Was the trailer going to clear? Gawd, only inches to spare. A Filipino sitting behind the wheel of the big Mack kept looking straight ahead. He was wearing aviator's goggles. I concentrated on my mirrors. It was taking forever. Now the trailer was past. Back in slowly. Step on the accelerator. Whew!

We kept driving for another two hours until we reached the town of Rahfa, where Steve cut left into a dusty parking lot. In less than a quarter of an hour the sky had turned from dusk to darkness and the town was alive with electric signs in Arabic script and people in nightshirts.

I fumbled with the gears, missed my shift into low range. The lever switch hadn't connected. Maybe I'd flicked it too soon. I hunted for fifth.

"Don't force it! Take it easy!" Graham yelled. "You'll bust the transmission!"

I let her coast, softly applying the brakes. Only when we stopped did I notice I was covered with sweat.

While Steve went into a small, modern hotel, I walked around the corner and bought kebab sandwiches from a man with an outdoor grill; Graham turned down my offer of one and built his own buttie. Not a woman was around, and the cafes, of which there were four, were about to close for evening prayers. After two pots of tea, we got under way, Graham back at the wheel. It was cooler, almost agreeable, and we continued down the Tapline for another three hours before pulling onto the left side of the road, under a microwave tower, where we decided to sleep that night.

As we brewed more tea we listened to the BBC World Service announce that Iran had raided the Iraqi oilfield at Kirkuk, causing major damage, which Iraq promptly denied. Kirkuk, which had started pumping in 1927, was the oldest oilfield in the Middle East. It was in Kurdish country not far from the Iranian border, and TIR drivers often wondered why it hadn't been attacked before.

I bedded down in front of the trucks till woken up at about 5:00 A.M. by a Bedouin tonka that had pulled off into the desert, almost running over me. As we had planned to set off before sunrise, I woke Steve and Graham.

We reached the road junction at the end of the Tapline, a mile south of Al Nuayriyah, and pulled into a sand-covered services area. It had a filling station with two diesel pumps, a general store, a local restaurant, and a mosque. British drivers call it Watford Gap because in the early days of Middle East trucking one homesick trooper, stretching his imagination back to Dover, had claimed it reminded him of the services area on the M1 near Rugby, in the green hills of Northamptonshire, about sixty-five miles north of London. We filled up with diesel: two hundred liters for twelve riyals, the equivalent of 2.40 pounds for one hundred liters.

After Watford Gap, Graham asked me to take the wheel again along the six-lane expressway from Kuwait, and at 1:00 P.M. we pulled into the Souks Supermarket parking lot on the outskirts of Dammam. Steve called Roger Hayes, who said he would meet us in half an hour. The supermarket was like a dreamland after being a prisoner of Saudi Customs in the desert at Ar'ar. There was everything one could imagine lined up in air-conditioned rows. Fresh dairy products, Double Gloucester cheese, Cheddar, Stilton, French Brie, Danish blue, fresh fruit and vegetables flown in daily from Holland, cereals, cold drinks, ice cream, a selection of meat, sliced bread, chocolate cakes, pies: everything our mouths had been watering for except beer and Beaujolais.

In the cafeteria we had slushpuppies and cheeseburgers and read the London papers. The censor had inked out the bare tits on page three and reports about the diplomatic storm brewing over what Sir James Craig, the former ambassador, had said about the Saudis in his valedictory report.

Roger Hayes arrived in the company Chevy and guided us to the Saudi Conduit & Coating Company's newly acquired factory. We squeezed the trucks around the back of the building, dropped legs, and unhitched the trailers. Roger suggested we park the units out of the sun in the vacant hangar where the oven was to be assembled. Radio Bahrain announced a high for the day of 106 degrees. "That's cool," Roger said.

Roger and his wife, Sue, were typical of the expatriate families that lived on the Saudi Gulf coast. In his late thirties, he had first come out to Dammam seven years before as an engineer with British Steel. The U.K. steelmakers had embarked on a joint venture with Saudi partners to build a steel plant at Al Khobar, which had paid for itself within six months of completion. Roger was a coachbuilder by trade and had helped design the ERF truck. His wife was a hairdresser.

"You're having dinner with me tonight. Sue can't join us. She has another engagement. But in the meantime, what would you like to do?"

"Swim in the Gulf," I suggested. Steve and Graham agreed. Roger said no problem. He'd take us to his favorite stretch of beach next to a military firing range. "They don't use it much," he assured us.

The strip of Gulf coast from Dammam to Al Khobar is regarded as Saudi Arabia's Côte d'Azur, and traffic along its so-called corniche is heavy. But once south of Al Khobar we saw not more than three or four people on the promenades and, beyond the pavement and amusement areas, the beaches were deserted. Roger took us on a detour to see what he called "the most dangerous stretch of road in the world," a four-lane expressway heading inland heavily traveled by industrial vehicles. Aside from the drivers who used it and their battered trucks, what made the road a killer was that it had been constructed on top of a causeway of sand, with no shoulders, so that if anything went wrong the only escape was either into the oncoming traffic or over the edge, down the steep embankment, onto the floor of the desert.

We sat on a side road, utterly mesmerized by the rolling chaos, watching the "beddie" drivers roar along above us in their "circus" trucks—brightly painted twenty-ton Bedfords or Mercedes—dodging larger tractor-trailer rigs, many unfit to pass European or U.S. safety standards. When we had our eyeful, Roger did a U-turn and headed back to the Gulf shore. He took us to Parrot Beak Bay. After bouncing down an unpaved track, he wheeled the Chevy onto the sand and we drove along the beach for a few miles, seeking a secluded spot. Any spot would have done, as we had the whole expanse of bay—a ten-mile curve of sand bordered by perfectly still, emerald green water—to ourselves. We changed and ran into the sea. After the dust and heat of the desert, it was like diving into a warm orgasm. The water was tepid, salty, and buoyant.

I think the three of us were reasonably disoriented by then. At least I was, and Roger tried briefly to explain something of the region's geography and history. Al Khobar was once a fishing port, but the government had built moorings for small craft alongside the new port of Dammam so that it was now little used by coastal dhows or fishing boats. Extending in an arc under the desert about six miles behind Al Khobar and running to the sea at Ras Tanura, thirty miles to the north, is a geological formation called the Dhahran Dome. In 1936 American oilmen working for the Arab-American Oil Company, better known as Aramco, sunk a test well into the dome and almost drowned in the resulting eruption of oil. Over the next twenty years nearly two hundred wells were drilled into the dome, most of them centered on Ras Tanura, which in 1939 became the first Saudi oilfield to export crude to the West.

Out of the sand at the western tip of the dome rose a suburban town to house the oil workers. Aramco employees named it Dhahran, after the subterranean pocket that they soon discovered contained a significant portion of the world's proven oil reserves. Officially Dhahran was a company compound with virtual extraterritorial status. It grew into a small city with a peak population of thirty-five thousand. The large ranch-style bungalows inside the compound are surrounded by manicured lawns, and many have tennis courts that Filipino gardeners daily water to keep down the heat. Except for the absence of anything resembling the Trinity River, Dhahran could easily be mistaken for a suburb of Dallas, with its own university, football stadium, and an intercontinental airport nearby. Some Americans born and educated inside the compound are now in their thirties and have never lived anywhere else.

Dammam, where the Hayeses live in a walled compound reserved for "expat" families not associated with Aramco, is on the coast ten miles north of Al Khobar. Today the three cities of Al Khobar, Dhahran, and Dammam form one large metropolitan jumble linked by a maze of beltways and expressways and pocked with ungainly industrial estates.

Driving back along the Gulf, we passed seafront domains belonging to royal princes, of which there are several thousand in the kingdom, and multimillionaire businessmen, members of Saudi Arabia's growing middle class. They have built themselves magnificent palaces inside landscaped compounds with swimming pools, marinas, and forests of palms. The water to sustain such opulence comes from four desalination plants. Graham was interested in seeing the largest of these plants because his brother, a plumbing engineer, had spent several years in Dammam helping to run it. The plant was truly grand, with four giant stacks towering over the inlet from the Gulf upon which it sat, a seeming marvel of science and technology until one considered that over the past seven years the process of converting salt water into sweet water had increased the level of salinity in the almost enclosed expanse of sea between the Saudi shore and Bahrain by 6 percent, killing much of the aquatic life.

Scientists from the University of Petroleum and Minerals in Dhahran are studying the phenomenon of the Gulf's rising salinity and have recommended better controls on coastal development. In addition to the estimated 170 billion barrels of oil still underground—enough to last for 120 years at normal production levels—the scientists point out that the waters of the Gulf are one of the country's most vital resources. Had this been appreciated sooner, the fifteen-mile causeway from Al Khobar to Bahrain might never have been constructed. Ecologists fear the causeway will have a negative impact on the Gulf's ecosystems.

On our way back to his home, Roger drove us under the causeway. Built by a Dutch consortium at a cost of 340 million pounds, it would be open for traffic in a few months. Already some enthusiasts had dubbed it "the Middle East's biggest maritime engineering feat since Moses parted the Red Sea." For most expats, however, it was a nonevent. Roger doubted many would use it. The rigmarole to obtain exit visas is so intense that few expats are able to take quick trips abroad, and those who do will almost certainly continue to use the daily Saudia 747 flight from Dhahran to Bahrain. Because there is a certain sense of urgency associated with air travel, Customs and Immigration formalities seem to be more relaxed at the kingdom's international airports. It takes but seven minutes to fly over to Bahrain and six minutes to fly back. The only drawback is that a return ticket costs sixty pounds, making it the most expensive flight per mile in the world.

The compound where the Hayeses rent a three-bedroom house for fifteen hundred pounds a month contains several hundred other expat families. Three more compounds just like it are on the same road. Their gates are guarded to keep out unannounced visitors. The layout of each compound is more or less the same, and they resemble southern Florida residential developments. This is not surprising, as they were built by the Bechtel Corporation, the largest civil engineering firm in the United States. Most homes have two-car garages, asphalted driveways, crabgrass lawns, and lush gardens. The homes are equipped with central air conditioning, refrigerators the size of closets, and the latest General Electric kitchens. They can be rented with pictures already on the walls, completely bare, or semifurnished, and with maid service if desired.

Sue Hayes regretted that the religious laws did not allow her to drive their four-year-old daughter, Louise, to kindergarten, but otherwise enjoyed the high pace of intercompound social life. She was a member of the International Women's Guild, frowned upon by the local authorities, and recently had joined the Al Khobar Thespian Society. She was unable to have dinner with us that evening, as the Thespians were rehearsing their Christmas presentation of *Mother Goose*.

Roger took us to the Oasis, a restaurant operated for the expat employees of the Tamimi Group, a local conglomerate whose interests extended from supermarkets to engineering. Standard fare at the Oasis was all you could eat from the salad bar, followed by T-bone steaks, ice cream, and cake. The carbonated drinks came out of stainless-steel hoses already chilled, but ice makers cranked out additional cubes free of charge. The atmosphere was a cross between Howard Johnson's and McDonald's, except that there were no waitresses, only a Filipino headwaiter and two busboys.

Over dinner Roger told us the story of his oven. A market survey had indicated a huge domestic demand for plastic pipes and conduits, another make-your-capital-back-in-six-months sort of thing, and when he spoke about it to his boss, Mr. Amimi, he said, "Go for it."

Roger went around the world obtaining quotes: Taiwan, South Korea, Japan, West Germany, Britain. Everybody said they could deliver within six to twelve months. That was too long, Roger decided. He went to Infrasystems, who told him they could build the plant in ten weeks and at a competitive price. He placed the order in June.

Then came the problem of getting the oven to Al Khobar. He could have shipped it by sea container and it would have arrived in the port of Dammam in six weeks, plus another two weeks for dockside handling and Customs clearance. The job required two forty-foot sea containers, and he was quoted a cost of three thousand pounds each. Roger wanted his first oven in operation within two months. He had a second, larger unit coming later. He asked about overland transport. He could find only three U.K. firms that were still offering regular overland freight services to the Gulf: Astran, Falcongate, and Whittle. He said he received the lowest quote and the best impression from Whittle. The quote he received was sixty-five hundred pounds per truck—more than double the cost of sea containers—but Whittle's sales manager said the material would be delivered to the factory in a month.

Roger opted for overland transport, to find that it took almost six weeks—only two weeks faster than sea freight, counting the time for dockside handling and Customs clearance. Of course, the six-week overland delivery time included the eleven-day delay at the Saudi border, which had cost him an additional two thousand pounds in demurrage. He was not, you might say, sold on the advantages of overland transport.

Roger in no way blamed us for the delay, although he felt that perhaps Whittle should have warned him that it might take longer. Clearly ten days in Customs was unacceptable, but that was the Middle East for you. What could be done? It was beyond our control, and for that matter his as well. And so, after everything we had been through, he wanted to ensure that the remainder of our stay would be as restful as possible. He saw that we got showers, clean laundry, and air conditioning if we wanted to sleep in a storeroom at the back of the factory. We were curious about many things, and he got us a *Gulf Directory,* which was a mine of information but didn't tell us anything practical about the route. The expressways around Al Khobar, Dhahran, and Dammam are even more confusing than Dallas. We told him that while trying to find our way that afternoon to our rendezvous at the Souks Supermarket we had stopped to ask directions at a police station that had a fleet of green-and-white patrol cars parked outside it. We gathered they were the traffic police. But we had also noticed blue-and-white police cars patrolling the roads, and we asked Roger about them.

"You want to say away from those fellows. They're the religious police," he advised us.

"Religious police?"

"Oh, yes. They make sure that shops shut for prayers, that people are properly dressed, that the drinking prohibition is respected, and that no women drivers take to the streets."

Women are placed on a curious pedestal in the kingdom. They may not pray alongside their menfolk in mosques. They are forbidden to enter a car unless it is driven by a member of their family or they are properly chaperoned. Any suggestion of a bare arm or leg brings a severe reprimand. Kissing between men and women in public is a punishable offense. Yet we had noticed that it was perfectly acceptable for men to hold hands and kiss in public.

With women virtually absent from public life, male rape can be a problem. Roger cited the case of a policeman who had abducted a Portuguese businessman. He took the businessman into the desert and sodomized and killed him. But even though it appears barren, the desert has its eyes and ears: Bedouin tribes roamed the empty spaces long before the Queen of Sheba reigned over them. A Bedouin identified the policeman, who was immediately arrested and beheaded.

Stonings of adulterers also occur but are said to be rare. Such executions follow a traditional pattern: A truck dumps a load of stones at the site. The stones are graded according to size. The religious police arrive with the condemned, who is buried up to the waist. The first volleys are with pebbles and gradually increase to deadly rocks. If the fornicator can wriggle free—very few are said to succeed—pardon follows.

However curious we found Saudi customs such as these, the crime rate is remarkably low compared to Texas cities like Dallas or Fort Worth, or, come to think of it, any Western industrialized metropolis. This partly reflects the fact that Saudi citizens have few wants. The Saudis have been told—perhaps it is written in the Koran—that they live in a land of milk and honey. To demonstrate it, the royal family makes life as pleasant for their subjects as possible. Schooling and medical care are free. Merchants are given land upon which to build homes. All except the new super-rich mandarins, who have their seaside domains the size of a city block, erect multi-storied mansions that they rent to foreigners for as much as twenty-five hundred pounds a month and then continue to live in tents in the desert.

One thing we found evident everywhere was the deepening recession that the Gulf war and falling oil prices had brought to the kingdom. Oil revenues have dropped 75 percent since 1981, the last boom year; so, too, have Saudi property values and, a logical sequel, the rents the merchants were formerly pulling in for their gaudy mansions. We saw several newly finished housing compounds that were completely empty, and supermarkets that had been forced to close for want of clientele. The American population in the triple-city complex alone has dropped from 35,000 in 1982 to a reported 12,500 in mid-1986. Many have been replaced by lower-paid Egyptians, Pakistanis, Indians, and Malaysians.

"In the last year, expats have been leaving in droves. Probably a decline of 30 percent," Roger said. "Before, you would call up a company and ask to speak to so-and-so. Now you ask, 'Is so-and-so still with you?' "

When Roger first arrived in Saudi Arabia, he met an American economist working for a Saudi bank. The economist told him, "By 1984 there will be a dramatic reduction in expat managers. By the end of the decade you will all be gone, replaced by Egyptians and Western-educated Asians. The economy will go steadily downhill as dependence on Middle East oil recedes. By the end of the century this country will be back where it began forty years ago, receding into the desert."

The exodus of foreign managers is of course not only a form of exporting unemployment, it is also saving the Saudi government a lot of money. During the boom years legislation was enacted providing foreigners with a state pension if they reached age fifty-five while on contract in the kingdom. The pension is based on the employee's last salary, indexed for inflation, and is payable anywhere in the world.

The one inconvenient fact about this is that while you are ticking off the years of service up to retirement age, assuming you are not chopped before then, the Saudi company that employs you literally owns you. You must at all times carry your *igtalla,* an ID booklet that lists your vital statistics, the name of your employer, and your visa data. Under the heading "Instructions for Residents", a copy of Saudia Airlines' inflight magazine, which I happened to pick up, gave these instructions: "All foreign visitors and employees when traveling within the kingdom are requested to carry with them a letter of consent issued by their employer or sponsor approving their travel plans, in addition to their regular registration certificate issued by the Immigration authorities. . . . An employee is prohibited from taking up a job other than with his sponsor's consent. Contravening this regulation will lead to a fine and other forms of punishment [i.e., expulsion]."

On Monday afternoon the last of the machinery was taken off the trucks. We went shopping along King Khaled Street in Dammam. We drove along the so-called corniche, a flat piece of road where the desert meets the sea. Roger pointed out the yard of one local entrepreneur who had bought a fleet of one hundred Mercedes bulk carriers for a single construction project. The project was abandoned in 1984 and the trucks were never used. The entire fleet was still standing there exactly as the vehicles had been delivered, with two years of desert sand on them and the tires rotting from exposure to the sun. Farther along the corniche, a housing estate the size of a self-contained neighborhood in any European town had been built but never occupied.

The Flour-Arabia Building and the 350-room Gulf Meridien Hotel looked like they were out of Dallas and Miami Beach, respectively. "Tampon Towers" behind the Gulf Center, is the nurses' residence. The gawdiness was similar to that of West Palm Beach. "But without the chicks," Roger observed.

"Without the chicks," I agreed.

"You can get anywhere from one to ten days in prison and a nine-hundred-riyal fine for jumping a red light," Roger warned. If he forgets to carry his *igtalla* with him it can lead to a ten-thousand-riyal fine.

We walked the six blocks of King Khaled Street between 4:00 P.M., when the shops reopened, and 6:00 P.M., when they closed again for sunset prayers. Steve wanted to buy a water pipe; Graham some kitchen copperware for Madeleine and T-shirts for Jennifer and Angela.

Dinner that evening was pleasantly middle-class. The Hayeses had invited three water-skiing friends. Roger owned a ninety-horsepower speedboat, and they usually spent their weekends camping at the beach. None of them ever went to church, as the religious authorities did not allow Christian churches to be built in the kingdom.

Roger introduced us to his guests. Gerry, he said, was the Dammam port manager. He was originally from Plymouth, England. His wife, Moira, was Scottish. Gunter was the manager of the 190-room Dhahran International Hotel. It advertises itself as "the most luxurious hotel in the Middle East, offering genuine Saudi Arabian hospitality, finest of international cuisine, five-star deluxe comfort, and complete business services." Gunter used to be the manager of the Mayflower Hotel in London.

A former civilian employee of the Department of Defense in Britain, Gerry had been in Saudi Arabia since 1982. He explained that the port of Dammam was built at the end of a five-mile causeway in the late 1970s. It was now the kingdom's second-largest port, after Jeddah. At its peak Dammam handled one million tons of cargo a week. No port in Britain is equipped to handle that much, he said. By comparison, I remembered that Salonika, Greece's second-largest port, handled all of eight million tons a year, and Greece's population was 20 percent larger.

"The infrastructure of this country was built in the 1970s," Gerry explained. "Before that there were no ports here other than Jeddah. Everything had to be brought in and an infrastructure assembled from scratch. First the ports were built and then through them came the materials and equipment that would build the roads, the petrochemical plants, the high-rise buildings, even entire cities in the desert."

The Saudis spent forty billion dollars on one petrochemical complex at Jubail, which they hoped would supply 5 percent of the world's needs. The Japanese-designed complex was shipped through the port of Dammam in two-thousand-ton modules. The modules were loaded onto giant flatbeds—tractor-trailers with twenty-four axles, each with its own motor. Straight roads had to be built out of the port to the factory site, fifty-five miles to the north.

Government spending on new projects was now around twenty billion dollars annually, down from fifty billion dollars in 1981. The only major project still under way, Gerry said, was a dual sixteen-hundred-mile pipeline across the desert from the Iraqi border to the Red Sea port of Yanbu.

Inevitably, conversation shifted to the Gulf war. When Iraqi forces invaded Iran on September 22, 1980, Saddam Hussein promised Iran's defeat in a mere three days. Abolhassan Banisadr, then president of Iran, vowed to crush the Iraqi army in two weeks. Since then more than a million persons have been killed in the war and there was no sign of it coming to an end. In fact, it was heating up.

Ten days ago two Iranian fighters made a rocket attack on the tanker *Umm Casbah* as it was calmly sailing down the coast from the Kuwaiti port of Shuaiba, bound for the United Kingdom with 765,000 tons of crude. The next day Iranian jets damaged an empty Kuwaiti tanker in another rocket attack, and on Wednesday the Saudi tanker *Yanbu Pride* was hit off Jubail.

Because of the war, most shipping now stops at Muscat, and their cargoes are trucked across the neck of the Oman Peninsula to Dubai for reloading on Saudi coasters. In theory, Saudi coastal waters are not in the exclusion zone. Iranian attacks against ships in Saudi coastal waters, however, have become routine. Gerry said the *Yanbu Pride* had been hit amidships by an Exocet missile.

"But the Iranians don't have Exocets," I replied.

"Oh, no? Then you must know more than I."

His point was well made.

Sue served us homemade chocolate cake for dessert.

20. TAPLINE

TUESDAY, October 14. At 7:30 A.M. fog was rolling in off the Gulf. The weather forecast predicted a high of a hundred degrees with light easterly winds. Right now it was a cool ninety degrees. The fog would soon burn off.

Radio Bahrain announced on the 8:00 A.M. news that the OPEC meeting in Geneva had entered its ninth day. Saudi Arabia had sent the spot-market oil price below sixteen dollars a barrel with her demand for larger export quotas. Although we didn't know it, that hiccup in the price of crude ended the twenty-four-year career of Saudi oil minister Sheikh Ahmed Zaki Yamani. Two weeks later he was sacked. The Saudi royal family, increasingly concerned by Yamani's attitude about oil prices, was uneasy by the drop in the kingdom's monetary reserves from an estimated one hundred twenty billion dollars to eighty billion dollars. The popular sheikh became their scapegoat.

The news report from Geneva also informed us that the Iraqi oil minister had informed the OPEC ministers that the Iranian raid on Kirkuk did not affect production and that the pipeline to Turkey was running at full capacity. The mosaic of trade was viewed from different angles in different places. Here the mosaic was centered on oil; in parts of Turkey it might once have been opium or sheep; in Syria and Lebanon it was guns. But in Saudi Arabia the locomotive was driven by crude oil and the fact that crude was not selling as briskly in the world markets as it once had indicated that the mosaic had taken another kaleidoscopic turn. Almost certainly the pieces would never revert to their former positions. They never do. The world was facing a modified configuration in terms of trade and economic structure. The

201

acid test would be how well this desert kingdom would adapt to the new mosaic. How competitive in world markets would the second generation of Saudi industries be? With the likes of Mr. Weasel guarding the flow of trade across its frontiers, how competitive could they ever be? Indeed, how competitive did the religious leaders of the country want them to be?

I filed these questions for further consideration while we recoupled the trailers. Minutes after the newscast had ended we pulled out of the Saudi Conduit & Coating Company yard. Traffic was still light as we turned onto the Dammam–Al Khobar expressway.

"She really feels light without the load on the back. Flying right along," Graham said. You could tell he was happy to be under way, heading home after thirty-one days on the road.

We passed the Petromin Building, headquarters of the Saudi oil industry, on our left, an ultramodern, sand-colored structure with blue-glass paneling and a palm court. "Turn right at the overpass," I told Graham, reading from Roger Hayes's instructions. The huge Al Khobar sports center, with two giant stadiums and covered gymnasiums that cost over a billion dollars, was now on our left.

After getting lost and ending up at the gates of the Prince Abdulazziz airbase, we pulled into the Souks Supermarket, where we stocked up again on food supplies: condensed milk, fresh meat, fruit and vegetables, and canned drinks for the refrigerator. By the time we nosed back onto the beltway it was after midday. Minutes later we passed Dhahran International Airport and turned right onto the expressway to Kuwait.

From what we could see from *Old Girl*'s cab, money—and lots of it—had been sprinkled everywhere to make the Saudi desert bloom. It seemed as if the whole 250 years of industrial revolution had been compressed into the last 25 years. Evidence of mismanaged resources lay everywhere: unused overpasses and irrigation canals, abandoned roads with new ones built alongside them, idle plants rotting in the sand and the sun, some never utilized and never likely to be.

Twenty miles north of Dammam a huge chunk of desert had been transformed into a carpet of green. A massive farming scheme stretched as far as the eye could see. Wheat, onions, tomatoes, and animal fodder grew in lush rows that dipped over the horizon. Mobile overhead sprinkling systems provided abundant rainfall at the push of a button. Since 1976, according to the official statistics, Saudi Arabia's wheat crop has jumped from six thousand tons to two million tons a year. As a result of projects like this, Saudi Arabia now grows more wheat than she consumes and has become a net exporter. Saudi milk production borders on 450,000 gallons per day, when only decades ago the Bedouin was content with milk directly from sheep, goat, or camel.

Over Radio Kuwait that morning came news that the Arab world would face severe food shortages by the 1990s. This prediction was made at a four-day conference in Kuwait City on the development of Arab food industries. The secretary general of the Arab Federation of Food Industries, Falah Jabr, told delegates that in this age of high tech and prosperity one third of the Arab world suffered from malnutrition. At present the Arab world produced only 40 percent of its cereal consumption, less than 30 percent of its sugar, 38 percent of its mutton and beef, and not even two thirds of its poultry, while Israel produced more food than it consumed or could sell abroad. According to one Jordanian trucker we met, Israeli fruit and vegetables used to find their way onto the Saudi market in unmarked containers brought in by foreign refrigerator trucks from Lebanon. This was supposedly a reason why foreign refrigerator trucks were no longer allowed into the kingdom.

We got off the Kuwait expressway and turned onto the Tapline road at Watford Gap, stopping at an Al Drees diesel station, where the pump jockey was an Indian. Graham took on five hundred gallons of diesel for fifty pounds. It would take us the eight thousand miles back to Blackpool. The tanks were so full they dripped.

Our strategy was to get as far north along the Tapline as possible before stopping for the night. We were hell-bent for home. "No more fooling around. No more fancy nights out with Robert," Graham half chanted, pushing a cassette of Elkie Brooks, which he had acquired on King Khaled Street, into the cassette player.

We drove up the Tapline through the dust and the heat, stopped to watch the sunset, then kept on driving into the night. We were itching to get out of Saudi Arabia. We would have driven the 735 miles of Tapline in one go if we could have stayed awake that long. Roaring down the road, Steve in front, we came up behind a slow-moving bulk carrier laden with cement. There was traffic coming at us. Rather than brake, Steve swung right onto what looked like hard shoulder and passed the bulk carrier on the inside. Graham plunged after him, and immediately we were engulfed in a cloud of dust kicked up by Steve's wheels. We were doing fifty miles per hour and suddenly couldn't see a thing.

"That's guy's a real head-banger. Can you see him?" Graham asked, his foot still on the floor.

"Nope."

Steve pulled back onto the asphalted surface, and the cloud cleared. We were heading straight for a road sign. Graham swerved at the last moment, missing it by an inch. He was laughing his head off.

We continued till 9:00 P.M., and then pulled onto the shoulder for an evening meal. I inaugurated the pressure cooker, preparing a beef, onion, and carrot stew. But there was a breeze blowing and we were running low on gas for the cooker. The stew took an hour and a half to prepare. "Too long," Graham complained. "We drivers can't spend that amount of time at the side of the road when we want something to eat. We have to have quick food, something easy to prepare, like out of a can."

Steve had conked out by this time, and attempts to awaken him were futile. We stopped where we were, in the middle of nowhere, for the night, hoping for an early start in the morning.

"Time?" I asked.

"Six o'clock."

Wednesday morning. The countryside was flat and grayish-brown. The Tapline was on our left. We drove for three hours and pulled into the parking lot at Rafha. While Graham and Steve attended to breakfast, I walked down the main street to change money at the bank. The street was dusty, the merchants sleepy. An armed guard stood outside the bank. He took no notice of me, though apparently laid-off expats, once they receive their exit visas, had taken to robbing banks before their departure. Previously, banks had been easy targets. They were subject to no particular security, as the Saudis themselves had no need to rob a bank.

Walking back, I attempted to take a picture of our two trucks parked in the distance, with a Saudi street scene as my foreground. I got my camera ready, but before I could snap the shutter a Nissan patrol wagon pulled up beside me with two policemen in it. The one nearest me asked in Arabic for my *igtalla*. I produced my passport and showed them the multi-entry visa. I then pointed toward the trucks and said, "Truck driver." They asked to see my camera. Reluctantly I let them have it. They got on the radio to headquarters, grunted a few times, and then motioned me to get in the back. I was under arrest.

At police headquarters they escorted me upstairs to a room where I was told to sit. Three policemen in khaki uniforms were also in the room, and they stared at me in silence. Finally one of them asked if I would like some *chai*. I said that sounded like a good idea.

"You truck driver?" the more surly-looking one, whom I suspected was the district intelligence officer, asked.

"Good truck driver," I said.

"Where you going?"

"Home."

"Where's that?"

"England."

"Oh. And where you been?"

"Dammam."

"Why you take pictures?"

"To show my children where I've been."

"Oh." He thought about that for a moment. "How many children?"

"Three."

"Oh. You like Saudi Arabia?"

"Nice place. Lots of sun."

"First time?"

"First time."

The tea came in little glasses with metal holders. It was sweet, black, and good.

"You like *chai?*"

"Very much. Possible to have another?"

That seemed to please him. He shouted instructions in Arabic to the *chai*-man, who hurried downstairs to heat up some more water on his Bunsen burner. After that, the intelligence officer went out and I was left with the two other officers, who observed me suspiciously. I looked around the room. It was bleak. Apart from the large desk and chairs around the wall, there were road safety posters with simple drawings and texts in Arabic and English. One showed a vehicle stopping at a pedestrian crossing with the caption, "Men Go First." Another showed two cars almost colliding and carried the slogan, "Don't Rush Out from the Right." Both looked like they had been designed by twelve-year-old schoolkids.

The intelligence officer returned and said, "You come." I was ushered into the chief's office. He sat behind a splendid desk, with a portrait of the king behind him. The Saudi flag—crossed sabers with Arabic writing above them on a green field—stood in one corner. He had my passport and camera in front of him. The two arresting officers were by his side. They explained in Arabic the circumstances of my arrest. The commanding officer may have been all of twenty-eight. He spoke English well, with a slight American accent.

"What are you doing in Saudi Arabia?" he asked.

"I'm a truck driver on my way home. I'm with two colleagues. Our trucks are parked down by the highway. We hope to get to Jordan tonight."

He flipped through my passport. "Your name is Mr. Robert?"

"Yes."

"Why were you taking pictures?"

"I didn't have time to take any. Your men were too quick. But I had wanted to take a picture of our parked trucks."

"You say you didn't take any?"

"I didn't have time."

"How do I know you're telling the truth?"

"Take the film and expose it."

"It is color?"

"Yes."

"We can't develop it here."

"Then confiscate the film. I don't care."

"But if you have no pictures of Rafha it doesn't belong to us. I have not the right to do that."

He was earnest and appeared concerned to render fair justice. "What religion are you?" he asked, having been unable to find it listed in my passport.

"Christian."

He thought for a moment. "Do you swear you have taken no pictures in Rafha?"

"I swear upon my soul."

"You know what the rules are in this country?"

"No."

"As a foreigner, you are forbidden to take pictures of police buildings, road accidents, or built-up areas."

I said I had not done any of that, stretching the point about build-up areas.

"Well, how is it in your country, then?"

I said that as far as I knew it was forbidden to take pictures of defense installations, Customs areas, or docks.

"So you see, it's the same here."

He seemed pleased by this, thinking perhaps he had demonstrated to me that Saudi Arabia was not a backward place but had laws and restrictions similar to those in Britain. He thought a while longer and then told me to wait next door. My second glass of *chai* arrived and I glanced through a magazine on road safety that was on the desk. Twenty minutes later the intelligence officer came into the office and handed me back my passport and camera, with the film still in it. "Come," he said. "I take you back." I got into his unmarked car and he dropped me beside the parked trucks. I thanked him and he took off without any acknowledgment.

Steve and Graham were seated in *Old Girl* wondering what to do.

"Holy shit," Steve said. "Where've you been?"

"Police station," I said.

"We know that. A copper drove up about an hour ago and said the Canadian was in calaboosh. Maybe two days," he told us.

I explained what had happened.

"Shit, let's get out of here," Steve said.

We were back on the road at 10:30 A.M. The desert on the left looked like it had been sprayed with crude to keep the sand from drifting onto the road. We saw some spectacular wrecks that morning: cars with their tires still on and no police paint sprayed over them, which meant that they were recent accidents, perhaps only a day old. We were averaging about sixty miles per hour although the speed limit was forty-five miles per hour.

The day before, Steve and Graham had remarked that they each had close to eight hundred pounds left in running money. "Never have I had so much left over," Steve said. They were also pleased to have received Roger's confirmation that they would receive a hundred pounds a day in demurrage (less 20 percent to Whittle) for time lost at the frontier.

So now it was rush, rush, rush to get back as quickly as possible, pick up another load, and head out again. "This is our fifth week out," Steve observed. "That's not too bad. We're catching up."

North of Ar'ar the desert was broken by mountains. Steve thought he had caught a glimpse of an Astran truck ahead, so he opened the throttle and pulled away from *Old Girl*. We had not seen another British truck, other than Leslie Massey's, since Ankara, twenty days ago, which was one measure of the depth of the Saudi recession. After an hour of racing through hills of sand, the desert became flat as a dish again and it was clear that no Astran truck was ahead of us.

At 5:30 P.M. we stopped at a service station on the outskirts of

Turaif and filled up with diesel. It was still dripping from our belly tanks. *Old Girl* had two and a half tons of diesel aboard. We parked for a tea break beside a Swedish VeebeTrans Scania with dual rear axles. The driver introduced himself as Tapi; he was carrying twenty tons of telecommunications equipment to Riyadh. He said we had a three-day wait ahead of us at the Syrian border. This worried Steve and Graham. We watched the Saudi sun go down for the last time, sipping Swedish filter coffee made by Tapi, and then got back on the road, heading west to Al Haditha.

Bam! Bam! Bam! We rattled over more speed-control bumps. The rattling of the empty trailer resounded through the cab like someone swinging a sledgehammer at it. We got into a jangle over a badly indicated fork in the road. Right to Turaif center, left to Jordan. Tapi said we would have to spend the night in no-man's-land, as Jordanian Customs closed at 6:00 P.M. It was already quarter to seven. No-man's-land, he said, was full of dead donkeys and stank. The donkeys—he meant sheep and goats—were transported into Saudi Arabia by Turks and Syrians, and their conditions of carriage were so cruel that more than a few died en route. As Saudi customs did not allow dead meat to enter the country unless slaughtered according to Koranic practice, the dead animals were tossed into no-man's-land and left there for the vultures.

After nightfall we entered mountains that in the moonlight looked eerily beautiful. Coming down a long hill we slowed to a crawl to swing around the wreckage of a Datsun pickup truck lying on its side, its headlights still burning, and a body beside it in the ditch. The vehicle had plowed into the back of a JCB. The Datsun had pushed the JCB across the road to the left-hand shoulder. The JCB driver was standing at the back of his vehicle, still wondering what had happened. The JCB's lights were on, but dim. He made no sign, and we assumed that the police were on the way. We continued.

Lights sparkled across the desert to our left. We wondered what they were: Nothing was indicated on our map. Around the next bend a police car with blue lights flashing had pulled a beat-up tractor-trailer loaded with used tires onto the desert, and we wondered whether the tractor-trailer was involved in the accident. We were about twelve miles short of the Jordanian border.

The BBC World Service announced that Iraqi jets had destroyed twenty-three Iranian C-130 transport aircraft on the ground at Shiraz Airport in southwestern Iran. Iran confirmed the attack but claimed

Iraq had hit an Iranair Boeing 737, killing three civilians. A grenade attack on a unit of young Israeli soldiers in the Old City of Jerusalem had left one civilian dead and sixty-nine injured. Israeli retaliation was expected.

We reached Al Haditha at 9:30 P.M. The Customs area was empty except for a pushy Jordanian driver and Stefan Nordquist, another VeebeTrans driver who was heading home after unloading in Jeddah. We cleared our Customs documents and prepared to move out of the gate. As Stefan still had paperwork to be processed, he said he would catch up with us at Jordanian Customs. The Saudi guard came over to inspect our belly tanks, which were still dripping diesel. He called to a second guard and told him to lower the barrier. Gruffly he told Steve we had to empty our belly tanks before leaving the country. Steve became excited.

"Chef," he said. "Can't do that. Need diesel to go home to England. Eight thousand miles, *Chef,* and no money."

Chef was unperturbed. He refused to budge. Steve persisted. *Chef* turned his back on Steve and walked back to the gate, where the second guard was sitting on a stool, watching with a deadpan expression.

"Fucking hell," said Steve. "They can't do this. I'm going to argue with that guy until either he throws me in the calaboosh or lets us through."

Steve started arguing with the guard, then pleading, and finally ended up on one knee, saying, *"Chef,* you can't do that; *chef,* please, no." He winked at the other guard, who started smiling. At that point, Steve knew he was making headway. Finally, *Chef* relented and requested a hundred riyals to let us through. Problem: We did not have any riyals left. Steve offered him ten pounds. *Chef* looked at the English bank note with suspicion. He had never seen one before. "How much worth?" he asked.

"Two hundred riyals," Steve told him, which was a lie. The guard stuffed it in his pocket and let us through.

"That son-of-a-bitch was laughing," Graham said as we rolled past the gate.

Stefan was not so lucky: He had to dump 230 gallons of diesel in the desert.

At 10:30 P.M. we parked on the side of the road behind a dozen Jordanian and Syrian trucks. Steve was elated with his antics. "I've a mind to tell Smithie I had to blow it out and make myself a few extra bob," he said.

We were too exhausted to think about eating. On the eleven-o'clock news we heard that Heathrow Airport had been besieged by Asians seeking entry into Britain before new visa requirements went into effect on the weekend. Customs officers were screening them carefully, causing huge delays. More than four thousand were being held in Customs while their travel documents were inspected. Those who couldn't be processed before the end of the day were lodged for the night in hotels near the airport at government expense.

"They're treating us like animals," a young Indian woman protested when interviewed by a BBC reporter.

"Animals," she said? Well, try driving a juggernaut on the Middle East run. Then she would know what being treated like an animal was really like. No one lodged us in hotels free of charge when we were delayed at a border.

The road was divided into two lanes, with a culvert between them. Abandoned in the culvert was a four-door Mercedes still in apparently reasonable shape. I bedded down in the dust by the roadside between the two trucks. The stars were bright and the evening warm. I smelled no rotting donkeys. Within minutes I was on another frontier.

21. WACKY RACES

THURSDAY, October 16. At 9:00 A.M. we re-entered the chaos of the Arab world, setting our watches back one hour. We were still in the desert, but the temperature was much cooler than by the Persian Gulf. Radio Amman said the expected range for the day was between sixty-three and ninety-five degrees.

After the relative orderliness of Saudi Arabia, we had returned to corridors full of unswept cigarette butts, confusion, and delay. The atmosphere at least was relaxed and the people were friendly. Four Customs officers inspected our papers and processed them one at a time: the triptychs for the unit and trailer, and our insurance documents. We were empty, so we had no cargo manifest.

Cabin control was pleasant—not so easy going, though, if you happened to be Syrian. The Customs police made Syrian drivers strip their cabs, and allowed them to replace their gear only after a search for weapons and bombs.

The Customs officer, when he got into Steve's cab, saw a postcard clipped above the dashboard of two chimpanzees hugging each other. "My wife and sister-in-law," Steve told the officer. He laughed. Behind it was a picture of Steve's redheaded girlfriend, Helen, posing on Steve's motorcycle in a black leather miniskirt, showing lots of thigh. That brought rave reviews from the officer.

It took us an hour to clear Jordanian Customs, and then we followed Stefan down the road to Azraq to fill our water containers. The desert was gradually changing, become greener as we approached the town T. E. Lawrence had called "the queen of the oases." Lawrence had made Azraq's fortress his headquarters during the winter of 1918.

211

A Jordanian airbase scarred the desert on the outskirts of the town. F-5 Tiger jets stood on the runway in front of hangars built into sand dunes. "It's a different sort of place altogether, isn't it?" Graham said. He compared the airbase to a Greek village, and it did have a more Mediterranean atmosphere. Stefan led us down a lane where there was a well and running water. We filled the containers and let the water from the hose run over our heads to wash off some of the dust.

Going out of Azraq we passed a detachment of desert police standing beside their camels. They wore red-and-white kaffiyehs and long khaki robes that fell to their ankles, with red-tasseled sashes, crossed bandoliers, and silver-mounted daggers thrust into brown leather belts. A road sign told us sixty miles to Amman and forty miles to Zarqa', our next destination.

For a while the road ran alongside the Hejaz railway that Lawrence and his Arab guerrillas had attacked and largely destroyed. It ran from Damascus to Medina, where the Prophet Mohammed is buried. The line was completed in 1908 and the trip by train then took three days when previously the fastest camel caravans covered the 780-mile distance in forty days. The steam locomotives were wood-burning, and during the ten years that the railroad operated they ate their way through the cedar and pine forests of southern Lebanon, Syria, and northern Jordan, denuding the hills with such thoroughness that the tree cover has never grown back. Jordan has repaired that part of the line that runs through that country, extending it south to the port of 'Aqaba, and now diesel locomotives do the work.

Arriving at Zarqa', we looked for signs of Dawson's Field, where in September 1970 Arab terrorism splashed into world headlines with the hijacking of three jetliners on the same day, almost simultaneously, to this abandoned World War Two airbase. After Zarqa' we crossed the Hejaz railway again, heading north toward Ramtha and the Syrian border.

It didn't take us long to cross Jordan. By 12:30 P.M.—hardly three hours after leaving Azraq customs—we were immobilized at Ramtha. The double line of trucks was at least three miles long, stretching to the white demarcation line painted across the hills to the northeast. Stefan estimated we would be in the Customs compound by nightfall, but a Syrian driver in front of us was less cheerful. "Maybe three days. Syrian Customs beeg problem. Syria no good," he said.

Every twenty minutes the line moved forward a few hundred yards. The Arab drivers would gun their motors, and some broke out across the dried cornfield on our right, trying to cut in at the top of the line. Few succeeded. Most of them coasted back, kicking up dust and sulking like disappointed children.

''They're nuts,'' Graham announced, and hardly had he spoken then the line began to move again. A couple of Jordanians had crept up on the outside and were trying to box us in. Graham wasn't going to give an inch and started yelling at them: ''Bloody head-bangers, get out the way!'' It was a battle of juggernauts. They didn't succeed, but I thought for a moment it would be daggers drawn until they peeled off like a pair of Spitfires and circled back through the cornfield to the end of the line. Finally, at 3:00 P.M., we entered the Customs compound. It was chaos. We had driven less than 150 miles, but that was it for the rest of the day. Our dreams of being in Turkey by Friday were shot.

Mohammed al-Jazar, regarded by many British drivers as the best Customs agent in the business, jumped on our running board as we inched forward and demanded in guttural sounds that we quickly hand him our *carnets de passage* so he could clear the truck and trailer through Customs. Mohammed was a deaf mute. He took me with him and showed me where the passport office was so I could get our exit stamps while Graham and Steve wound their way into a large parking area where the trucks filed into eight or ten lines abreast. This was pure insanity, as ultimately the lines converged again on a two-lane exit gate about five hundred yards away. This ten-lane parking area was in fact the entry pits for the Wacky Races that would begin on Saturday after a short warm-up tomorrow. Mohammed indicated with hand motions and his special talk that to get a better position on the starting grid we should cut right through a hole in the fence a bit farther along and drive across a depression into another compound where six Jordanian refrigerator trucks were already lined up.

Most, though not all, of the Arab drivers were in long jellabas with kaffiyehs wound around their heads. One in particular, whom Steve called Joe, was always smoking, always joking, and his white cotton nightshirt was immaculately clean. We couldn't figure out how, in this dust and heat, he managed to keep it so spotless.

We broke through the hole in the fence, but Stefan was unable to follow, as he was in a middle lane. Although it was after 5:00 P.M. and the exit gate had closed for the night, every time the ragheads thought the lines might move they started their motors and revved the innards out of them. For Stefan, caught in the middle of this pandemonium, the fumes were suffocating. Where we were parked a strong smell of sage filled the air, and it was relatively peaceful. Across the way they were at it again, blowing horns, gunning their motors, and then—bang!—a tonka ran into a back of another truck.

Mohammed al-Jazar still had not returned with our papers. This was a source of concern. The sun was now behind purple clouds, and we supposed we would not see him again that evening. But we had been told by Alex Durno that we could be sure Mohammed would not let us down.

The news on the radio was full of bloodshed and destruction. The Israelis had bombed Palestinian refugee camps near the port of Sidon in southern Lebanon in retaliation for Wednesday's grenade attack at the Wailing Wall. Iran was incensed over Iraqi strafing of a civilian airliner and promised to rain missiles on Baghdad. A tanker off Abu Dhabi was on fire and sinking.

The hour before dawn always is the coldest, and I was shivering. The driver of the Jordanian refrigerator truck behind us had woken me at 4:30 A.M. when he started his motor and began to move slowly to the front of the line. I had slept between the Volvo and Scania again, so when the Jordanian crept by, it felt like he was only inches from my ear. I woke Graham and Steve, as it had been agreed the night before that we would follow the Jordanian to the front of the line. His cousin was the guard at the exit gate. Graham started his motor and we inched up behind the refrigerator truck, squeezing into a space between it and another truck. Steve at first slipped into a space two truck lengths back, then decided this wasn't good enough and tried to move abreast of us. A Customs guard came out of the gatehouse and started giving him hell.

"Meester, you go back!"

The truck behind us was kicking up a rumpus because we both had passed in front of him. Steve tried to reason with the guard, but to no avail. The center lane had to be kept open, the guard said, and Steve was blocking it. Downcast, Steve prepared to maneuver the Volvo backward. The guard watched with satisfaction and then, smiling, said, "Meester, you go forward now. *Yallah! Yallah!*"

Astounded, Steve stepped on the accelerator and shot through the gate into no-man's-land, to the back of yesterday's line still waiting to move into Syria. He was now about twenty truck lengths ahead of us.

The sound of Steve's maneuvering and the guard's cries of *Yallah! Yallah!* had filtered back down the line, and at first two or three and then the full one hundred trucks in the Jordanian compound started their motors in anticipation of moving out. It was only 6:00 A.M. and there still was another hour of waiting, but the roaring of fivescore motors was shaking the ground we were standing on. And oblivious to the terrible din, Mohammed al-Jazar was walking toward us with our papers. He hadn't let us down.

At 7:00 A.M., which was 8:00 A.M. Syrian time, the line started to move. It was three miles through no-man's-land to the Syrian compound. We reached it five hours later, around 1:00 P.M. The sun was beating onto the bare Syrian hills, and it was miserably hot. The roadside was littered with wrecked cars and trucks. Dead goats and sheep had been left in the ditch, and the smell at times was nauseating. Observation posts and gun emplacements studded the hillsides. There were some olive, poplar, and pine trees, and a boy playing a flute guided a herd of black goats among them.

The Golan Heights were to our left. We listened to the news reports on Radio Amman about Israel rescuing one of its pilots shot down in the raid on Sidon. The copilot was still missing. Iran attacked Baghdad again. The rocket was aimed at the main telecommunications center, where Jean-Louis Gautier had delivered equipment two and a half weeks before, but Iraqi officials said it hit a school and a mosque. We later heard from a trucker returning from Baghdad that it had hit the central post office.

Coming into the Syrian compound, there was a scrap pile of ruined cars and impounded trucks with their best parts scavenged off them. Along the western perimeter the car carcasses had been bulldozed aside and an eight-foot-high wall erected to hide them from sight. Our most immediate concern was to find out which convoy we would join. The Syrians require all foreign trucks to transit their country in military-escorted convoys. There are various stories about why they insist on this. One version is that a Swedish truck was caught smuggling weapons to the Muslim Brotherhood during the Hama uprising of 1982. Another was that a TIR truck loaded with dynamite had tried to blow up the palace of Syrian president Hafez al-Assad. Whatever the real reason—probably just a desire to keep track of foreign trucks and prevent them from being used by foreign intelligence services—we had to join a convoy heading north to the Turkish frontier. We hoped we would be assigned to the one leaving at 3:00 P.M.

The Der'a Customs compound was immense, disorderly, and littered with filth. It rivaled the Iraqi Customs compound at Wadi Ar'ar for general squalor. Cars went through on the western side of the compound, trucks on the eastern side; administrative buildings, a bank, and a restaurant were between the two. The cargo compound, nearly a mile long, had never been completed. Curbstones lay in the middle of unpaved lanes, and the central walkway had man-sized holes in them. The place was alive with a jumble of uniformed and semi-uniformed officials, while tractor-trailers and tonkas played Dodg'em amid the dust and garbage.

We passed two parked West German trucks pointed in the direction of Jordan. One of the drivers, we were told, was in prison. He had been carrying six thousand deutsche marks in running money he had not declared when entering the country (apparently this was a new requirement). We had no intention of declaring our foreign currency for fear of having it taken. The authorities arrested the West German driver and confiscated his cash. The West German ambassador was attempting to negotiate his release.

A second deaf-mute Customs agent offered to handle our paper-work. He was still in his teens, but because he seemed to work harder than the other agents, who were loafing around, we gave him our papers. Graham and Steve had to pay eighty pounds each for a transit visa (as a Canadian I received a free visa). A rubber stamp applied next to the visa stated: "The visitor is required to exchange U.S. $100 upon his entry in Syria."

We needed proof of having changed a hundred dollars or its equivalent in another hard currency before the Customs police would stamp our entry into the passports. Without the entry stamp you are not allowed out of the compound.

The problem about changing money at the only bank in the compound was that there was only one teller, and he had to fill out three forms for each exchange transaction. This took more time than it should have because access to the teller's window was barred by about two dozen ragheads and Turks who were already waiting and who let all their friends into the line in front of you. We realized at this point that no hope remained of making the 3:00 P.M. convoy. Changing money took over an hour; then the Customs police shut down for lunch.

Stefan got into the compound three hours after us. In the crush to get out of the Jordanian compound he had run into the truck in front of him. Damage, fortunately, was minimal. It was hot and dusty and I wanted a shower more than anything else in the world. We were parked at the far end of the cargo compound, and every time we walked from the truck to the Customs buildings we had to thread our way through the litter of abandoned tires, old inner tubes, sections of hose, pieces of wire, yesterday's dinner, tin cans, turds, pools of diesel, and plastic bottles.

The Davies Turner agent came over and told us he had not seen another British truck come through Der'a in over two weeks. ''Trucking's finished,'' he said. We'd heard that before on this trip and were beginning to believe it ourselves, as least as far as running to the Middle East was concerned.

Syria was a land bridge for traffic to the Gulf. Before convoys were imposed, it took one day to drive from the Saudi border through Jordan and Syria into southern Turkey. Under normal convoy conditions it can take between three and five days. We would get there on the fourth day tired, tense, and dirty. The strain was immense, and for this we were charged forty-five pounds in ''convoy fees'' per truck. We were assigned to the 3:00 A.M. convoy.

A guard came at 2:30 A.M. and thumped on all the cabs in our line. We were given ten minutes to get ready for departure. Minutes later a Nissan Land-Cruiser belonging to the military police led the first trucks out of the compound into Der'a's main street. Our destination was Bab al-Awa, with a day-long stop at Homs, north of Damascus. The rules of the convoy, listed on the back of the paper stuck to our windshield, were no overtaking, no stopping, and a minimum fifty-yard distance between each truck.

We drove half a mile out of the compound and parked in the deserted street to give the back half of the convoy time to form. We were thirty-five trucks. Behind us were two Bulgarians, two Romanians, a Hungarocamion, and a Lebanese. The rest were either Turks or Jordanians. Der'a had once been the junction of the Jerusalem, Haifa, Damascus, and Medina railroads and the navel of Turkish defenses in Syria. In a building near the old railroad station, Lawrence was sexually assaulted by the Turkish governor.

At 3:45 A.M. the convoy roared to life. The first leg of the Wacky Races had begun. We went like *Gangbusters* through Der'a, which was larger than I had expected and stretched over several hills. Every second lamppost had a half-tone portrait of Hafez al-Assad on it, and broken-down Raba dump trucks were abandoned on every other corner. A road sign told us sixty-six miles to Damascus. The moon was partially covered by high mist rolling over Mount Hermon to our left. After five minutes the road narrowed into a two-lane highway across a flat, green plain. The road was straight and bordered by cedar, pine, and plane trees and a few houses.

After seventy minutes of flat-out driving and fighting off the ragheads who kept trying to crowd us off the road, we began the long descent toward Damascus. Although we had been cruising at a steady sixty miles per hour, the convoy had split into at least three sections. We were following Steve, who was following a Jordanian refrigerator truck that seemed to know its way. Behind us were four more trucks. We hoped the refrigerator truck driver knew where he was going because we surely didn't and we had completely lost the front section of the convoy.

We had turned onto a dual highway leading to the airport, and could see the lights of the Damascus suburbs on the hillsides to the left. Suddenly the Jordanian refrigerator truck did a U-turn across the center island. We followed Steve in the same maneuver, and the remainder of the platoon followed us. We were now heading for the center of Damascus, which claims to be the oldest continually inhabited city in the world. Along this road, two hundred yards from the railroad line to Der'a, stands a gaunt black building guarded by plainclothes policemen with submachine guns. The building looks like an inverted pyramid, each floor longer and broader than the one beneath it, and has a forest of antennas on the roof.

Built by East Germany, it is the headquarters of Syria's secret police, the Mukhabarat. Experts say it has more floors below ground than above and that Mukhabarat agents torture the supposed enemies of the Syrian state in underground cells. Amnesty International has reported that on one of the subterranean floors each room has a special instrument of torture. The most notorious is said to contain a device that forces a metal spike into the prisoner's anus.

We drove by a brightly lit mosque, and to our left were the old walls and a gate. It was 5:30 A.M. when we passed the bus station, and it was humming with activity even at that hour. We turned northward onto the Homs expressway. Twenty miles later we passed a turnoff across the desert to the ruins of Palmyra, where in Roman times trans-Arabian caravans met those from the East to exchange their wares, making it at that time one of the great staging centers of trade. Today it is wasted and abandoned, a victim of its own folly and the ever-changing mosaic.

Dawn streaked the eastern sky as we drove up a barren valley with mountains on either side. At 7:00 A.M. we pulled onto a paved shoulder twenty-four miles south of Homs and waited forty minutes for the convoy to regroup. Once the Land-Cruiser had herded us back together, we moved out again and eighteen miles later were directed left across the highway into a TIR park that could easily hold one thousand trucks but was empty when we arrived. The park had just been opened; a drivers' rest house was still under construction, but there were three sinks and three squatters' lavatories in an adjoining unit. We were told we would start again at 8:00 P.M.

Graham, exhausted from the strain of convoy driving, went for a piss against the back axle. When he got back, he was shivering.

"Funny it gets this cold and they don't have that much green stuff growing around," he said.

Steve joined us to discuss breakfast plans. I wasn't hungry, but I was interested in visiting Homs.

"How about eggs, sausage, and beans?" Steve asked.

Graham examined the eggs, bought four days before in Dammam. He smelled the shells, then shook them. The refrigerator, even installed in Steve's truck, hadn't been working that well. "These eggs are fucked," he said.

"Whizz 'em," Steve suggested.

Graham opened the window and tossed them out. "We'll just have sausage and beans."

"And how about fried spuds?"

"Aye."

As they started cooking, Steve noted, "It's going to be six seeks before we're back."

"This job ain't worth a carrot," Graham said. "Could have done two Greeks in that time."

I left the two of them and walked back to the entrance gate, which was guarded by soldiers. They wanted to know where I was going. "Homs," I said. The officer grunted. I thought there was a bus stop across the road, but the four men in jeans I had spotted were carrying submachine guns and randomly stopping the traffic, demanding ID cards and searching vehicles. An unmarked police car was parked on a side road. The chief of this ragtag detachment came over and asked if I was a *kamyon* driver. I said yes. He wanted to know where I was going. I said Homs.

"One moment," he told me.

He went out into the road and stopped the first passing car. It happened to be a taxi driving a businessman from Damascus to Homs.

He asked in Arabic if they would take me into the city, six miles away. No problem. I thanked him. He smiled and we parted.

The businessman was born in Saudi Arabia and spoke perfect English. He offered me some Syrian pastry, which I declined, but I asked him to recommend the best restaurant in Homs. Without hesitating, he said the Toledo.

He was knowledgeable about the history of Homs and I regretted we did not have more time to talk. He confirmed that the city had its place in the mosaic. Surrounded by a fertile plain, like Damascus and Palmyra it had been an important relay stage for traffic from Egypt, Palestine, and Arabia bound for more northern lands. Roman emperor Heliogabalus was born here and showered favor on the city. It fell to the Arabs four centuries later.

The streets of Homs were crowded. But the city itself, like much of the rest of Syria, was in an advanced state of decay. Everything seemed to be crumbling. A large section of the town center was in ruins, apparently leveled for redevelopment that never developed. Syria, striving to achieve military parity with Israel, had doubled its military might since the October 1973 war. Syria's armed forces counted ten divisions, 450 combat aircraft, and a very aggressive air defense system. But the country was almost bankrupt.

People stared at me. Army officers turned when I passed them on the sidewalk. Druse women in long black robes, some with tattooed faces, carrying their children through the marketplace, cast glances in my direction. In the main street I spotted a photographer with a box camera on a wooden tripod. The camera was an Agfa and predated the First World War. I asked him how much he charged for a picture. Ten Syrian pounds, he said. A deal. He claimed he was himself a First World War veteran, which would have put him in his mid-eighties. It was possible. He had a gray moustache and green eyes. The camera was entirely hand-operated, with no moving parts, not even a shutter. There was a lense connected to a wooden box by a leather bellows. The lens could be moved along two rails on a small wooden platform, and under the wooden box was a drawer lined with lead that contained a developing solution. Under the tripod was a bucket of water.

He lined me and the camera up like a man with lots of experience in such things. First he shot a negative, which he developed, washed, and tacked to a board. Then he suspended the board in front of the lens and shot a positive, with the same elegant hand action, removing the lens cap, waving it above his head for two passes, then replacing it.

The photo rendered a clouded image of someone with long, unkempt hair and a ragged beard, looking mightily uncomfortable. It sent me looking for a barber shop. The shop I found had a picture taped to a mirror of the owner standing under the Eiffel Tower. I figured this meant he spoke a few words of French. He had in fact mastered maybe six words of it in all, but he was affable and sat me down in one of the two chairs. There was no sink on the counter in front of the chair. He sprayed some water on my head from a hand-held plant humidifier and tried to run a comb through my tangled hair. Impossible. He took me to the back of the shop where, behind a screen, there was a tiny sink with cold running water. He had me kneel on the floor and sprinkled detergent over me and set to work. I was drenched by the time I got back in the chair. I watched as he chopped away, cutting hair, beard, and moustache down to a uniform quarter inch, and he was very proud of his work. He charged me twenty Syrian pounds, which meant I still had more than eight hundred Syrian pounds left and a half day to spend it in.

The barber turned out to be the neighborhood black marketeer. People came in and slipped him money, whispered in his ear, and he would point to a laundry bag; the other barber's chair, which was covered with used towels; or a cupboard, and they would fish out whatever they were after and leave. A policeman came in. ''Oh, boy,'' I thought, ''now both of us are going to the calaboosh.'' Not at all. The policeman wanted two packs of Gitanes, French cigarettes. Syria had been a French mandate for twenty years. Again, the mosaic of trade.

Feeling cleaner, I bought a French-language newspaper and wandered down the street to a coffee garden where the locals played backgammon and dominoes and smoked water pipes under spreading eucalyptus trees. I ordered coffee, was offered a shoeshine for my tattered sandals, which I declined, and read my newspaper. It was three days old and carried wire-service reports of the Iranian raid on the Kirkuk oilfield and an interesting item about a high-level French security official visiting the head of Syrian Intelligence in Beirut.

At one o'clock I walked across the street to the Toledo. It was doing good business. The owner found me a table and informed me in French that the midday special was a mixture of rice, green beans, and lamb, with a tossed salad on the side. To go with it I ordered a Laziza Pilsener brewed in Lebanon. It was a welcome change from *camion cuisine*.

After lunch I bought a grilled chicken for thirty Syrian pounds and found a taxi to take me back to the TIR camp. Stefan had arrived with the midmorning convoy. Two other convoys had also come in: the southbound from Bab al-Awa and the one from the port of Tartus. It was 4:15 P.M. and Steve and Graham were finishing their dinner of ersatz hamburgers and pressure-cooked cabbage and potatoes. I gave the chicken to Stefan.

Our convoy now numbered sixty vehicles, including several Greeks, two Poles, and one West German. We had first seen the German truck at Evsoni on our way down, had seen it again when it passed us at Watford Gap, and had met again at Der'a. At 9:00 P.M. the white Nissan passed down the line, the convoy officer checking each vehicle against a list on a clipboard. At 9:50 P.M. we began to move out of the compound. We drove for a few miles, stopped on the shoulder while the convoy regrouped, then set out again, bypassing Homs. Although the convoy regulations said no passing, the Jordanians and Turks all wanted to get to the front of the line, which obviously wasn't possible, but it meant that the second heat of the Wacky Races was under way. As we passed the Homs oil refinery on the right we were three trucks abreast. When we got halfway into a sweeping left-hand bend I could see a solid line of taillights stretching a mile and a half in front of us, and I estimated we were somewhere in the middle of the convoy.

Graham had *Old Girl* going flat out just to keep his place in the convoy behind Steve. To prevent others from crowding in on us, he had to stay glued to Steve's tailgate. Then Steve would accelerate to prevent someone from cutting in on him, or to overtake a slower vehicle, and the pressure would be on us again. Graham had *Old Girl* doing more than sixty miles per hour. Each time we passed or repassed a Jordanian truck, the driver got mad and flicked his lights. Racing down an incline through a cut in the mountains, we overtook a Jordanian refrigerator truck. The raghead didn't want to let us back in. He was edging us farther and farther to the left as we approached a viaduct on which the four lanes were separated by a crash barrier that suddenly rose in the middle of the road. Graham hadn't seen it and hit the edge with his front left wheel. I thought it was going to tip us over. Graham was never more cool. He kept *Old Girl* under control and straightened her out. The refrigerator truck driver was fit to be tied. Then, once on the viaduct, the convoy came to a pounding halt. We locked the brakes and smelled the burning rubber, then saw the reason for the sudden stop: Halfway across the bridge a tonka tanker had overturned, Lord knows how, and it was blocking the left lane. As we crept by, the driver was standing beside his vehicle, stunned but alive. An odor of spilt diesel invaded the cab.

We arrived at Bab al-Awa in total confusion at 2:00 A.M. The Wacky Races were over. A swarm of Customs agents descended upon us, all wanting to handle our papers for a small fee. We parked in lines six or eight deep, sixty trucks squeezed into a small compound. We would be cleared in the morning. But our agent, Mustafa Awad, had already told us we would have to pay *baksheesh* to get through with two and a half tons of diesel.

22. EFES KONTROL, ADANA

I rolled out of the back of Steve's van at 7:00 A.M. to a cold, crisp morning. Mustafa Awad told us we had to get in line for diesel control. Graham refused to budge. "I think this lad is putting us on," he said. So we stayed put, missing an opportunity to make an early break.

Around 8:00 A.M. half a dozen vendors of honey-sweetened warm milk appeared in the compound. For one Syrian pound each they sold glasses of the sweetened milk with a hard sesame seed roll to dunk in it. It was delicious.

While waiting for Graham and Steve to pay the fifty pounds for excess diesel and extract themselves from the traffic jam, I chatted with two Austrian army officers who were with the U.N. Peacekeeping Force on the Golan Heights. They had driven to Bab al-Awa in a U.N. station wagon to intercept a Yugoslav truck carrying a full load of Austrian beer, wine, and schnapps for the October 26 celebrations of Austria's national day. Last year the truck carrying the national day goodies had been held up at the frontier and arrived two weeks late.

On the far side of the compound was a British bus which had been transformed into a camper. It was pulling a speedboat on a trailer and had two motorbikes tied to the back. The bus was owned by a British couple who were traveling with their children to Saudi Arabia, where the husband had accepted a job. The Syrians would not let the vehicle into the country because it had no *carnet de passage*—the temporary import papers issued by national automobile clubs—and the Turks wouldn't allow it back into Turkey because they had granted its owner a one-way, one-time transit permit only. The owner was distraught. "No one," he said, "will listen to reason."

"Try *baksheesh*," I suggested. "In the Middle East that's the only reason that counts."

"I have, but it doesn't work." His right eye twitched and he looked like he hadn't slept for a week. "We've been bounced back and forth five times now," he said. "The only solution is to dump her with all our gear and fly back to London."

We were ready to move so I left feeling sorry for him, but wondered why he hadn't better researched the travel documents he needed before leaving London. Or maybe he had but was given the wrong information. Graham asked me to get our passports stamped while he and Steve parked the trucks on the far side of the Customs house and settled their accounts with Mustafa Awad. They were talking to him in the cab of the Volvo when two well-dressed men started walking toward the trucks. Awad said we had better clear out: They were the secret police. Graham hurried over to *Old Girl* and started her up.

"Put that damn camera away. We've got trouble," he said.

We drove under a stone arch known as the Virgin's Gate and stopped at the last Syrian checkpoint, a hundred yards down the road. The officer commanding the gate looked up at us and asked, "How many days in Syria, meester?"

"Two days."

"Enjoy your visit?"

"Beautiful. Can't wait to come back."

"Friends are always welcome," he said.

Satisfied, he waved us through. We drove into a defile that had ruins strewn around and led us between bleak and well-worn mountains. We were in Syrian no-man's-land and the road was full of potholes.

"The road that no one wants," Graham called it. The defile had a haunting beauty to it, rendered more mysterious by the impressive ruins of a Crusader fortress hidden in one of the bends. Midway through this majestic but lonely valley, the bankrupt Syrians were building a monumental Customs complex, though it looked as if work on it had been suspended.

We entered Turkey at Cilvegözü, which British drivers call Silver Gazoo. It felt as if layers of tension had been peeled off our backs. Graham shouted and I felt like crying with relief. We were back in the civilized world!

The Turks had just completed a new Customs complex of their

own. It was simple, functional, and clean. As we entered, I jumped out of the cab and went to the gatehouse window. *"Bos?"* the border guard asked. "Empty?"

"Yes, *bos,"* I replied.

"English?"

"Yes."

"Exit where?"

"Ipsala," which is what Graham had told me to say.

The guard gave me a police control sheet with our registration number—FGV 150T—written on it. "Passport control, transit papers, cabin control, and out," he said.

As Graham parked *Old Girl,* the local Young Turk came out of the Customs house and greeted us. Maybe a dozen trucks were in line ahead of us; more soon arrived. Steve made the fatal mistake of telling Young Turk that the triptych for his truck had expired.

"You have problem, Mr. Steve," Young Turk said.

"You can fix it," Steve assured him.

"Maybe, but you will not go through today. Colleagues yes, but you no."

Young Turk told Steve he would have to get a new triptych issued by the Automobile Association in London. For this, Steve would have to go to the Turkish Automobile Club in Iskenderun in the morning and have them telex London for the AA's authorization to issue a new triptych. Steve was crestfallen. He had meant to renew the triptych at Dover, but there had been so much hassle over the manifest mix-up that he hadn't had time.

"But *gumruk chef* won't notice," Steve said.

"Mr. Steve, maybe not notice right away. But if *kontrol,* then I am responsible. They send *me* to calaboosh. Not you."

Stefan caught up with us and together we cleared Customs and parked to wait for Steve while he tried to plead with *gumruk chef* to let him through. Stefan, meanwhile, treated us to a Swedish breakfast: coffee, cheese, *knäckerbröd,* and herring.

"Steve should never have opened his mouth," Stefan said.

"Young Turk would never have noticed a thing," I agreed.

"The trouble with Steve is that he's too eager to give money away. We didn't need Young Turk anyway. You see, Steve's still a bit green in some ways. He doesn't think it through before going ahead with something," Graham said.

Toward midday, Steve walked over to us, downcast. "Nothing

doing. I'm stuck. In the morning I'll take a taxi into Iskenderun." The city was thirty miles away. Graham said we couldn't wait. We were obliged to go on.

We transferred the refrigerator back to *Old Girl,* left Steve with some extra teabags and sugar, and departed Silver Gazoo Customs. I rode in Stefan's Volvo F12 Intercooler; it had a hugely spacious cab and offered a Pullman ride compared to *Old Girl*'s bounce. Very quickly the barren mountains gave way to a broad plain with reddish soil. Plane trees lined the road, and it seemed very much like France, with neatly cultivated fields and Mediterranean-style villages. We were in a province of Turkey known as Hatay, which from 1922 to 1938 had been a French mandate.

We drove up the side of Kizil Dagi (Red Mountain) to the village of Bagras, where we passed the ruins of a tenth-century castle. We stopped nearby so I could take some pictures and met two young men holding hands. They asked if I would photograph them. I did and questioned the about the castle. They made me understand that it was a dark and sinister place, much feared locally and not often visited. It had been, I later read, a Templar stronghold until it fell to Saladin in 1188. Once through Bagras we descended toward the Mediterranean coast. The sea was deep blue, and after weeks in the desert it looked incredibly inviting.

On our way into Iskenderun, which had the appearance of a French colonial city, Stefan and I discussed what made long-distance drivers put up with the life they led. It was the challenge, he said, and the thrill of being able to tell the people back home about places they would never visit and things they would never see.

"You can never describe what it's really like. Words just don't capture it. And anyway, nobody would believe half the things that go on."

Stefan had made his first trip to the Middle East in 1983. But, he said, the life of a diesel gypsy had taken its toll. "It's hell being alone on the road. In the long run it drives you crazy."

Divorced, Stefan has a five-year-old daughter whom he rarely sees. "I won't make the same mistake again," he said. He has a new girlfriend now and wants to settle down. He was prudent on the road. He had learned never to be in a hurry, but drove long, steady hours. On their way to the Middle East, the Swedes drive through Eastern Europe. They take a ferry to Gdańsk in Poland and come down the Trans-European Expressway through Katowice, Zilina, Bratislava, and Budapest. They get paid for each day on the road. Their pay stops when the truck is back in the depot at home. Stefan handled his own Customs clearance to save money. It took him a bit longer, but he was paid by the day, so it didn't matter. When alone in the cab, he thought about Sweden and his girlfriend, and increasingly about what he will do after he stops driving.

We passed a Roman aqueduct in the plain near Dörtyol, north of Iskenderun, where, in 333 B.C., Alexander defeated Darius at the Battle of Issus. We reached Toprakkale at 4:00 P.M., branching left on the road to Ceyhan. It felt good to be back on familiar territory. Passing Ceyhan, we looked out at Yilanli Kalesi, the Castle of Snakes. We reached Oryx's garage on the outskirts of Adana as a huge orange sun disappeared behind the horizon. Parked in front of Oryx's was a blue MAN belonging to Rhenien Transport from Stuttgart. Its driver, Gerhardt—we never did get his last name—was happy to see us. He carried a bottle of Metaxa around with him and offered us a swig. The harsh-tasting brandy reminded me of the night we had spent at Evsoni with Bob Anderson, Gordon Durno, and Terry Grant a month before. Gerhardt had delivered twenty-three tons of bottled water to the PX supermarket at the U.S. Air Force base up the road. He swore the bottles were filled with quality German tap water.

The two coin collectors were quickly upon us. These young kids bum coins from the drivers and make collections out of them that they sell to American servicemen. They were pretty smart kids, but when you've just gotten off the road and are tired and dusty, you don't want them bugging you. They can be very persistent. They told us that four British trucks had returned from Iraq yesterday and left for Ankara this morning. We asked who the drivers were. The coin collectors knew most of the British regulars by name. They had never seen these ones before. They concluded, therefore, that the four belonged to a "new company."

To gain some peace, I pulled out my change bag and let them rummage through it, telling them they could each choose any three coins they liked as long as they didn't take the German five-mark pieces. They emptied the bag and debated at length which were the best ones, then replaced what they didn't want and handed me back the bag.

While I went for a shower at the back of the BP station they snuck away my sandals and polished them. When I got out of the shower the sandals were on the ground and the coin collectors were waiting nearby for my reaction. The sandals literally shone. "For you, it's free," they said, beaming. They were good kids.

On his way down, Stefan had ordered leather jackets for his girlfriend and uncle from one of the shops on Airbase Road. After Graham had showered, we took Gerhardt with us to pick up the jackets. They cost eighty-five dollars each and appeared to be well crafted. More important, Stefan was pleased with them. By then it was time for our first *Efes kontrol*. The evening was warm and we sat at a table outside the newly opened Piknik Bar and ordered a round of the golden Pilsen.

"Might have another one of those," I said. Even Graham agreed. We had three more rounds and then ordered kebab dinners.

Ten thousand Americans live at the Adana airbase. It is the largest U.S. military facility in the Mediterranean. Its greatest notoriety came from the fact that Francis Gary Powers took off from here on his ill-fated U-2 flight across the Soviet Union in 1960. The base was pretty much a front-line operation, and the Piknik Bar was overflowing with American Air Force personnel. A table of about twenty of them were helping their sergeant celebrate because he had been awarded some sort of medal. "They are, as you say, whooping it up," Gerhardt observed. The noise finally whooped us out of the place, and at 10:00 P.M. we rolled across the street to our trucks, ready for bed.

23. CAIRO GOES TO SCHOOL

NOW that we were clear of the Middle East, Graham's first concern was to get to the Telex Motel to find out whether King Leon had a backload for us. The quality of the backload and the amount of waiting involved in getting it would make the difference between whether our trip was financially rewarding or marginally disastrous. Graham expected the backload would be from Yugoslavia, which was his usual route home.

We left Oryx's at 8:00 A.M. and immediately got snarled in Adana traffic. The car in front of us on the bridge over the Seyhan River stalled every time it came to a stop and one of the passengers had to hop out, lift the hood, and jiggle the carburetor to get it going.

After the Tarsus TIR *kontrol* we stopped at a fruit stand and purchased ten pounds of locally grown bananas, grapes, apples, pears, and tangerines for fifteen hundred Turkish lire (1.50 pounds) while Stefan went in search of eggs and *ekmek* for our breakfast. We stopped three-quarters of the way over Tarsus Pass, on the side of a mountain, for bacon, eggs, and coffee. My stomach was growling, so I went for a walk in the woods, along a path covered by a carpet of pine needles with volcanic rock outcroppings on either side and flashes of russet, green, and gold bursting through the trees. I was wondering whether Alexander might have trod this path, when a loud-hailer started calling, "TIR *kamyon musmuv*. TIR *kamyon*, you leef now."

About a quarter of a mile up the road the *trafik polisi* had set up a checkpoint and were pulling everybody over for a document inspection. We packed up, expecting to be fined when we reached the checkpoint, and sure enough, an officer in the middle of the road directed us onto the shoulder.

"Where goink, Meester?"

"Ipsala," I said.

"Ah, very gut. Any Marlboros?"

I looked across at Graham. For once he didn't have a cigarette dangling from his mouth. "Don't smoke," I said.

"Ah, yes, but *kollege* smokes."

Now, how did he know that? We gave him a pack of Marlboros from the carton we had purchased duty-free at Silver Gazoo. He was happy about that. "Okay, you go," he said, and he waved us back onto the road.

"Nice sort of fellow," Graham remarked.

We continued climbing toward the top of the pass. "Look at all those blue bottles," I said as we approached a bend at the foot of a long incline.

"Never mind the bottles, look at the truck."

"Where?"

"There, off the road, in the bend."

A red tonka carrying a load of blue gas canisters had lost its brakes coming down the incline and tipped over onto its side, spilling hundreds, if not thousands, of bottles down the hill and into the ravine.

"Must be empties. None exploded," Graham said.

The driver was sitting on one of the canisters beside his truck, looking the other way. Except for his pride, which was no doubt severely bruised, he was unhurt. We gave him a toot on the airhorn, but not even that stirred him.

On the north side of the pass it had snowed down to six thousand feet (the pass is at 4,521 feet) and the tops of the mountains were gleaming white. We rumbled across the plain of Konya, stopping at International TIR Services to have the metal locker fitted that Graham had ordered on our way down.

"Half hour," the boss promised when we asked how long it would take to mount the box on the tractor chassis.

Two hours later the job was done and we were on the road again, heading for Aksaray. Roadwork slowed us to ten miles per hour at the entrance to the town. Some of the potholes could have swallowed a small car, and even *Old Girl* had to skirt them with caution. It was dusk when we pulled into the Aksaray TIR *kontrol* twenty minutes later.

We left for Ankara at 6:15 P.M. with the BBC World Service telling us that Iraqi warplanes had bombed and strafed Iranian troop and ammunition trains heading for the front. Tehran claimed that the Iraqi jets had hit a stationary goods train, killing one civilian.

We pulled into Telex TIR Park at 9:30 P.M. and were greeted by a smiling Ali Baba. The yard was more crowded than the last time: two Stolk International trucks from Holland, a French truck, a couple of Alpine Turks, and four unmarked British trucks, one of them with the right side of the cab scrunched in.

Upstairs, three English drivers were watching *Life of Brian* on the TV. They drove for Brooks Transport, whose depot is at Purfleet in Essex, on the far side of the Dartford Tunnel. They had just returned from Baigi, the Iraqi oil refining center, where they had delivered a load of chemicals needed to repair the inside of a defective reactor vessel. It was a one-off job, said Rod Brookstein.

The mystery of the "new company" whose four trucks had preceded us by a day at Oryx's was thus solved. Rod and his three companions, John, Terry and Mickey, were the first British drivers we had seen since September 29, when we had said good-bye to Leslie Massey at Fallujah outside Baghdad.

Graham checked the noticeboard. There was a message from Pam Aspden, Leon's assistant, to contact her for backloading instructions. Graham would telex in the morning.

Rod, a South African married to an English girl and living in Swanley, Kent, England, had been a Middle East driver in the 1970s until his firm, run by the Brooks brothers, dropped out of the Asian market to concentrate on Eastern Europe and Spain. He said he was amazed by the changes along the route. He hardly recognized parts of it. Their fourth driver, Mickey, had the face of an aging cherub. He was asleep.

"What happened to Mickey's cab?"

"A Turk swerved to miss the bumps in Aksaray and ran into him. Head on."

Although it was clearly the Turk's fault, Mickey had been fined a thousand pounds. The police officer explained, however, that the money would be refunded at the frontier. What the reasoning behind a refundable fine was we couldn't determine.

Rod and John had not seen anybody along the road but shared our impression that Iraq was about to crumble. When the Brooks squadron returned north from Baigi, the line to get through Zahko Customs started at Dahuk, forty-five miles away, and numbered more than one thousand trucks. The Iraqi cops were offering to escort drivers to the head of the line for *baksheesh*. Rod had noticed that Terry was starting to edge out of the line. He ran up to him and asked, ''Where the hell do you think you're going?''

Terry explained why he had the cop sitting beside him in the cab.

''Are you crazy? Get that thing out of there. He'll skin you alive once around the next bend. Take everything you've got.''

Terry told the cop to get down. The cop shrugged and went to the next driver in the line, a Womble, who accepted for a carton of cigarettes. When Rod and the others got to the diesel checkpoint at Zahko a day and a half later, the Womble was only half an hour ahead of them.

''Fat lot of good it did him.''

Aytekin Atik was pleased to see us. ''How did it go?'' he asked. Not too bad, I told him as I checked into one of the Telex's upstairs rooms. A comfortable night in a reasonable sack was high on my list of priorities. We retired early to bed, my first time between sheets in a month.

Next morning—Tuesday, October 21—I rose early to get my laundry done. The washing facilities were on the third floor, next to the showers, and with luck my clothes would be dry by noon. As I turned the corner I almost bumped into the Vicar. He was standing stark naked and dripping wet, wondering where he had left his towel.

''Cairo's looking for you. He wants to take you to school,'' he said by way of a greeting.

When I had first met Tony Medding the year before, he had come storming through the door at the National Hotel in Belgrade, covered with grease, a roll-your-own cigarette dangling from the side of his mouth, a pouch of tobacco in his shirt pocket, and a wallet chained to his belt bulging from his back pocket. Medding was hopping mad.

''I almost rammed some fuckin' Yugo up the ass. Had no damn lights. Brakes jammed and I had some trouble unfreezing them, didn't I?'' he had said.

After Tony had cleaned off the grease, he sat down at our table at the National, ordered a beer from George, and started to talk. He was about to turn forty and had been driving to the Middle East for twelve years. He had hoped then that it would be one of his last trips, but here he was, still on the road more than a year later. He had twelve thousand pounds in the bank and needed another four thousand pounds to buy the tenancy of a pub. He was divorced, rarely saw his two kids, but said he and his ex-wife, Irene, would remarry as soon as he stopped driving. The incentive was there, but Tony still loved the road. "Once you leave the depot, you don't have no foreman on your back," he explained.

Tony was one of the more sensitive drivers on the route. He was interested in everything that occurred along it, and over the years had built up a network of friends for whom he had done favors or had helped out at some time or other. He knew about the Lion of Amphipolis and the Castle of Snakes as well as every bend going over Tarsus and down Zahko Mountain. He knew who should get *baksheesh* and shouldn't, and he never had a bad word to say about anyone. We had driven with him last year from Belgrade to Baghdad, and it had been an education.

Graham, Tony, and I had breakfast downstairs, waiting for Cairo to appear. Tony, who drove a Prior refrigerator truck for Charlie Leadham, had rolled in at 3:00 A.M. from Izmir. He was carrying seven tons of chilled meat from the U.S. bases at Ankara and Adana.

"My last trip to Baghdad was a strange one," he said. Gary Leadham, Prior's operations manager, had received a telephone call from a lady in London. She wanted to know whether Prior still accepted loads for Iraq. She said the customer was willing to pay fifty-two hundred pounds for a Baghdad, but it had to be done really quick. Gary asked it tomorrow would be soon enough. She said fine and gave an address off Covent Garden.

Gary told Tony to drive up with a forty-foot refrigerator truck and check it out. The woman had said her customer would provide all the necessary documents, including an Iraqi manifest, and arrange Customs clearance. It was a computer, she said, and it had to travel dust-free under controlled temperature. She insisted that the refrigerator truck carry no other cargo.

Tony arrived at 9:00 A.M. from Folkestone and parked outside, practically blocking the street with his juggernaut. He walked up the stairs of a grubby building and introduced himself to a receptionist. "I'm Prior's driver for the Baghdad load."

He was told to wait, and after a few minutes an attractive dark-haired woman in her midthirties, wearing a tight-fitting skirt and a jumper that wrapped around the curves of her breasts, came out of an office. She asked Tony where he was parked. She took note and told him to wait at the truck. About half an hour later a delivery van pulled up and loaded a couple of boxes into the refrigerator truck. They weighed less than half a ton and covered not even a quarter of the floor space. The van drove off. Tony secured the boxes at the front of the refrigerator truck and went back to the office.

"When is the rest of the load coming?" he asked.

"That's it!"

The woman went down into the street and watched him lock the refrigerator truck, then peeled off twenty-five hundred pounds in running money from a wad of bills. He was given the travel documents. "The consignee is the Ministry of Defense, Baghdad. When you get to Zahko, call this number." She explained that the computer was the first of its kind to print out in English and Arabic. "Be careful with it, now. A lot depends on it." She gave him a bedroom smile that suggested he should call when he got back.

When Tony arrived at Zahko he telephoned the contact number and was told to wait at his truck until a liaison officer appeared. He wasn't required to clear customs. He was given a military escort to Baghdad, unloaded his shipment, and was back at Habur, Turkey, within forty-eight hours.

"It was magic. If every trip was like that, this would be a pleasant way to earn a living," he said.

Tony was going to deliver half the sides of beef he had on board in Ankara that morning, which meant he would be back at Telex by about three o'clock, and he hoped we would still be there. Graham was doubtful, as he expected Pam would be dispatching us to someplace like Sarajevo or Zagreb.

"Hey, Robert, good to see you," Cairo said when he appeared at 8:30 A.M. "You come with me this morning. Okay?" I looked at Graham. "I take you to my English class. Teacher's very nice. She asked me to bring one of my English friends to speak to the class."

Cairo was one of the authentic characters along the route, a sort of brother-confessor to many of the drivers. When he first went to work at Telex Motel one of the English drivers thought he looked Egyptian because of his curly hair and swarthy complexion and called him Cairo. The name stuck. His real name was Adnan Güven, and he was from the city of Erzurum in Turkey. He held a master's degree in archaeology and had been invited to study for his doctorate at the University of Vienna when his father died. As he was an only son, with a mother and two younger sisters to look after, he had to find a job.

The Telex Motel opened in 1980 and was advertising for a night manager who could speak foreign languages. Cairo went to see the owner, who was impressed by his qualifications and hired him on the spot. At the time less than ten trucks a night parked at Telex Motel. He became friends with several English drivers, and soon they made it a regular stop. The English attracted the Dutch and Scandinavians, and then the Germans and French started coming. Most of the Eastern Bloc drivers stay down the road at a Bulgarian TIR park.

To earn more money, Cairo applied to the Ministry of Transport to become an air traffic controller. They sent him to the civil aviation department's navigation school, where he was told he must perfect his English.

The Ministry of Transport enrolled him in a nine-month English course at the university. He had thirty hours a week of classes. The only problem was that they began at 9:00 A.M., five days a week, and the third time you arrived late they expelled you. Cairo, therefore, didn't want to be late. We took a taxi to the university. On the way he explained that his teacher's name was Emel. "Cute," he said. "About thirty, unmarried." She had been to the University of Washington for a three-month teaching course. From what I could gather, her students liked her.

The modern-languages section of the university consisted of three nondescript buildings on the western limits of Ankara. They were gray and had a semipermanent air to them, like they had been built thirty years ago pending the construction on the same site of more splendid facilities. Probably they would still be there in another thirty years.

Cairo had wanted me appropriately dressed. I had only a clean pair of overalls, open shirt, and a sweater, and could present myself no neater than that. "Okay," he said, shaking his head. The rest of the class—thirty-two in all—were government employees. They came in sports jackets or business suits, and the four women in skirts, one with a matching jacket that looked very rue Faubourg St. Honoré.

Emel took roll call. She asked if I would address the class. I spoke slowly, first introducing myself and then explaining that I was writing a book about long-distance truck drivers. I told them where we had been and what we had seen. They were alert listeners, but shy when it came to asking questions. It was difficult to understand some of their English. They were eager to know my impressions of Turkey: what I thought of the *trafik polisi;* what Turkish words I had learned; how we were treated at border-crossing points; and they were surprised when I said that I found Turkish roadhouses clean and agreeable places at which to stop.

At the midmorning break, Emel took me to the professors' lounge and introduced me to the other staff. I was served tea and noticed, while talking to a French teacher, that Emel had been taken aside by a matronly looking woman. When the bell rang for the resumption of classes, Emel came over to me and apologized because I could not come back to the class. She would send my sweater down with Adnan.

Cairo, when he arrived to pick me up a few minutes later, said that Emel had been told off by the director for having admitted a foreigner to her class without permission. I had to leave. Cairo was in no hurry, though, to return to class. He had been out on the town with Senator Karagülle the night before and complained of a hangover.

While waiting for a taxi, we talked about the drivers and it was clear that he lived in a trucking world. What he learned in class during the day, he practiced on the drivers at night. Not surprisingly, he was first in his class.

At the height of the Middle East boom, more than a hundred trucks stopped at the Telex each night. Now there were rarely more than twenty. "Big trouble," he said. "Maybe we have a war."

At the Telex Motel, he said, the drivers find a family atmosphere. "It's important to them that they feel they are part of a big family. We encourage them to treat it like their home.

"Here the drivers let off steam. They have two thousand miles behind them when they arrive in Ankara and all the problems that go with driving big trucks over that distance. After they've been on the road for several days, they want to talk and drink. When they drive they have nobody to talk to and they never drink."

Every Christmas, Cairo organizes a big party for the drivers who are caught on the road and must spent the holiday away from their families. He gets the kitchen staff to cook a couple of turkeys, and the drinks are on the house. There is singing and laughing, and everybody has a good time.

For Cairo, there are three princes among the drivers, and one is now dead. The most professional, he said, is Dick Snow. "Snowie knows everything about the road." Another knight of the tribe is Tony Medding. But the most gentlemanly of all had been the Welshman Dai Hobbs.

Hobbs had one bad-luck trip in his career, and that was his last one. He had driven a load to Saudi Arabia in early December 1985 and was coming back through Jordan when he had an accident and smashed his truck. He had been running with another driver, named Frank. They loaded Dai's unit onto Frank's trailer and got it back to Londra

Camp, where Dai's brother, Robert, who also drove for Rollie Mason, a well-known Welsh hauler, was waiting with news that Dai's divorce had gone through. Dai, who had been trying to make it home for Christmas, sat down in the bar and started to drink. By the time the evening was out he had consumed a bottle of vodka and was paralytically drunk—so drunk he couldn't get into his own cab on Frank's trailer, and he slept instead on the bottom bunk in his brother's DAF. In the morning, Dai was dead. He had literally drowned in his own sorrow. The funeral was in southern Wales. The church overflowed with mourners, most of them Middle East drivers.

When I got back to Telex Motel, Graham was chomping at the bit. He was also in a foul mood. The instructions from Leon Ashworth were to pick up twenty-one tons of wine from the Vinimpex winery at Shumen in northern Bulgaria, fifty-six miles from Varna, on the Black Sea coast.

"What about Yugoslavia?" Graham telexed back.

Bulgaria or nothing.

But his police paper said exit at Ipsala, not Kapikule, which was the border-crossing point with Bulgaria.

Too bad.

Twenty-one tons was too heavy for *Old Girl*. How about eighteen?

Eighteen okay. Where's Steve?

Stuck at Silver Gazoo.

"Come on. Let's get going," Graham grumbled.

"What about Tony?"

"Can't wait. I want to be backloaded on Friday so we can be in Dover on Tuesday. Otherwise they won't load us till Monday. We'll lose three days."

Stefan had already gone ahead. He wanted to get home to see his girlfriend.

We left Telex at 3:00 P.M. The sky was pregnant with autumn clouds. Graham was hoping to cross Bolu Pass before dark. An hour later we paid our three-thousand-lire toll to get up Death Valley. In addition to the Iranian wreck, still there, a tonka had crashed through one of the tollgates.

At 4:15 P.M. we passed a Davies Turner truck heading east. He flashed his lights in greeting. Fifteen minutes later we passed an Astran Ford.

"Hey, that's Bob Hedley on his way out again," I said.

"Anything coming?"

I had to lean out of the window to see around a slow-moving tonka. "Truck coming down. You can't pass."

"Say when."

"Now." It was like flying on instruments. Only I was the instrument.

We reached the top of Bolu at 5:40 P.M., after passing Bob Mattingly's DAF. We now had a descent of 2,970 feet in three miles. Darkness was falling. The sky was painted in deep purple and orange brushstrokes. At 6:00 P.M. we pulled into the Düzce TIR *kontrol* park for the obligatory one-hour rest.

The night guard came over to us. "Are you staying or going on?" he asked.

"Going on," Graham answered.

"Do you have any English books or magazines? If you don't it doesn't matter," he said with a sigh. "There is nothing I can do about it. But if you do, I would be grateful." He had curious elocution, so that his words seemed to bounce along.

"Sorry," Graham said.

He walked away. "Pleasant chap," was Graham's comment. We almost felt bad not being able to give him an old paperback or even a Sunday supplement.

We were preparing to leave when Robin Fraser drove in on his way to Jordan with another load of Mars Bars. It was good to see him. We chatted for a few minutes until another guard came over and started agitating. "In five minutes you'll have to pay sixteen hundred lire for all-night stay," he said.

"Any rain ahead?" Robin asked.

None. The roads were dry. So we left.

In the town of Düzce it started to drizzle. Very lightly at first. Graham said there was so much hot rubber on the road surface that it was like a skating rink in the rain. A road sign told us that 120 miles remained to Istanbul. They would take us four and a half hours to drive.

As the tonkas mostly have bald tires, they crawled along at ten miles per hour. A lot had pulled off to the side of the road. A few had slid into a ditch.

"The Turks are frightened to death of this, aren't they?" Graham said.

On even the slightest incline the traction wheels started to spin. "Wish I had a load on to hold her down," he mumbled.

Twelve miles from the Bosporus Bridge the storm struck. Rain bounced off the road in golfball-size drops. At 11:20 P.M. we were back in Europe. Eight cars had piled into each other because of aquaplaning. A bus had gone off the road on the right. It was like a war zone. Flooding had caused many vehicles to stall. *Old Girl* plowed through. At midnight we entered Londra Camp. British row was full. Nine Dow Freight trucks, one Falcongate, several French trucks, the four Brooks Transports, one Stolk International, and Stefan. We were too late for an *Efes kontrol*.

24. A RIDE FOR A RIDE

WEDNESDAY, October 22. We had been on the road twenty-nine days, and all but seven of them had been with Steve Walsh. Steve, more than any of us, had been looking forward to our return to Londra Camp. With autumn well advanced, it was, he said, the height of the bird season. By this he meant that it was the time of year when the English, Aussie, and Kiwi girls (from New Zealand) start heading north for the winter after spending the summer along the Aegean or Mediterranean coasts.

As Chris Lawrence had observed, they weren't the type of girls who ''come out here on their mother's arm and expect Pullman service.'' A good number of them turned up at Londra Camp in search of a ride home.

Steve had explained while cleaning his cab at Ar'ar Customs, putting fabulous effort into making it look invitingly neat, ''It's a ride for a ride.''

Homeward-bound drivers hurry to Londra Camp as fast as their wheels will carry them during the bird season to see what's available. When we arrived, the place had been cleaned out. The last of the flock, a Kiwi on her way to Hungary, had been taken on board by Martin, off Brooks Transport.

There had been a gathering of British drivers at Londra Camp over the weekend. Ian Cook, a Lancashire lad who drove for Stolk International out of Holland, had been among them, and he was talking with Alan Wood about Richie Thorne's latest antics. Alan, known to some as The Romancer, drove his own Volvo F12 and had arrived at the weekend with a load of Land-Rovers for Istanbul and Adana. Alfie

241

Jones had also been present and Richie had made him sing "The Band Played 'Waltzing Matilda.' "

By the time we arrived, however, the party was over. Alfie had left on Monday, Richie on Tuesday. Ian, who had run to Istanbul with Richie, said, "Being with him is like sitting on a time bomb, waiting for it to explode." Richie had been alternately friendly and belligerent, back to his former self, the terror of bars from Dover to Dubai.

We had met Alan Wood in Ankara last year. He had driven the Middle East route for ten years, but stopped because of the "hassle" of going into Saudi Arabia. Every Middle East driver we met used that word—"hassle"—to describe the problems of dealing with Arabs, but especially the Saudis. The aggravation, upset, restrictions, discrimination, stupidity, and prejudices were lumped together into that one word. The hassle, as Gordon Durno had said, "knocks the ass out of the job." Iraq and Syria were the other two countries that drivers feared and detested, but nowhere to the same degree as the Saudi hassle.

Alan, from Slough in Berkshire, England, would not drive his black "snatchback" any farther than Adana. "That's it, as far as I'm concerned." Beyond Adana there was a steady deterioration of working conditions. He admitted he treated his truck like a mistress and didn't want to put her through the treatment.

"When they cut holes in her, rip out the paneling, and cut into the upholstery, you want to strangle them. It just churns up your stomach," he said.

"A truck is like a woman. When she's running well, she's a dream. When she's not, she can be a perfect bitch. Treat her well—keep her clean inside and out—and she loves it. Treat her badly and she'll never let you forget it."

Alan, who had been a diesel gypsy since age twenty-one and knew no other life, had turned forty that month and was fearing he might be getting too old for the job. He had had only one accident in his career, driving through Yugoslavia, and he didn't want another. He had knocked over three trees in a blinding rainstorm, wrote off the truck, and had a six-inch gash in his leg. He was taken to the hospital, where a doctor, cigarette between his teeth, sewed it up. He was fined thirty pounds and released. His wife, Leslie, was Middle East export manager for Tempco and he had brought her to Istanbul on his last trip. They had two teenage children.

His feelings toward the Saudis were summed up in his story about

Dave Talford, who had worked for Payne Transport. Talford was driving down the Tapline when a Saudi car coming the other way had its hood fly up. Vision obstructed, the driver ran under Talford's trailer and killed himself. Dave was arrested and spent five and a half months in prison, where he picked up a case of dysentery. Nobody knew where he was until a couple of English drivers saw the roof of his van sticking up over a building and asked questions. They reported their find to the British embassy. The embassy staff intervened and eventually won his release. The judge who sentenced Talford told him, "It was your fault. If you had not been there the accident wouldn't have happened."

"Dave drives only to Greece now," Alan said.

The Brooks team was in good spirits in spite of the fact that John had burned out his clutch going onto the Bosporus bridge and had to be towed across by Rod. When they called Purfleet for backloading instructions—they had four loads of tires to pick up in Romania—they were told that their companion, Keith Shaw, whom the Romanians had placed under "truck arrest" at the Romanian border for having killed a cyclist, had been released. After a three-month investigation, the police determined that the accident wasn't Shaw's fault. The cyclist had been drunk and had veered into the front of the truck without warning. Shaw, who had been traveling slowly, only nudged the bicycle and thought he had merely bowled the cyclist over.

The Romanian police had not been gentle with Shaw. They arrested him and seized his tacho. His blood test showed no trace of alcohol. They had an expert decipher his tacho. The expert found that Shaw had been traveling at twenty-nine miles per hour in a twenty-five-mile-per-hour zone. The accident occurred within two hundred meters of a level crossing. The Romanian authorities imposed a twenty-thousand-pound fine. Lawyers for Brooks Transport negotiated a 50 percent reduction of the fine, which the firm paid, and Shaw was finally released.

Graham was still worrying about our exit from Turkey at Kapikule, which the British drivers call Kapik. He was unhappy, too, over the fact that Pam Aspden, Leon's assistant, would not give us Steve's backload, which was not as far afield. "It means we have an extra six hundred miles to drive," he said. As it turned out, when she learned that Steve was detained at Silver Gazoo, she gave his backload to Richie, who was now only two days ahead of us.

As for Alfie, we didn't know where he was. He had left Londra on Monday with two Aussie girls. "Alfie doesn't go the way the telex tells him, but the way the girls are going,'' Ian Cook said. The girls wanted to see Kavala beach. Alfie was supposed to be backloading in Bulgaria.

We left Londra Camp at midday, branching right on the road through Thrace to Edirne. Gibbon called Thrace a ''wasteland,'' Nagel thought it ''rather unattractive,'' and Paul Theroux, watching the countryside flick by his window on the *Orient Express,* had decided it was ''a dreary monotony of unambitious hills.'' But I found it fascinating. The weather was bright and the visibility sharp after the previous night's storm, and clouds raced by like giant airships, casting suggestive shadows across the hills. The countryside was totally different from the mountains of Anatolia, which we had driven through the day before. It was wide open with few trees—like the fields of central France or parts of Britain, except not as green.

Coming out of the town of Ulas, the road narrowed and dropped into an unexpected depression. Two Yugoslav trucks had met there, head on. The one on the left side of the road had its cab smashed to a degree that surely ruled out the driver's survival. The one on the right was in a ditch. The scene was deserted. It seemed a strange quirk of fate that the two Yugos had to come all this way into Thrace to meet head on like that. The chances of it happening must have been about a billion to one.

In the town of Babaeski we crossed a humped bridge barely wide enough for a juggernaut. How it supported *Old Girl*'s weight was a miracle of Ottoman engineering. The bridge was perhaps four hundred years old and had been built to sustain ox-drawn carts or, at worst, the sultan's cannons.

On the outskirts of Edirne, once called Adrianople after Emperor Hadrian, who founded it around A.D. 125, we stopped to buy eggs, fruit, butter, and soft drinks. An English-speaking policeman walked by and said we should be on our way. He was pleasant and kept on walking, assured that his request would be obeyed. We didn't disappoint him.

The approach to Edirne was dominated by a four-spired mosque with a broad central dome. It had been built in 1575 by the great Ottoman architect Mimar Sinan for Sultan Selim I. Sinan, who was eighty when he finished it, considered the mosque his finest work. According to legend it has 999 windows and a dome slightly larger than Hagia Sophia. Its four spear like minarets could be seen for miles down the road.

Edirne used to be of great strategic importance. It guarded the crossing over the Maritsa, where it is joined by the Tunja River, and in A.D. 378 on an unmarked battlefield twenty miles to the north the Goths so thoroughly defeated the main Roman army that it was a miracle the empire survived. The battle was one of the milestones of military history, pitting Gothic horses against Roman legions. The barbarian cavalry drove the Roman foot soldiers into a box and slaughtered two thirds of them, including Emperor Valens. On that August evening more than sixteen hundred years ago the sun set on the glory of the legions, the foundation of Roman power, and for another thousand years cavalry remained supreme on the field of battle.

Edirne, which counted eighty thousand inhabitants at the turn of this century, had become prosperous under the Ottomans as a center of silk manufacture and a city of trade through which passed the weighty caravans that plied the Zarigradski Drum from Constantinople to Belgrade and Budapest. Since the collapse of the Ottoman Empire, the city has shrunk and trade has passed it by for other destinations.

Once out of Edirne, we drove along the west bank of the Maritsa, leaving Thrace for the Balkans. The river was lined with poplars and the countryside was more varied, the farms appearing richer and more colorful. Half an hour later we reached Kapikule Customs. A rug merchant showed us his selection of machine-made tapestries in bright acrylic colors as we waited to be admitted to the Customs compound. Once inside, we found the exasperated members of the Brooks team. It had taken them six hours to reclaim the accident deposit paid in Aksaray. We noticed that Mickey had replaced the damaged DAF's right-side head lamp, missing since the accident, with a tiny Citroën 2CV head lamp purchased in Istanbul.

Graham was braced for nastiness from the Customs police. It had been nagging him since Ankara. He had been careful to stop at all seven TIR *kontrol* stations along the road and not to miss any, as westbound trucks sometimes did. His concern paid off.

The police officer at the checkout counter was giving Mickey, who was in front of us, a hard time. Mickey had missed the Ankara TIR *kontrol*. He was acting dumb and, with his cherubic smile, hoping the copper would give up.

"Stamp missing Ankara TIR *kontrol*," the officer repeated.

"Aksaray okay," Mickey said.

"*Ja, ja*, Aksaray *gut*. Ankara *nix gut*."

"Habur police said not needed."

"No, no. Mushav."

"Sorry, mate, don't understand. I've got four of the fuckers."

"Mushav fumphff," he said, like he was trying to blow the sheet away, at the same time holding up five fingers to indicate that *fumphff* meant a numeral and not a breeze. "Fumphff," he said again. He grabbed Graham's TIR *kontrol* sheet and looked at the stamps.

"Ah-hah! Here *ist gut,*" he said triumphantly, stabbing at the Ankara stamp on Graham's sheet. He showed the paper to Mickey. Then he started counting them. "Fumphff."

"Oh, five stamps. I see. Okay, I go now."

"Meester, you pay ten thousand lire."

Mickey had to go to the bank to change money to pay his fine. The police officer was so pleased to have made himself understood he never noticed that Graham's place of exit was marked as Ipsala. He filed the paper and gave us our exit voucher.

We moved out of Turkish Customs after nightfall and drove into the Bulgarian compound at Kapitan Andreevo.

"Quick, roll your window up!" Graham shouted as he edged *Old Girl* into an open-ended hangar through which the roadway was funneled. We were squirted from every angle with a DDT solution. It was the foot-and-mouth washdown. After exiting from it, the truck smelled of chemicals.

"That was a close call," I said.

"I forgot once, and I can tell you I got it all over me, in my ear, on my glasses, everywhere. It was no joke."

We arrived in the Bulgarian compound as the Customs guards were changing shifts. We had a two-hour wait for trailer and cabin inspection and to get our transit visas. We were sitting in the cab listening to the BBC news when there was a tap on the door. I looked out. A professorial-looking man with hair over his ears, about fifty, a sharp nose, and angry eyes was standing by the front wheel. "Been out long?" he asked.

I got out and said hello. He introduced himself as Martin Stratton from Fosters Booth. He said he had been in a convoy of three other Whittle trucks but had been detained at the frontier and was stuck overnight. He was driving an extendable lowloader, parked down the road, that looked like a ship of war. He was carrying presses for making diesel engine blocks from the recently closed British Leyland plant at Bathgate in Scotland. British Leyland had sold the presses to the Turks, and he was taking them to a new plant on the Black Sea. "Pretty soon," said Martin, "the Turks will be selling British Leyland engines to the British."

Martin claimed he was the victim of bureaucratic injustice. He hadn't wanted to bow to it, but attempts to convince the Bulgarians of his logic had cost him a day and come to naught.

"They have a weighbridge office here for a weighbridge that doesn't exist. They let me into the country without questioning my weight. Then when I arrived here there was a message from traffic control in Sofia saying that I looked heavier than forty tons. I told them to put her on a weighbridge. They said, 'Sorry, we don't have one.' I told them I'd go back to the weighbridge at Sofia. They said, 'No, you have a thirty-hour transit visa. Not possible. You must pay.' "

The overweight tax, according to a notice in the weighbridge office for the weighbridge that didn't exist, was equivalent to 351 pounds sterling for a six-axled rig.

At first Martin thought he could sit it out, but he didn't want to kick up too much of a fuss because he was overheight and overlength and they hadn't cottoned to that. He phoned Whittle to see if the customer would pay. King Leon said it wasn't Whittle's concern. "You're on your own on this one, I'm afraid," Martin said King Leon had told him.

"Come, look at this," Martin said, taking my arm and walking me across the compound to the Customs house. The building, a low rectangle containing a series of offices with counters in front for passport control, cargo clearance, and one marked *Brückenwage buro,* looked like it had been hastily erected some twenty years ago as a temporary measure and never removed.

"Look," he said, pointing to a sign on the back wall. It was also in German.

Taxen für Schwertransport

38–40 T.	
mit 4 achsen	*320 leva*
über 4 achsen	*120 leva*
40–45 T.	*470 leva*
Über 45 T.	*700 leva*
Für Uberdimensionierte	
Transporte	*400 leva*

Achsen, I knew was German for axles. "What's *leva?*" I asked.
"That's what they call their money. A hopeless currency. Nobody,

not even the Wombles, wants it. Not real money at all—just pieces of paper. And they have this funny exchange rate, you know; 470 leva equal 351 pounds. Not 350 pounds flat; there's that extra quid built in there. As they don't accept coin, and since they don't give change in sterling, you have to change another bank note. This gives you some leftover *leva,* which you're not allowed to take out of the country. It's all a game.''

He showed me his manifest. It said:

unit [unloaded] net	13,230 pounds
trailer [empty] net	17,640 pounds
load	48,819 pounds
gross weight:	79,689 pounds
	or 39.84 tons

The weighbridge on leaving Bathgate had registered 83,658 pounds (or 41.82 tons). The difference between the manifest weight and weighbridge weight was his personal gear, tools, and a full load of diesel. But with six axles, he was just within the limit.

"Come and have a coffee when you're through. I'll tell you all about it.''

I thought I had already heard everything. But Martin wanted to talk. He was alone on the edge of the Balkans and needed company to calm his nerves. We got our thirty-hour transit visas, paid the road tax, and went through the rest of the rigmarole. The Brooks team was having some problems. Minor stuff. But an Iranian driver who was going through Customs with us, and who spoke English with an American accent, helped translate. He also spoke Turkish and some Bulgarian.

Reza, the Iranian driver, had been a fighter pilot in the Iranian Air Force and had learned to fly F-5 Tigers in the United States. He resigned his commission because he was over forty, and to escape being redrafted had become a TIR driver instead. His wife was Austrian; she had moved back to Vienna, and he visited her on his trips through Austria. Their twelve-year-old son lived with his parents in Tehran. When he returned home on his last trip, his son told him he was going to join the Revolutionary Guards and fight for Ayatollah Khomeini. Reza said he cuffed his son and told him: "I do all the fighting in this family.'' He later told his son if he did well in school, he would take him to see his mother in Vienna. Reza said he planned to enroll him in an Austrian school as soon as possible.

We were standing in line, waiting to get our passports back from the visa office. I was leaning against the wall when I noticed etched by the window in tiny handwriting: "Peter the Plater plated in Kapik and liked it."

We were cleared at 9:30 P.M. and drove one hundred yards down the road till we came to the cafe where Martin Stratton was parked and waiting. A full moon lit his man-of-war, and the temperature had dipped below freezing. We could see our breath as we circled the blue Mack. It had a Union Jack painted on the front and Fosters Booth Traction, his company, on both doors. Martin and his lowloader specialized in so-called abnormal loads.

Inside, the cafe was crowded. We found a table and ordered coffee and plum brandy. The waiter wanted four *leva*. We discreetly slid him a ten-deutsche-mark note. He loved it. According to the official exchange rate, one deutsche mark was worth 0.4 *leva*. But we got six *leva* back.

Martin explained he had received a call from Whittle asking if he wanted to transport some machinery to Turkey. He was told it was three crated pieces within regulation sizes, but because of weight distribution the load needed six axles. He agreed with the terms as quoted, but when he arrived at Bathgate to pick up the machinery he discovered it was four loose pieces and one crate. He had to extend the trailer by a meter, so he was now overlength and marginally overheight. He would have been overwidth, but he made the crane shift one part of the load to meet the requirements. They threatened to charge him extra crane time for doing it. He covered the load with canvas so its silhouette looked like a modern sculpture, and hid the extension on the trailer under the sheeting so that only a sharp eye could detect its extra length.

He told King Leon he would not go through Hungary because he would be caught on the weighbridge, and got an extra hundred pounds added to the freight charges to cover road taxes in Austria. "The client isn't pleased," Leon told him.

He entered Bulgaria at Kalotina, coming from Nis. He had helped the Customs officer measure the load, placing the yardstick on his toe and lifting it when the officer climbed to the top of the sculpture to get its heights, and shifted it down a good ten inches from the end of the trailer when he measured its length. Relieved, he thought he was in the clear all the way through to Turkey.

Driving on the beltway around Sofia, he was spotted by the highway police, who telexed ahead to warn the weighbridge officer at

Kapitan Andreevo. When he arrived at the border he was taken into the weighbridge office and shown a telex in Bulgarian that listed his registration number and said, according to the translation he was given, that he "seemed" more than forty tons.

He argued about it for the rest of the day, and when finally he decided there was nothing to do but pay, the foreign-exchange counter had closed and he was stuck till morning. The tax would leave him short of running money, and he worried about making it back home. He said he would have to find a Turk or an Iranian to run with.

"Why?" I asked.

"Because they feed you."

The Brooks team, who had taken the last free table in the cafe, was having a minor dispute. Mickey and Terry wanted to stop for the night, have a warm meal and something to drink, while Rod was pushing them to drive on. Rod, as usual, won. His road experience gave him seniority.

I looked at my watch. It was 11:15 P.M. "We stopping here?" I asked Graham.

"Not bloody likely," he grumbled. "Want to be loaded tomorrow."

We wished Martin a safe journey to Istanbul and shifted out. The road signs were in Cyrillic script, which didn't help, and we got lost in the town of Haskovo at about 1:00 A.M. Out of the night a police car marked KAT came screeching to a halt beside us. The officer in the passenger seat got out and came over to my side of the cab. He asked what the problem was. I had the map out and said we were lost.

"Where you go?"

"Shumen," I said.

"By Stara Zagora?"

"Yes."

"Straight. Always straight," he said, pointing down the road.

Highways in Bulgaria are narrow and bumpy, like the asphalt has been applied from a toothpaste tube. We bumped along, got lost again at Stara Zagora, but found a road sign to Burgas on the Black Sea. Somewhere around Sliven we pulled onto a paved shoulder and stopped for the night. It was 2:30 A.M.

There was frost on the ground. I found a flat, grassy patch and collapsed under the stars.

25. ENGLISH OKAY

GRAHAM reasoned that if we could arrive at the Vinimpex depot before 10:00 A.M. we would be loaded that day, Thursday, giving us an extra twenty-four hour margin for our planned Monday arrival in Dover.

It had been a cold night and I was impatient to see the countryside in daylight. Around 6:00 A.M. I knocked on Graham's door and told him it was time to head out. I had on four layers of clothing and was shivering. Only a week before we had been complaining of hundred-degree heat.

Graham woke slowly as I filled the kettle and prepared to brew tea. Three teabags in the pot, water on top, a five-minute stew, then a quick stir. "Hey, there's a dead fly in the pot!" I said, surprised.

"Well, didn't drink much, did he," Graham observed.

Within an hour we were heading east toward the Black Sea, into a bright sunrise that promised a warm autumn day. We were traveling down the Tunja Valley, named after the river on our right that would shortly sweep to the south and fall into the Maritsa at the gates of Edirne. For five centuries Bulgaria had been a prized province of the Ottomans, only gaining its independence in 1908. Its valleys were fertile and its farmers said to be among the most industrious in the world. Its roses are as famous as its tobacco, and it is a net exporter of grain. Its wine-growing tradition, dating from the seventh century, has made it the tenth-largest wine producer in the world. But Bulgaria, a country the size of the state of Ohio, or a bit smaller than England, and with a population of nine million, sells most of its wine abroad; it is the fourth-largest wine exporter. Its biggest customer is the Soviet Union,

251

but the Russians pay in rubles, which doesn't help Bulgaria's foreign-currency account.

To capture as much foreign exchange as possible, the Bulgarians have set up roadside "free shops" that sell foreign goods—anything from whiskey to washing machines—for hard currency. One result is that this encourages Bulgarians to scrounge foreign currency wherever they can. Trucks or cars that passed us often made frantic signs that they would change money at black-market rates. The problem was, with only thirty hours to transit the country, on what do you spend the *leva*?

We entered Karnobat at 8:00 A.M. This quaint-looking market town had churches with bulbous spires and plump women in long skirts and kerchiefs who looked like they had just stepped out of a Brueghel painting. Some had brooms of twigs and were sweeping their front steps. Flocks of geese scattered out of the road and a sow trailing a litter of piglets herded them underneath her as we passed.

Leaving Karnobat, we turned north toward Shumen, sixty miles distant, and began to climb through an oak forest into the Planina Mountains. The mountains were not high and, other than the poor road conditions, offered no impediment to *Old Girl*. White doves rushed in and out of the trees. There wasn't a soul around, and it seemed an appealing place to spend a few hours on a warm autumn's morning. But Graham was in a hurry and we were soon over the hump, descending toward Shumen. The countryside looked like Lombardy, with tall poplars turning orange and yellow. As we neared the winery, Graham freshened up with his battery-powered shaver.

We pulled into the Vinimpex yard at 9:30 A.M. The woman manager told us we were to load at another winery six miles from Shumen, in the village of Xah Kpym. One of the workers showed us the way.

The winery at Xah Kpym employed perhaps thirty people. Most of them were lined up on the loading dock to greet us. Graham swung *Old Girl* around and backed her up to the dock. We opened the back and as soon as we had swept out the van the Vinimpex staff got to work. They joked with us and wanted to exchange rubber tire patches for cassettes of the latest Western hits. They were not looking for *baksheesh* but wanted to exchange goods, albeit the goods they were offering belonged to the cooperative. The manager asked if we wanted to buy white wine for thirty deutsche marks a case. We bought two cases. It was not going to be a dry trip home.

About eight hundred thousand Bulgarians, or about 9 percent of the population, are classified as "ethnic Turks." Ankara has made a lot of fuss in recent years with assertions that the Bulgarian authorities have killed or imprisoned several thousand ethnic Turks because they refused to adopt Bulgarian names. Turkish truckers transiting Bulgaria were restricted to the main TIR routes so they might no longer visit relatives in out-of-the-way ethnic Turkish villages. We saw no signs of this, nor did we look for any. The only "ethnic" Turk we met was at the Vinimpex winery, and he seemed to be on top of the world.

He had very shyly asked Graham for a cassette but had nothing to offer in exchange. Until then we had resisted attempts at barter, but this fellow somehow seemed more earnest. He told us his wife and daughter also worked at the winery. He was jovial enough and didn't bother us, although he returned every twenty minutes or so and asked, "You no have tape?"

Graham handed him an old Phil Collins cassette. Our friend was transported into an orgasm of joy. He came back ten minutes later from a shed behind the loading platform with two liters of freshly bottled white wine, which we stored in a corner of the lower bunk. When this operation was completed he walked back to the main bottling plant, stopping every few yards to shout, "English okay!"

Not long afterward he was back, wanting to know if we had any more cassettes. He had been tippling in the shed, where the workers had their own vat of wine. I found him a Willie Nelson cassette, and he grinned in appreciation. Moments later he was back with two more liters of wine. "English okay!" he said.

A little while later he was back. "Cum, cum," he motioned. I went with him toward the bottling plant. He introduced me to his wife and nineteen-year-old daughter. We smiled at each other because we could not make ourselves understood with words, except for the "English okay!" The daughter fished under her apron and produced two wrapped pieces of bubble gum. She handed them to me, blushing.

"Tankoo," she said so softly I almost missed it.

Graham had gone to sleep in the cab, so I went for a walk on a road that led northward, out of the village. The sidewalks were bordered with roses and covered overhead by a latticework of vines laden with grapes. They appeared to belong to nobody, or rather to the village, and I sampled them as I walked. They were green, pulpy, and sweet. I passed a church that was boarded up and a graveyard that still received corpses for religious burial, judging by the freshly turned graves, floral sprays, and newly erected crosses. I walked about a mile up the road, turned around, and came back. I could have been in France. The roadsides were lined with trees and acres upon acres of tall, healthy-looking vines stretched out on either side. The Shumen area produces six million liters of wine a year, as much as all of Beaujolais.

When I returned to the winery the loading was completed: fourteen thousand bottles of wine. Shutting the tailgate, I noticed that the spare tire rack at the back of the van had come loose. The foreman indicated we should drive down to a shed by the gate where they kept their welding equipment. Within minutes it was fixed. A tractor pulled in with a load of grapes. The workers plied us with bunches of the freshly picked fruit. We received our consignment receipt, which we had to take to Sofia, where a Vinimpex manager would issue us with a TIR carnet. We shook hands all around and parted.

"Time?" Graham asked as we turned left out of the gate.

"Two forty-five."

"She's feeling a little heavier now," he said after we had been running a moment. "Doesn't pull up the hills like she used to.

"I must admit," he added, "it's nicer when she has eight or nine tons on, just enough to hold her down. When she's like this, it's hard work for nine hours driving. They said she had eighteen and a half tons on, but it feels like more than that."

He was, nevertheless, in good spirits, happy that we were backloaded and homeward bound on the last leg of our trip. This was our thirty-ninth day out, and I for one felt very tired.

"There's four women over there digging the road up, and the cows are eating the sunflowers," he observed.

As we drove, he calculated his profit. The backload paid fifteen hundred pounds. But he had 675 pounds in trailer rental to settle and another 450 pounds in ferries. Plus the running expenses and overhead.

"So if you knock all that off you don't get much out of it," he noted. He would clear twelve hundred pounds for the trip. "It's just not worth it. For a normal Greece, I usually get anywhere between fourteen hundred and eighteen hundred pounds and it's two and half weeks' work."

His target for the Saudi trip had been twenty-three hundred pounds. He was a thousand pounds short. Madeleine would be worrying. "To make a Saudi Arabian drive pay, you'd have to do it in four weeks."

We bypassed the city of Veliko Trnovo, which straddles a deep gorge curling around two promontories that are connected by a high causeway. On one of the promontories stands the ruins of Baldwin's Tower, where the Latin emperor of Constantinople is supposed to have been imprisoned. The city, once a Roman garrison town, was the medieval capital of the Bulgar Empire.

At 6:30 P.M. we stopped on a paved shoulder surrounded by forest for an in-cab meal. Night was soon upon us, and I slept most of the way through the mountains to the Sofia ring road. By 11:00 P.M. we were parked beside a German truck in the Sofia TIR park next to a motel and snack bar that remained open all night.

"Damned if I'm going to freeze again tonight," I told Graham. "I'm going to ask for a room at the motel."

"Fine by me," he said.

The girl at the reception desk didn't look very friendly. "Do you have any rooms?" I asked her.

She said that she did and asked to see my passport, which she flipped through until she found my Bulgarian visa.

"Sorry, can't give you a room," she announced after examining the visa.

"Why not?"

"Your visa expires at 1:00 A.M. this morning."

I started to protest.

"If you want to extend your visa, you must go to the nearest police station."

There was no point in arguing with her, and I was not about to go to the nearest police station. Fuming, I steeled myself for another night in the Bulgarian cold, this time on tarmac, under the trailer. I unhitched the board from the back of the unit, unrolled the insulation mat, and laid out my sleeping bag. I was cold, tired, and dirty. Fully dressed, with my woolen hat pulled down over my ears, I crawled into bed and within minutes was asleep.

Sleeping under a trailer in a Bulgarian TIR park can be dangerous. I was woken at 6:00 A.M. by what I thought was a piece of ice breaking off the top of the van. I heard it go sponk! on the pavement and felt the moisture of what I supposed were ice particles brush across my face. I opened half an eye. A crumpled beer can lay six inches from my head. The German next door had tossed the nearly empty can out of his cab, and it had literally bounced by my nose.

I went into the snack bar and ordered a coffee. We had to wait till the Vinimpex manager drove out from the center of Sofia with our TIR carnet. It gave me time to reflect. For all I had seen of Bulgaria, it struck me as being perhaps fifty years behind the rest of Europe, but a clean and tidy country where people seemed warm, the night receptionist excepted. The Vinimpex manager, when he arrived at about 8:30 A.M., confirmed this impression. And where else could you find the streets lined with roses and with grapes growing over the sidewalks?

The Vinimpex manager was sleepy-eyed after a night out on the tiles and dived into his tiny cup of coffee, ordering a second and then a third before Graham or I had managed one. He was a bachelor in his midthirties and said his parents were beginning to despair that he would ever marry. Life in Sofia, he said, was too good as a bachelor. There was a party every night. He spoke excellent English.

He asked if we knew whether other trucks were on their way through Turkey. "We're desperate to find trucks going to England."

We said maybe another Whittle truck was going to Plodiv. He didn't think so, however. Whittle had sent a Tansleam truck to Plodiv yesterday. From this we supposed Richie Thorne had picked up Steve's load.

"Year-end wine sales are booming," he said. All of a sudden the British tippler had discovered Bulgarian wines. "We sold thirty-two thousand cases in January, as opposed to twelve thousand the year before. Now it's thirty-two thousand cases a week. We need every truck we can get."

"Why don't you use sea containers?" I asked.

"We do. There's a sea container service from Varna to Felixstowe every ten days. It takes twelve days for a container to arrive. But we fill our rush orders by truck. And now we have nothing but rush orders. We're having trouble keeping up with them."

Bulgaria's largest customer, the Soviet Union, used to buy 250 million bottles of wine a year. Bulgaria, however, had become one of the principal casualties of Mr. Gorbachev's anti-alcohol campaign. As a result of the clampdown on alcoholism, exports to the Soviet Union had declined by 40 percent.

We left the TIR park at 9:30 A.M. after discovering that we had developed a slow leak in the back right trailer tire. Another magnificent autumn day seemed assured, although the wind had changed, and with only twenty-four miles to drive to the Yugo border we decided to have the tire repaired in Yugoslavia.

"There's a KAT behind us," Graham said.

"Alley or Angora?"

"Bulgarian, you twat, and he's going to pull us over so make sure that wine is out of sight."

The prowl car overtook us, but kept on going, showing no interest in a yellow Whittle truck. On our left was the cobblestoned surface of the old Zarigradski Drum. Only eight miles left to the frontier. We entered the Dragoman Gorge and passed under the Orient Express line. Above us the trees were bright daubs of color like an Impressionist painting. At Customs our paperwork was quickly stamped and returned, but at passport control the officer said something to me in Bulgarian.

I shrugged. "Don't understand," I told him.

"Moment," he said. "I call *chef*."

Chef wanted to know why we were twelve hours beyond the visa limit. "TIR drivers," I said. "We loaded in Shumen yesterday."

He did a quick calculation, Shumen being the other side of the country. "Okay," he said.

We got a seal on the van, and into Yugoslavia we went. On the far side of the Dragoman, bad weather was being pushed toward us by strong westerly winds that shook the van and made *Old Girl* gurgle. We had traversed into another world. Though both countries have Socialist economies, their monetary policies are vastly different. Exchange controls are severe in Bulgaria, and the *leva* is one of the most restricted currencies in the world. The Yugoslavs, on the other hand, are allowed to hold bank accounts in any currency they want— drachmas, dollars, dinars, it's all the same.

Frontiers are artificial barriers to the free flow of people and trade. Here at Gradina we had a prime example. Yugoslavs travel by the busload to Bulgaria to buy clothes and other items that are cheaper there than at home. They are attracted by the "free shops" where they can buy supposedly duty-free American and West European goods. The Yugoslav Customs guards have a field day with their own nationals when they reenter the country. They treat them like animals. The travelers have to lug their bags into the Customs house and wait in line for an inspector to go through them. While we were there the inspector turned every bag upside down, emptying its contents. He sorted through them, pushing what didn't interest him onto the floor, which was littered with cigarette ash and butts. The travelers said nothing. A woman went around with a broom and swept the trash into little piles. Then she would find a piece of cardboard and pick up every fourth or fifth pile. The piles nearest the door she swept outside. Anything too big was left on the floor. A woman inspector in a brown uniform surveyed this chaos, waiting for body-search customers. The guard at the desk sent her an old drone as broad as she was tall. I swear I saw him wink. The female inspector was unamused. She escorted the drone into a dark closet and came out minutes later, still unsmiling.

A score of Turkish truck drivers were going through Customs with us. The procedure was to hand all cargo papers through a window and receive in return a number written on a piece of cardboard, which became your file number. When your file was processed it was passed to the cashier behind a neighboring window. He would call out your number. He might call it out in German, Yugoslav, or any other language in which he knew how to count. Rarely English. Graham lost his card and was in a tizzy trying to find it. This cost us an hour. He finally decided to build a new one. We cut out a square of cardboard from the back of my pad and wrote "21" on it—his original number. Graham went to the window where the cashier was already processing file No. 32. He handed in his number and smiled. The cashier looked at it, frowned, got file No. 21, and asked for sixty pounds in road tax. He then gave back our documents, stamped and ready to go.

We put our watches back one hour to Yugo time, which was midday, and decided to try the restaurant opposite for a quick bite. The waiters were having their lunch; no one would serve us. We went to the men's room. The toilets were overflowing with shit. It was putrid and disgusting. We knew we were back in Yugoslavia. In spite of the filth and the surliness, it felt good.

We drove to the next village, where I bought bread and garlic sausage for lunch. The sausage gave off an aggressive aroma. Graham got mad. "What's the matter?" I asked.

"I hate garlic!" he said and punched open the roof vent. I remembered he wouldn't even keep fresh onions in the cab, but tied them to the front of the trailer. I assured him it was delicious, which it was, but he sulked until we found a *lastiki* repair shop that vulcanized tires.

The owner of the *lastiki* shop said it would take half an hour to repair the tire. As usual, it took two hours. Rain started falling as we swung back onto the road. A detour took us through the hills south of Pirot, with twenty trucks, mostly Turks, ahead of us. Turkish drivers don't like the rain. The road was not sufficiently wide to allow us to overtake them. Speed was reduced to ten miles per hour. The line bunched together and we crawled up the hills in low range, wheels slipping and *Old Girl* giving out sighs and groans. These were tiny hills, really, but were presenting us with tremendous problems.

"This is hard work," Graham said. He was tense. We descended into a trough. The Turk in front of us slowed before attempting the next hill rather than taking a run at it. Perhaps he feared the truck in front of him wouldn't make it. Graham exploded.

"Gaw on, get going! Get on with it, you crazy twit!" We were in third. The Turk pulled onto a bit of hard shoulder, probably hoping to get a better grip. Graham pulled around him, *Old Girl* protesting as he built up the revs. The Turk had to swing back onto the roadway, but couldn't because we were alongside him. He was going to miss his gear change. He had to stop. He was furious. He was yelling his head off at us, blowing his horn and flashing his lights. He was in the mud and had lost all momentum. His wheels were spinning. He had thrown it into bottom gear. Now he was behind us again, making all the signs and manifestations of one very mad Turk.

The trailer on the Turkish truck ahead of us was sliding into the banked corners even though the driver inched his way through them.

"This is damn frightening," I said.

"Try it in winter."

And we, too, slid around the hairpin going down the mountain to Bela Palanka, where we rejoined the Trans-European Expressway. We came through the gorges to Nis, where the road became a four-lane expressway again, with 144 miles left to Belgrade. I took out a bottle of Bulgarian wine and sat back to enjoy the ride.

"The trouble with those Turks is that when they get off tonkas and get into these big trucks they don't know how to drive. They miss their gear changes, panic in bad weather, and do all the wrong things. Show them something like the Pirot detour and they fall to bits," Graham remarked.

I didn't say anything.

26. BEER, GEORGE, PLEASE

"HELLO, George, you're back," the waiter said to Graham and I as we walked through the door of the National. "This means big celebration."

We saw Neville Woolridge sitting at a table by the door, smiling. "Maybe too true, George. Maybe big celebration," I told the waiter as Graham went over to say hello to Neville.

"Good, George. I bring you beer."

Neville, an owner-driver from Colchester, England, was on his way to Greece, thinking he was going to be alone on a Friday evening at the National, which was an unusual occurrence. I had met Neville, also known as Small Eyes, last year with Graham at Chris's in Evsoni. Neville was laid back and cool, always smiling, an observer rather than a doer, and a wise one at that. He had made his last trip overland to Pakistan ten years before, and he had stopped running to the Middle East about six years ago. He didn't like the hassle. He was a Greek specialist now, and he could make it from London to Athens in four and a half days. He knew all about Metaxa. I could attest to that.

"Where you been?" he asked.

"Saudi Arabia."

"How was it?"

"Not worth a carrot," Graham said.

"Could have told you that."

"Seen anyone?"

"Not a soul."

"Any news of Ossie?"

"He's out of the hospital."

"Damn, it was him, then."

Ossie MacIntosh, Neville said, had been asleep in his bunk when a German truck barreling down the autobahn at fifty-five miles per hour had a blowout, lost control, veered onto the paved shoulder, and drove smack into the back of Ossie's trailer. Ossie was thrown out of his bunk. His truck was pushed into the one in front of him, which rammed the car in front of it. Another seven cars were damaged. The last in the line was pushed out onto the autobahn. The German was killed instantly; Ossie was taken to the hospital with concussion, broken ribs, an injured spine, and internal lesions. His truck was a write-off.

George appeared with the beers. Ten minutes later he was back. "You want order dinner, maybe?"

"What have you got, George?" Neville asked just for the form.

"You want nice mixed grill?"

"Pork chop?"

"Yes, we have very good pork chop, George."

"Okay, George, pork chop."

"And you, George?"

"I'll have a pork chop," Graham said.

"Three?"

"Do you have *cevabcici*?" I asked.

"What is this, George? Where you think you are? In Serbia? For you we have very good steak and chips."

"I'll try the pork chop," I said, giving in.

"Good, George. Always difficult." And he hurried away to the kitchen.

Halfway through dinner Mark, a new Falcongate driver on his first trip past Dover, walked in. He was nervous. He was on his way to Greece. The operations manager at Falcongate had given him only five hundred pounds in running money and told him to go via Austria. Mark had already paid over three hundred pounds in tolls and transit taxes and was only two thirds of the way there. He was worried about getting home again. His roof vent wouldn't shut and the night heater didn't work. He spent last night in the Alps, shivering himself to sleep. "This is no life," he said. "Darn near froze to death."

We finished our dinner and were on our first round of slibovic, the Yugoslav plum brandy, when we heard a voice behind us ask, " 'Scuse me, are you chaps English?"

We turned around. Steve Walsh was leaning against the door. He had backloaded seven tons of suitcases in Plodiv and had come through Gradina only hours behind us. He was grinning from ear to ear.

Steve's arrival called for more slibovic. He was pleased with himself for having caught up with us, and we were happy to see him. But under the smiling mask was a hint of uncertainty. He was not his usual cocky self.

He had to draw money in Turkey because it had cost him 150 pounds for the new triptych. Smithie, his foreman, had not been pleased. The taxi ride from Silver Gazoo to Iskenderun had been an adventure that cost him another thirty pounds. The driver was such a maniac that Steve had to take the wheel and do most of the driving himself.

There had been no girls at Londra Camp when he arrived there Thursday, and he didn't have the time or the money to wait for some to show up. He had to make up the time lost at Silver Gazoo if he wanted to save his job and reputation, so he had left Londra Camp before sunup that morning.

He had acquired a new tapestry to hang on the backboard of his cab, replacing the Stars and Stripes. It was one of those black, crimson, and silver jobs with a pastoral motif that the roadside seller at Kapik had been selling. Steve had been waiting in line to get into the Turkish Customs compound as the rug merchant went through his act, folding and unfolding different tapestries. One caught Steve's eye and he asked the merchant for a closer look. The merchant wanted five thousand Turkish lire (five pounds) for it. While Steve was making up his mind, a copper came along and told the carpet seller to buzz off. No hawking was permitted at the entrance to the compound.

"But, but—" the merchant protested, trying to retrieve his merchandise from Steve. The copper didn't want to know about it. He unhitched his billy club and started bashing air. The line moved and Steve wound his way into the compound. When he got out of the truck to clear his papers there was no sign of the carpet seller.

In Gradina, Steve went to the border restaurant for some grub and was approached by two Turkish drivers, who showed him their CMRs. They were carrying hazelnuts to London and wanted instructions on how to get to the warehouse where they were unloading. Steve knew the place and was able to draw them a map. They then showed him a telex with instructions to pick up a Baghdad load at the Davies Turner depot in London. Did Steve know how to find this address? they asked. Steve knew very well, but he told them he had no idea.

We had two more rounds of slibovic. George was serving them in half-size tumblers. We were in decompression, and Neville was smiling sagely at us, realizing what was happening. The cork went "pop" and suddenly the tension was out of the bottle. We were relaxed for the first time in forty days, in a good mood, backloaded, and on our way home. The dangers were over—or almost.

"What you carrying?" Neville asked.

"Eighteen tons of Bulgarian wine."

"You're kidding."

"Good stuff, too. You want to try some?"

The question was superfluous. We went out to *Old Girl* and sat down on the curb as Graham handed out four bottles. Before Neville had the fourth bottle uncorked, Steve had finished the first and Graham was well into the second. It all seemed terribly hilarious, though it was only a banal curbside party.

"Oh, no," Steve said. "We've got company."

Creeping down the lane was a police car with two coppers in it. By this time we were overcome with hysterical laughter and didn't care who it was or what they wanted. They stopped and looked at us, no doubt wondering what we could be doing in the middle of a cold autumn night sitting on a curb and in fits of laughter.

The copper driving the patrol car wound down his window. "Problem?" he asked.

"No problem," Steve said. Graham, in the cab, was doing an imitation of me looking for my notebook. He was screaming in a high-pitched voice, "Wherzit? Wherzit?" The cops started laughing.

"Party," Neville said.

"Here, for you," Steve said, handing them each an unopened bottle of wine so that they could share our good cheer. They accepted the bottles in the comradely spirit in which they were offered. To return the gesture, they asked: "You want gurlls?"

"Sure, sure," we told them. We didn't care who joined our party; the more the merrier, and if we finished the two cases in the cab we still had 1,180 more in the van. We had actually noticed two hookers plying their trade down the lane, by the Shell station. The coppers drove slowly off in that direction but never returned.

Graham was looped out of his mind. He stumbled into the woods opposite the hotel and came back moments later looking gray and having trouble focusing. The party had ended. I had taken a room for the night, and the others returned to their trucks.

Saturday, October 25, dawned full of promise. Except that Graham was still dizzy. And that his newly vulcanized tire had gone flat. One trailer tire weights 180 pounds, and the prospect of changing it was not inviting.

"What are you doing in the woods?" I asked.

"Looking for my false teeth."

"What are *they* doing in the woods?" He was on his hands and knees, feeling around in the grass.

"They must have fallen out last night when all the slibovichie stuff came up."

We went into the hotel for breakfast. Frederika, a blond Danish refrigerator truck driver with a Dolly Parton chassis, was sitting with another Danish driver at the table opposite, smiling knowingly. She and her companion had come in from Athens during the night and were on their way home, empty.

"She's a real looker," Mark said. "Do they have many like that on this run?" He was beginning to think that the life of an international freight driver was not that bad after all.

"Come on then, Graham, let's get that tire changed," Steve said after a leisurely breakfast.

We walked Neville and Mark to their trucks. Neville had a green Transcon with a yellow-sheeted trailer. It looked smart from a distance, but when you got closer you saw she had been through the wars. "Got a bit of metal worm, here," Steve said, running his finger across patches of rust along the top of the grille.

"She's been over the mountains a few times," Neville said.

With Neville and Mark gone, Steve changed into a pair of overalls and began organizing Graham. As Graham was still feeling weak, Steve did most of the tire-changing. We brewed a last pot of tea together and prepared to set off.

As Smithie had unlimited Austrian permits and didn't mind the extra transit tax, Steve was going home on the more direct Ljubijana–Salzburg route. Graham had decided to take the longer TEM route through Hungary and Czechoslovakia into East Germany. Then it was a quick dash across West Germany to the Rhine, through Holland, to Zeebrugge.

Steve left half an hour ahead of us. Graham took his time firing up the motor, then at 1:00 P.M. we waved good-bye to Frederika. Graham was singing, "All I want for Christmas are my two front teeth."

27. UP THE TEE

WE had a four-hour run to the Hungarian border through a countryside rich in autumn colors and scenes: Saturday laundry hanging in front of cottages; trees whose golden leaves had fallen; goats tethered by the roadside; a miniature donkey on a village common; shrines decked with flowers; bossy white geese chasing schoolgirls through a field; hay stacked like houses; chickens as big as turkeys; brown-and-white cows entering an arched barnyard.

As we approached Sabotica, Graham noted, "It's drawing in." The day was almost over; the sun was getting weaker, and evening was coming on, though it was only 4:00 P.M.

We got through Yugo customs in twenty minutes. An Alfred Hitchcock film was playing on television in English, and the Customs guard invited us to stay and watch it. We thanked him but said we had to move on.

Hungarian Customs at Röszke took an hour and a half to clear. "Act as daft as an Englishman and you can get away with anything," Graham remarked. He was worrying about our axle-weight distribution.

Four years ago, when he came through Röszke for the first time, with a full load of Greek wine, he knew he was overweight and was low on running money. He parked on the Yugo side of the border till midnight, and when nobody was around moved slowly to the border and raced across the weighbridge: Boom, boom, boom! Clatter-bang, bang-clatter!

A guard came running out of the weighbridge house, screaming, "No, no! You must go slowly, slowly!" and told Graham to go around

265

again. This time he rolled his front axle over slowly, then accelerated for the four other axles. Again the guard came out, furious this time, and a Customs woman in the weighbridge office window was shouting and waving a card at him.

He was sent back a second time and repeated the same maneuver. Both of them ran out and started shouting at him. He was sent back again. He went a little slower, waiting till he got the tractor's back axle over before accelerating. They finally gave up and waved him through. "English dumb," the woman said, tapping her head.

This time we went over the weighbridge slowly, slowly. A woman guard came out and said we were overweight on one axle. She indicated that a bribe would lighten the load.

"You do it," Graham said. "But be careful."

"Does she speak English?"

"A little," he said.

I went over and asked her, with a wink, "Are we really overweight?"

She didn't look at me but lowered her eyes to see what was in my hand—a twenty-dollar bill. She glanced down the line of trucks. No one in sight. I almost jumped when she squeezed my hand as she took the note.

"Well!" I thought, never having been picked up by a weighbridge lady before. "Do you live around here?" I asked.

"Must go next truck." And back she went into the weighbridge house.

We got another seal on the van, but no cabin control. We were, however, charged five deutsche marks in overtime. When we got to the gate the guard there asked if we had any chocolate. He was about twenty and seemed a nice enough lad. We didn't have any chocolate, but I gave him the last of the lighters with the ladies on them. He smiled and put it in his pocket.

On the well-surfaced Hungarian roads we made good time. Sipping chilled Bulgarian wine, I was able to sit back and reflect. Apart from the Arab countries, we had hardly been harassed by police this trip. We were stopped a dozen times in Turkey, only once in Yugoslavia, and in Bulgaria the KATs gave us directions. Except for the controls around Plzeň, we were neither molested nor bothered in Czechoslovakia nor, when we got there, in East Germany. Hungary was much like Greece. You rarely so much as see the police.

Our return coincided with the thirtieth anniversary of the Hungarian

Revolution. It began on October 23, 1956, sparked by students demanding political reforms, and was savagely crushed by Soviet tanks thirteen days later. In Hungary there is no longer any fear of the state apparatus, such as still exists in Czechoslovakia. People speak their mind. Private enterprise is tolerated, producing a form of goulash communism that has contributed to the highest crime, divorce, and suicide rates in the Eastern Bloc.

Approaching Kecskemét, we were followed by two Hungarocamions. They were racing to get home for the weekend. It was dark, and for a while they stayed on our tail. Then the lead Hungarian pulled out to pass. He couldn't and tucked himself back in behind us. A car was coming down the tree-lined road toward us, and beyond there was a right-hand bend. When at last the road was clear, Graham signaled with his right indicator that it was safe to pass. The Hungarian steamed by, and as soon as his trailer had cleared the front of our cab, Graham flicked his headlights once, which in truckers' code means "Thank you for passing me safely."

The Hungarocamion winked his back indicators—first the right and then the left—which is the customary way of saying "Thanks for your help and good luck."

British and most European drivers use a code of headlight and indicator flashes. One flash of the headlights at an oncoming truck is a form of greeting, usually reserved for someone you know or at least another Brit. Two flashes at an oncoming vehicle means that the coppers are lying in wait ahead. Austrian, Balkan, Turkish, and Middle Eastern drivers are not code-users, though sometimes a Turk or a raghead will indicate the road is clear for overtaking by putting on his *left* indicator.

Every time an overtaking truck responded with a "Thank you" wink it left me with a warm feeling. It was reassuring that someone else out there spoke our language, even though he might be a Frenchman or a Dane. On a return trip it also meant we were getting closer to home.

At 8:00 P.M. we turned left into the Windmill parking lot. It was the tallest windmill I can remember ever having seen: easily five stories high and perfectly restored. We parked behind some Turkish trucks and noted that half the Brooks team was there and a Dow Freighter. Because of a windmill's structure the ground-floor room was circular, with booths around the wall and a bar in the center, where the shaft once had been. A kitchen was downstairs, connected to the ground floor by a dumbwaiter. The restaurant and bar were operated by a manager, two waitresses, and a barman.

We joined Rod and John of Brooks Transport in one of the booths. They had come through from Romania, leaving the other two behind. Terry, angling for one more night with his Kiwi before dropping her off in Budapest, had been dragging his feet, and little Mickey seemed to be in a daze since his shunt in Aksaray.

"Mickey," John said, "has trouble getting up in the morning, and he doesn't like driving at night."

"That must be bad news if you're a long-distance driver," I ventured.

"Not necessarily," Rod replied. "Other than that, he goes like *Gangbusters.*"

Steve Crewe off Dow Freight joined us. He had taken a load of Rothman cigarettes to Greece and was on his way home to Manchester with seven tons of Yugo textiles. "And Manchester used to be the textile capital of the world," he said with a sigh.

Drivers' fare at the Windmill is steak, eggs, and chips. I had goulash and some Bull's Blood wine while Steve Crewe told us about another Dow Freight driver known to the fraternity as Billy Butterbum. Billy had entered Hungary from Yugoslavia and was parked on a paved shoulder, emptying his cab of a few days' accumulated trash, when a Hungarian police car drove up. A police captain got out and walked over to Billy's truck.

"Why are you dirtying our country with your trash?" the police officer asked.

"Because Yugoslavia's full," Billy replied.

The showers at the Windmill are beside the toilets in a shed at the back. Among the graffiti on the wall I noticed, "Peter the Plater plated in Kecskemét and liked it."

"Peter comes through Kecskemét all the time. He has a refrigerator in his cab and buys his meat here," Steve Crewe said.

He described Peter as a shy person until he has had a few drinks. Then he becomes boisterous, vulgar, and sometimes hilariously funny. His abnormally long tongue had become his trademark. Recently divorced, the romance of the road had taken its toll on his personal life.

Late that night we heard that Britain had broken off diplomatic relations with Syria. The decision followed the trial in London of a Syrian-sponsored terrorist, Nezar Hindawi. He had been found guilty of attempting to plant a bomb on an El Al aircraft with 380 people on board at Heathrow Airport. The evidence showed that Hindawi had been supported by the Syrian embassy in London and official agencies in Damascus. He was sentenced to forty-five years in prison. We pitied any British trucker who was on his way through Jordan in hopes of transiting Syria. Syria had instantly closed its frontiers to all British commercial traffic and ordered the British embassy in Damascus closed.

Church bells woke us on Sunday morning. After a Windmill breakfast of eggs, ham, toast, and coffee, which cost us five Deutschmarks each, we started north again, running with Steve Crewe as far as Prague. Steve drove a new MAN named *Manning Grey,* after an English racehorse. All Dow Freighters are named after racehorses or secretaries. As I wasn't sure of the common denominator between the two, I asked Steve what it might be.

"The foreman thinks they bring him luck," he said.

Dow Freight Services, out of Swindon, England, is known in the trade as a class carrier. The company has about fifty trucks in its international division, making it the largest privately owned haulage firm in the United Kingdom. For one client—Massey Ferguson—Dow Freight carries forty-five loads each month to Istanbul.

But the foreman's luck was soon to run out. In May 1987, the Manchester Crown Court sentenced Roger Dowsett, Dow Freight's managing director, to eighteen months in prison for conspiring to use unregistered vehicles, forging international road permits, and falsifying journey sheets. His clients were said to be none too happy with the news, and his drivers risked being put on unemployment because of it. His lawyers filed an appeal.

Driving to Budapest, we noticed that snow fences had already been erected along the eastern side of the highway, and though it was only October 26 it felt like it might snow tomorrow. Graham was more cheerful than I had seen him in a long time. *Old Girl,* he said, was pulling like a dream. "If she runs like this for the next four years, it'll do."

We arrived on the outskirts of Budapest at 10:30 A.M. in an absence of traffic. The city looked happy. I had first visited Budapest in 1966, ten years after the uprising, and it was drab and battle-scarred then. But now I could see buildings and squares by the Danube that I had known twenty years before, and they had been richly restored; their facades were healed and smiling. The streets were so clean they could have been in downtown Zurich.

We crossed the Danube on the southernmost of Budapest's eight bridges. On the far side we joined the expressway north to Tatabanya and Györ. Since entering Hungary—indeed, since Istanbul and even Ankara—we had been following the Trans-European Expressway (TEE). At this point it was six lanes wide and other than us had not a soul on it. "It's Sunday, that's why," Graham informed me. On our left was the Hotel Wien, a world-famous brothel and truck stop. It is a modern eight-store structure with a large parking lot, but from the outside it has nothing other than a large neon sign on the roof to recommend it.

The Trans-European Expressway was a rather cunning scheme to build a modern expressway down the backbone of middle Europe from the Baltic to the Bosporus, then link it with the two arms of the Trans-Asian Expressway, one on the banks of the Tigris and the other at Gürbulak, on the Turkish border with Iran. Six thousand miles of high-capacity roads.

The Romans used to build their roads first, and the legions followed. The Trans-European Expressway was promoted and planned under the auspices of the U.N. Economic Commission for Europe. The project has been jointly financed by the U.N. Development Program and ten participating countries. The Soviet Union was not a participant, but the project was instigated by members of the Warsaw Pact, which the Soviet Union controls. According to a U.N. pamphlet describing the project, the Trans-European Expressway will be completed in the 1990s. The project's central office is in Warsaw. The expressway, the pamphlet added, will ease trade between Europe and the Middle East. From memory, the Soviets had said something similar when they built a superhighway south to Kabul in 1964. But they had built that one without U.N. assistance.

The Trans-European Expressway also has a number of branch roads that feed into it—or feed from it, rather, through Austria to Italy, Gevgelija into Greece, and from Prague to Bonn and Paris.

"Against the background of an enormous increase in goods transported by road between Europe and the Middle East, the growing role of the private car in international tourism, the Bosporus Bridge providing access to western Asia, and the maritime links to North Africa, the importance of the Trans-European Expressway can only increase," the pamphlet predicted.

We reached the Hungarian-Czech border at Vamosszabadi in the early afternoon. For some unexplained reason, the frontier crossing between Hungary and Czechoslovakia is always one of the slowest in Eastern Europe. We had a five-hour wait ahead of us. The Hungarians and the Czechs shared the compound. The Hungarians were quickly done with us, but it was the Czechs who made us wait for the return of our cargo papers and passports. Dozens of Turkish drivers were mingling around. We were sitting along one wall and the Czech Customs guards, enjoying one of their frequent breaks, were seated along the opposite wall. One of the Czech guards was a small blond woman showing a lot of thigh. She was rather plump but saucy-looking, and by no means unattractive.

Graham started, "I wouldn't like to be married to her. She'd have me for breakfast."

Steve Crewe: "She looks like a real bitch."

Graham: "Can you imagine being in bed with her?"

Steve Crewe: "Oh, a ball-buster, all right."

They kept at it for a good fifteen minutes. And she was staring at us all that time.

A plainclothes inspector came out of a back office and gave some instructions in Czech to the guards. "Cabin control," somebody said. We moved outside. "Has the Englishman come through Turkey?" we heard the woman guard ask her colleague, *in English,* and with a Brooklyn accent to boot. He nodded affirmatively.

"Whittle driver!" she called out.

Graham went pink, then white, and back to pink. He didn't know where to put himself.

Cabin control was serious. One of her male colleagues sifted through everything we had. Next they announced they wanted to open the van. Graham was obliged to break the seal, unlace the canvas, and pull it aside. Another man, in overalls, arrived with a German shepherd. The dog jumped in, had a sniff, and came out. "Okay," the woman said, "close it."

Ours was not the only truck singled out for this treatment. Steve Crewe, as he had not come through Turkey, was spared. But three Turks were tested. One of them was carrying a load of onions. Steve Crewe's eyes lit up when he saw them. He went over to the Turkish driver and said, "I say, we're having a cab party tonight. I'm making curry. Could you spare a few onions?"

The Turk handed him a stringbag full.

We went back into the Customs building to pick up our TIR carnets and passports. Graham insisted that the Czech officer mark on the carnet that the seals had been broken for inspection, which he did. We resumed our previous positions, looking at the thighs of the woman inspector who had managed to raise her skirt, after crossing and recrossing her legs, to a few inches short of her waist.

Neither Graham nor Steve Crewe said a word.

We heard somebody shout, "Hey, you guys!" We looked up. It was Black Billy Hall, on his way to Istanbul. He had seen us from the far side of the compound and risked his very life to circle the building and come in to greet us.

"Billy, what are you doing here?" I asked. The question was stupid. The answer was self-evident. We had met Billy the year before, in Istanbul. His White Road Commander 2, which he called *Silver Bird,* had a bumper plate on it that said, "It's hard to be humble. But I drive the best." Billy was wearing a cowboy hat and was looking like a movie star, or maybe a cowboy in a Marlboro ad for *Ebony* magazine.

"I saw you so I had to come over and say hello," he said.

Ludlow Hemsley Hall, managing director of Ludhost Limited, from Woodley near Rading, England, was without a doubt one of the legendary figures of the Middle East route. A kinder, more conscientious trucker was hard to find. Trained in the British army, the son of a Jamaican psychiatrist who was retired and living in Toronto, he had stopped running beyond Adana after being shot at by Iraqi deserters as he was driving back from Basra two years before.

His White was built to American specifications, except that it had front-wheel brakes. "It's a man's truck," Billy said. "You guys don't understand." Other truckers called it *Council House on Wheels.* He kept a picture of his twelve-year-old son on the dashboard and another of his wife, a nurse, taped to the ceiling over his bunk. "It keeps me out of trouble," he always said.

"What's the news of Ossie?" Graham asked.

"Should be back on the road soon. Getting a new Transcon. The insurance is paying."

Our passports were ready. We said good-bye to Billy and moved out of Customs. It had started to drizzle, making it slow going over the mountain behind Bratislava. Coming down the last stretch in a left-handed bend, we saw a house with a tarpaulin covering one side. Steve Crewe said that Sammy Thorne, Richie's brother, had gone through the wall a few months before.

We pulled into a service area and parked beside a Romanian truck.

Its driver was pleased to see us. He was on his first trip out of the country and had lost his running companion. He had a load for Strasbourg and asked how to get there. After Steve Crewe gave him instructions, he returned to his truck, pulled the curtains, and retired for the night.

Steve Crewe made two batches of curry: one not too hot for Graham, and one, very hot, for the rest of us. It was pure delight. After dinner, I found shelter under a concrete structure beside the service station, which was closed, and laid out my gear. There was a lot of movement on the concrete shoulder during the night: trucks pulling in, roadside conferences, door-knocking, the sounds of cargo being transferred between vehicles, and other seamy events. I was glad nobody found me. It remained in my memory as one of the five most unpleasant nights of the trip.

28. THE CHANGING MOSAIC

"I'M cold and want to get going!" I called to Graham from outside the locked cab at around 6:00 A.M. There was ground fog and drizzle. Graham rolled out of his bunk and, once he had stowed his bedding, Steve Crewe and I got in and made tea. The three of us watched the Romanian next door get out of his cab, walk in his pajamas around to the back axle for a pee, then return to the cab. Before climbing back in he removed his pajamas, not to reveal his birthday suit but a full set of work clothes. He got back in the cab and warmed up the motor for ten minutes before moving off on his way to Strasbourg.

"Cor, did you see that? That's one to tell the wife. She won't believe it."

Chris Crewe was a social worker, and she plotted Steve's progress on a wall map in her office. He said she had promised before they married that April never to ask him to come off the road. But Steve Crewe was unlike other drivers I had met. He not only loved the road and was a master of its lore, he also treated his fellow drivers more like an anthropologist might treat a lost tribe of aborigines. He knew all their dirty habits, their idiosyncrasies, their ways of talking and letting off steam. He fascinated me with his road trivia, and with Graham's blessing I rode for the morning with Professor Crewe. As we got back on the Trans-European Expressway the BBC announced from Luxembourg that Sir Geoffrey Howe would ask his Common Market counterparts to impose diplomatic and trade sanctions on Syria.

"There's one for you. The only trade sanctions will be against British trucks going through Syria," Steve commented.

He was probably not far off. Syria, from a trade point of view, was really the pimple on the elephant's ass. Syria's shortage of foreign exchange and the country's state-controlled economy had made it a market of limited attraction. The country's 10.6 million people had no money to spend on imported goods. In 1985, Britain's exports to Syria totaled eighty-one million pounds, and economic activity had fallen since then. By comparison, British exports to Saudi Arabia totaled 1.256 billion pounds in 1985. So loss of Syrian trade was not a problem to the truckers who carried British exports to the Middle East. The problem was the closing of a land bridge to and from Saudi Arabia and the other western Gulf states. One other land bridge existed— through southern Iraq. But, as we had experienced, that one, too, was becoming less and less practicable. Another shove by Khomeini and it might close altogether. Of course, Turkish trucks could still get through Syria. It looked like more British cargoes would be going to the Gulf on Turkish wheels, which did not augur well for owner-drivers like Richie Thorne.

When we reached Prague services at 11:00 A.M., we stopped for breakfast and said good-bye to Steve Crewe, who was taking the road west, to Waidhaus. We continued northwest, to the East German border at Voitanov. We crossed into East Germany at Schönberg and were subjected to a thorough going-over by a pink-cheeked East German border guard in his early twenties who had nothing else to do. He uncovered the dismantled CB. Truckers are allowed to use one CB band in East Germany provided they buy a CB permit for ten Deutschmarks (East Germans use West German marks for administrative matters). Usually nobody bothers to buy a permit because there is no one they can talk to on the CB band.

Our young German friend was more interested in my books on the Middle East. From the discussion we had—severely limited by my pidgin German and his kitchen English—it seemed that he was fascinated by Lawrence of Arabia and had a special interest in Assyrian history. Once cleared, our route took us around Jena, Weimar, and Gotha. We entered West Germany near Kassel and the Fulda Gap, with some Saudi diesel still in our belly tank. We were the only truck in Customs, and yet nobody was interested in us.

We pulled into the service area outside the Customs compound and went into the all-night diner for our first meal in Western Europe since September 15. Two Falcongate trucks were parked at the far end of the service area, but their curtains were pulled and we didn't disturb them.

I slept under the trailer again, and it was freezing cold in the

Hessian hills. But at least I had the restaurant to go into when I couldn't stand the cold any more. At 7:25 A.M. we began our dash to the Rhine. When we left, the two Falcongate trucks were still snugly parked, curtains drawn.

"Three more countries and we're home," Graham said. We crossed the Rhine at one o'clock, and twenty minutes later we were at the Dutch frontier. Graham handed in the TIR carnet to get it stamped.

"What vintage is the wine?" the Dutch Customs girl asked.

"I dunno. Last week, I think."

We blew the last of the Saudi diesel into the running tanks on a paved shoulder at 2:00 P.M. as rain began to fall, and we crossed into Belgium at 3:40 P.M. Customs in the three Benelux countries are nonexistent. A man sitting in a kiosk waved us through. Saudi Customs had taken ten days to clear, Belgian Customs only ten seconds.

Now began the race for Zeebrugge, hoping to catch the 7:00 P.M. ferry. "This is what T-form Charlies do all the time: chase ferries. They've been out three days and they're eager to get back home," Graham said.

We arrived in the Ro-Ro Haven of Zeebrugge at 6:00 P.M. The Townsend Thoresen dispatcher told us that with luck we might get on the 6:00 A.M. ferry. We were pissed off, especially when we learned that Steve Walsh made the 4:00 P.M. ferry. So we went to the East Enders Pub for a drink and ran into Alfie Jones, Rod Brookstein, and his friend John, as well as two other drivers. The East Enders Pub claims to serve "the finest English breakfast this side of the Channel." It includes Lancashire black pudding.

We were loaded onto the 6:00 A.M. ferry, which arrived in Dover at 10:50 A.M., U.K. time. We headed for The Barnacles, where Steve Walsh, Steve Crewe, Pat Searle, the Brooks duo, Alfie Jones, and a supporting cast of dozens were gathered telling war stories and catching up with the news of other drivers. Graham telephoned Madeleine to let her know we were back. He returned with the look of a man who was tired but pleased to know that he had a wife and two daughters at home who were eager to see him and relieved he was safe.

Peanut had found a new job, driving for J. J. Smith. Coming through Rozvadov, opposite Waidhaus on the Czech side of the border, Steve Crewe saw Wolfgang Myer, the German Geordie, parked by the roadside. Wolfgang said he was waiting for Peanut. They had been running together. Peanut had a load of red diesel in his belly tank and had offered to sell some to Wolfgang. Wolfgang agreed, but told Peanut they would transfer it on the Czech side of the frontier. They got to Waidhaus together, but Wolfgang was cleared through ahead of Peanut. He assumed Peanut would catch up with him on the Czech side. He had been waiting five hours.

A Whittle driver came through while Steve Crewe and Wolfgang were chatting and announced that Peanut had been arrested by the West Germans for bending his tacho needle and carrying red diesel. When Steve Crewe arrived at Waidhaus Customs, he saw Peanut's blue Volvo parked with the curtains drawn. He made inquiries and was told Peanut was in custody.

Border crossings have always been a trucker's biggest hazard, and only one driver, Terry Smith of Dow Freight, and perhaps Andrew Wilson Young, knew how to turn a Customs compound into perfect pandemonium and get away with it. Terry Smith had once been a vaudeville ventriloquist. He still performed, but only when on the road, so to speak.

One time Steve Crewe was going through the Romanian-Hungarian border with Terry. Ahead of them was an F-Troop truck on which a Hungarian inspector was about to place a seal. As Terry walked past, he threw his voice toward the F-Troop trailer. "Let me out!" a voice inside the trailer cried. It caused minor havoc.

"You hear about Billy Murray, of Dave Freight?" Professor Crewe asked me.

"No."

"He hit a submarine on the M6."

You might ask how that could be possible. I did, and I was told that the Ministry of Defense was transporting the submarine by road to a naval depot. Murray had the misfortune to run into the back of it. "Caused a million pounds' worth of damage, it did," the professor said.

Pat Searle, known as The Bear because of his shaggy brown beard, and Mick Eckersley, an old Middle East hand, held the view that the roads had improved so much it has taken most of the challenge out of the Middle East run. They still do occasional Baghdads but complain that the Turk has taken over most of that work. Otherwise it's East Europe and the Balkans.

"With the new bypass around Prague it's nowhere near as interesting," Pat said. "You used to drop down into the city, go through an old section of town near the station and then under a four-meter bridge. If you didn't go through it with your wheels in the right-hand gutter you ripped off the sheeting on top of your van. Coming home, the only way was to take it on the wrong side of the road. This meant making an illegal turn, then crossing over to the far side of the road and sneaking through. Usually a traffic cop was waiting for you at the other end. He would fine you, even though he was well aware that you had to take it that way.''

The run down Cizre Hill on the disappearing road used to be another extraordinary challenge. "It really got your adrenaline running," said Mick. "Now it's just an easy ride down a gentle gradient. Nothing to it anymore.''

The Middle East drivers sense they are a dying breed. Most have been reduced to T-form Charlies, a category of trucker they used to despise. The spectrum of viewpoints about what lay in store for the long-distance trucker went from the realistic approach, expressed by Terry Grant over a glass of Metaxa at Evsoni—"trucking's fucked!"—to Richie Thorne's more romantic vision: "Another route will open up, maybe to China. Otherwise we'll all be fuckin' bankrupt.'' They were, all of them, victims of the changing mosaic.

China, to me, seemed a remote possibility. The Soviet Union, maybe. But the only certain development that will bring back good times on the craziest Route 66 in the world is an end to hostilities in the Gulf. Once peace between Iran and Iraq is reestablished, millions of dollars will have to be spent on rebuilding the ports and oil terminals that seven years of war have destroyed. The city of Basra is now in ruins. Iraq's second city, with more than one million inhabitants before the war, will have to be rebuilt entirely. Once Iraqi and Iranian warplanes stop shooting up shipping, investment in the Gulf will take off. Cargoes will again roll overland; trucks will have to carry them because the ports have been bashed to hell.

Unless, of course, the Iranian ayatollahs decide to bring their revenge to the western shores of the Gulf. Shiite fanatics have already attempted to blow up Sheikh Jaber al-Ahmad al-Sabah, the Kuwaiti emir, and have bombed Kuwaiti oil wells. But if the ayatollahs do push their "border conflict" too far beyond the Shatt al-Arab we might be talking about World War Three, in which case the only traffic likely to be rolling down the Trans-European Expressway will be Soviet tank transporters.

The one person who had hardly said a word during our Barnacles barnstorming was Steve Walsh. He looked downcast. When he had telephoned Blackburn, the foreman told him he would collect only nine hundred pounds for the trip, which hardly seemed an adequate wage for seven weeks on the road under the conditions we had come through. Smithie, moreover, had sold one of his Volvos to buy a second news vendor's store. Maybe he had seen writing on the wall that others had missed. Steve was not even sure he had a job to go home to.*

We were cleared out of Her Majesty's Customs at 6:45 P.M., eight and a half hours after logging in. That put H.M. Customs on an efficiency par with the Iraqis and Syrians but not quite as good as the Czechs. The Port Authority policeman at the gate as we drove out of the docks asked Graham if he had been drinking.

"Eh? Certainly not."

"Aw right. Thought I smelled beer on your breath. You haven't been drinking at all, then?"

"No, not at all," which was the truth. Graham had consumed maybe thirty teas and two packs of cigarettes during our wait for Customs clearance, but not a drop of anything alcoholic.

It was nice to be home.

We arrived at the vintner's warehouse in southeastern London at 9:30 P.M., ready for unloading in the morning.

Thursday, October 30. Graham backed *Old Girl* to the loading dock, unzippered the back, and lowered the tailgate. Four bottles fell from a damaged case and smashed on the ground. After two thousand miles from Shumen along roads that were not always the easiest, this was the only damage suffered by the total load of 14,160 bottles.

We were under way again by 11:00 A.M. The pressure was still on. We had to get the trailer back to Preston before 5:00 P.M. or pay another fifteen pounds' rent, which Graham wanted to avoid. We lumbered under the Blackwall Tunnel, built in 1897, hugging the right wall all the way, missing oncoming traffic by inches. By midday we were on the M1 north, and we arrived at the Haydock trailer rental yard with twenty minutes to spare.

Graham phoned home to say we would be there within an hour.

"The road is a lonely place. You have nobody to talk to. It's not like other jobs where you can stop and have a chat," he remarked on our way to Blackpool.

---

* Steven Walsh was laid off when he returned to Blackburn and found a job driving for Montgomery Transport, an Irish company.

I knew something had changed in my appreciation of juggernaut drivers. I knew that from now on whenever I saw a juggernaut, I would pay its driver the fullest respect. Their work conditions are among the roughest that exist. Their responsibilities are enormous, not only to the owner of the cargo entrusted to them and to the shipper who contracted the load, but above all to the safety of other road users. They get the job done, keep the road open, and ferry exports to their destinations safely and in reasonable time. There is little money in it for them, and they feel they are unnecessarily hassled by the ministry of this or that, by policemen, by other road users, and by every Customs service from Dover to Timbuktu. Yet the truckers I met had the kind of hearts that, running home empty, should they see a stranded East German motorist with his family by the roadside in Yugoslavia, their car having broken down, they would load the car into the van and carry it, the owner, and his family back to the East German border without charge. You don't believe it? Well, it actually happened.

They are modern merchant-adventurers.

Mad Mick Moody, the owner of the blue Scania who drove under contract for Astran, told me one day as we drank tea and listened to the wind whistle through the Cilician Gates, "I was born in the wrong century. I should have sailed with Sir Francis Drake. I've climbed mountains, been to sea, fought in wars, but nothing is as challenging as driving to the Middle East."

"There's nothing nicer when you're on your way home than turning off at the next junction," Graham said. "They always say that the last mile home is the longest."

A strong wind was blowing off the Irish Sea. It rocked *Old Girl* as we parked in front of the red brick house on South Park Drive. Jennifer and Angela were waiting in the living-room window. They ran out to help us unload. Jennifer was so happy she had tears in her eyes. "Silly goose," Graham chided her. After tea, Graham brought out the Saudi copperware, the T-shirts from Al Khobar and Adana, and the other souvenirs from places that now seemed so far away.

Next day he drove me to Preston, where I was to catch the intercity express to London. We had lunch together at a greasy spoon: homemade steak-and-kidney pie, choice of vegetables, and tea, all for three and a half pounds for the two of us. In silence.

At the station when we shook hands, Graham said, "It won't be the same anymore. I'll have no one to chat with. Take care now, I'll miss you."

INDEX

45